Thomas Richardson and Sons

The Parochial Garden of the Soul

Containing Devotions for Mass and Benediction ; the Rosary ; bona mors ; and Way of the Cross...

Thomas Richardson and Sons

The Parochial Garden of the Soul
Containing Devotions for Mass and Benediction ; the Rosary ; bona mors ; and Way of the Cross...

ISBN/EAN: 9783337248789

Printed in Europe, USA, Canada, Australia, Japan

Cover: Foto ©Lupo / pixelio.de

More available books at **www.hansebooks.com**

THE PAROCHIAL GARDEN OF THE SOUL:

CONTAINING

DEVOTIONS FOR MASS AND BENEDICTION;

THE

ROSARY; BONA MORS; AND WAY OF THE CROSS,

VESPERS FOR SUNDAYS, AND COMPLIN;

DEVOTIONS FOR

CONFESSION AND COMMUNION, AND FOR VISITS TO THE BLESSED SACRAMENT;

DEVOTIONS FOR THE SICK;

MASS AND PRAYERS FOR THE DEAD;

PRAYERS TO THE SACRED HEART, TO OUR BLESSED LADY, AND TO ST. JOSEPH;

HYMNS, LITANIES,

VARIOUS OTHER DEVOTIONS, AND THE CONDITIONS FOR GAINING INDULGENCES.

London:
THOMAS RICHARDSON AND SONS,
26, PATERNOSTER ROW; AND DERBY.
1877.

COPYRIGHT RESERVED.

Nihil obstat.

A. Canon M'Kenna.

Imprimatur.

✠ Edwardus,

Episcopus Nottinghamiensis.

Die 29 Januarii, 1877.

CONTENTS.

Mass.—Instructions for Mass, page 26.
    Prayers before Mass, 36.
    The Asperges before Mass, 49.
    Devotions for Mass, 51.
    Prayers after Mass, 112.
    Prayer for the Queen after Mass, 111.
    Litany of the Mass, 114.
    Invocations after Mass, 300.
    Mass for the Dead, 341.
    Manner of Serving at Mass, 123.

Benediction.—O Salutaris Hostia, 174.
    Tantum Ergo, 175.
    Adoremus in Æternum, 178.
    Hymn to the B. Sacrament, 179.
    Litany of the Blessed Virgin, 184.
    Divine Praises, 180.
    Ejaculations to the B. Sacrament, 172 & 179.
    Acts of Adoration to Jesus in the Blessed Sacrament, 182.
    Quarant' Ore, or Forty Hours Devotion, 181.

Vespers—For Sundays, 143.
    Anthems for particular periods of the Year, 167.

Complin, 155.

Rosary of the Blessed Virgin, 404.

Way of the Cross, 378.

Confession—Devotions for Confession, 244.
    Examination of Conscience, 249.
    Affections and Resolutions, 266.
    Act of Contrition, 265.
    How to go to Confession, 271.
    Short form of Confession, 273.
    Prayer after Confession, 273.
    Satisfaction, 276.

CONTENTS.

Communion—
- Devotions for Communion, 277.
- Manner of receiving Communion, 285.
- Aspirations after Communion, 286.
- Acts of Devotion, 289.
- Invocations after Communion, 300.

Indulgences—Explained, 190.
- Plenary—for England, 191.
- Indulgenced Prayers, 194.
- Devotions for Jubilees and Indulgences, 196.

Sacraments—Instructions on the Sacraments, 241.
- Manner of Baptizing an Infant, 243.
- Penance, 243.
- Holy Eucharist, 277.
- Extreme Unction, 314.

Litanies—Litany of Jesus, 350.
- ,, of the Blessed Virgin, 184.
- ,, of the Saints, 219.
- ,, of the Mass, 114.
- ,, of the Sacred Heart of Jesus, 394.
- ,, of St. Joseph, 431.
- ,, for a Happy Death, 337.
- ,, for the Dead, 323.

Prayers—Morning Prayers, 11.
- Night Prayers, 229.
- Evening Devotions, 219.
- Prayer on entering a church, 48.
- Universal Prayer, 140.
- Thirty Days' Prayer, 419.
- Prayer to the Holy Family, 140.
- Prayer before a Crucifix, 301.
- Prayer of St. Ignatius, 392.
- Prayers before and after Instructions, 47.
- Occasional Prayers, 24.
- Prayers at Meals, 23.
- Memorare, or the Prayer of St. Bernard, 449.

Devotions for the Sick—
 Daily Prayer in Sickness, 302.
 Acts of Virtues in Sickness, 305.
 The Holy Viaticum, 310.
 Extreme Unction, 314.
 Prayer before Extreme Unction, 315.
 Prayer after Extreme Unction, 318.
 The Last Blessing, 319.
 Preparation for Death, 311.
 Litany for a happy Death, 337.
 How to assist the Dying, 321.

Devotions for the Dead—
 Mass for the Dead, 341.
 Litany for the Dead, 323.
 Prayers for the Dead, 332

Special Devotions—
 The Sacred Heart of Jesus, 393.
 Our Lady of Perpetual Succour, 425.
 Seven Sorrows of Mary, 429.
 Sorrows and Joys of St. Joseph, 432.
 Bona Mors, 437.
 Way of the Cross, 378.
 Sacred Thirst Confraternity, 448.

Miscellaneous—
 The Seven Penitential Psalms, 204.
 The Miserere, 217.
 Psalms of Adoration, &c., 131.
 Canticle of the Three Children, 129.
 Canticle of Zachary, 138.
 Jesus Psalter, 357.
 Acts of Faith, Hope, Charity, 38.
 Act of Contrition, 265.
 Te Deum, (English) 418.
 Act of Consecration to the Sacred Heart of Mary, 417.

Hymns—Come, Holy Ghost, Creator, come, 235.
  Come, Holy Ghost, send down those beams, 236.
  Faith of our Fathers, 356.
  Hail, Queen of Heaven, 449.
  Hail, Holy Joseph, 436.
  I rise from dreams of time, 450.
  Jesus, the only thought of Thee, 354.
  Jesus, my God, 266.
  Jesus, my Lord, my God, 179.
  Immaculate, Immaculate, 424.
  Look down, O Mother Mary, 423.
  Litany of the Passion, 447.
  O come and mourn with me, 392.
  O turn to Jesus, Mother, turn, 204.
  Sweet Saviour, bless us ere we go, 228.
  To Jesu's Heart all burning, 402.

Latin Hymns—
  Alma Redemptoris, 167.
  Ave Regina, 169.
  Dies iræ, 343.
  Lucis Creator, 152.
  O Salutaris, 174.
  Tantum ergo, 175.
  Regina Cœli, 170.
  Salve Regina, 171.
  Stabat Mater, 374.
  Te Lucis, 152.
  Veni Creator, 238.
  Veni Sancte Spiritus, 239.

Feasts and Fasts—
  Table of Moveable Feasts, 7.
  Days of Obligation and Devotion, 8
  Fasting Days, 9.
  Abstinence Days, 10.

Table of Moveable Feasts.

Year of our Lord.	Ash Wednesday.	Easter Sunday.	Whit Sunday.	Corpus Christi.	First Sunday in Advent.
1877	Feb. 14	April 1	May 20	May 31	Dec. 2
1878	Mar. 6	April 21	June 9	June 20	Dec. 1
1879	Feb. 26	April 13	June 1	June 12	Nov. 30
*1880	Feb. 11	Mar. 28	May 16	May 27	Nov. 28
1881	Mar. 2	April 17	June 5	June 16	Nov. 27
1882	Feb. 22	April 9	May 28	June 8	Dec. 3
1883	Feb. 7	Mar. 25	May 13	May 24	Dec. 2
*1884	Feb. 27	April 13	June 1	June 12	Nov. 30
1885	Feb. 18	April 5	May 24	June 4	Nov. 29
1886	Mar. 10	April 25	June 13	June 24	Nov. 28
1887	Feb. 23	April 10	May 29	June 9	Nov. 27
*1888	Feb. 15	April 1	May 20	May 31	Dec. 2
1889	Mar. 6	April 21	June 9	June 20	Dec. 1
1890	Feb. 19	April 6	May 25	June 5	Nov. 30
1891	Feb. 11	Mar. 29	May 17	May 28	Nov. 29
*1892	Mar. 2	April 17	June 5	June 16	Nov. 27
1893	Feb. 15	April 2	May 21	June 1	Dec. 3
1894	Feb. 7	Mar. 25	May 13	May 24	Dec. 2

NOTE.—*The years marked thus * are leap years.*

A TABLE OF ALL THE FEASTS
OBSERVED BY THE CATHOLICS OF ENGLAND.

The Days of Obligation are in Small Capitals.
The Days of Devotion are in Italics.

ALL THE SUNDAYS IN THE YEAR.

JANUARY.
1 THE CIRCUMCISION, or New Year's Day.
6 THE EPIPHANY, or Twelfth Day.

FEBRUARY.
2 *The Purification, or Candlemas Day.*
24 *St. Matthias.*

MARCH.
19 *St. Joseph, Spouse of the Blessed Virgin.*
25 THE ANNUNCIATION of the B. V. or Lady Day.

APRIL.
23 *St. George, Martyr.*

MAY.
1 *SS. Philip & James.*
3 *The invention or finding of the cross.*

JUNE.
24 *The Nativity of St. John the Baptist.*
29 SS. PETER & PAUL.

JULY.
25 *St. James.*

26 *St. Ann, Mother of the Blessed Virgin.*

AUGUST.
10 *St. Lawrence, Mar.*
15 THE ASSUMPTION of the Blessed Virgin.
24 *St. Bartholomew.*

SEPTEMBER.
8 *The Nativity of the Blessed Virgin.*
21 *St. Matthew.*
29 *Michaelmas Day.*

OCTOBER.
28 *SS. Simon & Jude.*

NOVEMBER.
1 ALL SAINTS.
30 *St. Andrew.*

DECEMBER.
8 *The Immac. Conception of the B. Virgin.*
21 *St. Thomas.*
25 CHRISTMAS DAY.
26 *St. Stephen, Mar.*
27 *St. John.*
28 *Holy Innocents.*
29 *St. Thomas of Canterbury.*

MOVEABLE FEASTS.

Easter Sunday, *Monday*, and *Tuesday*.

Ascension Day, or the Thursday forty days after Easter.

Whitsunday, *Monday*, and *Tuesday*.

Corpus Christi, being the first Thursday after Trinity Sunday.

FASTING DAYS.

The forty days in Lent.

The Ember Days, at the four seasons, being the Wednesday, Friday, and Saturday of the first week in Lent, of Whitsun Week, of the third week in September, and of the third week in Advent.

The Vigils or Eves of Whitsunday, of Saints Peter and Paul, of the Assumption of the Blessed Virgin, of All Saints, and of Christmas Day.

All Wednesdays and Fridays in Advent.

N.B. When any fasting-day falls upon a Sunday, it is to be observed on the Saturday before. If the feast fall upon a Monday, that eve is kept upon Saturday.

ABSTINENCE DAYS.

The Sundays in Lent, unless leave be given to the contrary.

All the Fridays of the Year; but if Christmas Day fall upon Friday, it is not a day of abstinence.

N.B. That the Catholic Church commands all her children upon Sundays and Holidays of Obligation, to be present at the great Eucharistic Sacrifice, which we call the Mass, and to rest from servile work on those days, and to keep them holy.

2ndly, She commands them to abstain from flesh on all days of fasting and abstinence; and on fasting days to eat but one meal.

3rdly, She commands them to confess their sins to their pastors at least once a-year.

4thly, She commands them to receive the Blessed Sacrament at least once a-year, and that at Easter, viz., between Palm Sunday and Low Sunday.

The fourth Council of Lateran, Can. 21, ordains,—"That every one of the faithful of both sexes, after they come to the years of discretion, shall, in private, faithfully confess all their sins, at least once a-year, to their pastor; and take care to fulfil to the best of their power, the penance enjoined them: receiving reverently, at least at Easter, the Sacrament of the Eucharist, unless, perhaps by the counsel of their pastor, for some reasonable cause they judge it proper to abstain from it for a time; otherwise let them be excluded out of the Church whilst living, and when they die be deprived of Christian burial."

THE PAROCHIAL GARDEN OF THE SOUL.

ON PRAYER.

"Watch ye, and pray, that ye enter not into temptation." (Matt. xxvi. 41.)

"Is any of you sad? Let him pray. Pray for one another, that you may be saved; for the continual prayer of a just man availeth much." (St. James v. 13, 16.)

"Ask, and you shall receive; seek, and you shall find; knock, and it shall be opened to you." (Matt. vii. 7.)

"Daniel knelt down three times a day, and adored, and gave thanks before God." (Daniel vi. 10.)

"It is certain that there is no means of grace more generally useful than prayer; and therefore we ought to entertain a great esteem and love for it, and to use every endeavour to pray well." (St. Vincent of Paul.)

A MORNING EXERCISE.

At your first waking in the morning make the sign of the cross, saying, In the name of the Father, and of the Son, and of the Holy Ghost. Amen. Blessed be the holy and undivided Trinity, now and for ever. Amen. *Or repeat the following:* In the name of our Lord Jesus Christ crucified I arise; bless me, O Lord, defend me, preserve me, and keep me; and after this short and miserable pilgrimage bring me to life everlasting. Amen. *Then adore God, and make an offering of your whole being to him, for that day and for ever. Then say the following prayers.*

TAKE NOTICE.—If you have not time to say these prayers at home, then say the Our Father, Hail Mary, and Apostles' Creed, going to your work or at your work.

The Lord's Prayer.

OUR Father who art in heaven, hallowed be thy name: thy kingdom come: thy will be done on earth as it is in heaven. Give us this day our daily bread; and forgive us our trespasses, as we forgive them that trespass against us: and lead us not into temptation: but deliver us from evil. Amen.

The Angelic Salutation.

HAIL, Mary, full of grace, the Lord is with thee. Blessed art thou amongst women, and blessed is the fruit of thy womb, JESUS. Holy Mary, mother of God, pray for us sinners, now and at the hour of our death Amen.

The Apostles' Creed.

I BELIEVE in God the Father Almighty, Creator of heaven and earth. And in Jesus Christ his only Son our Lord, who was conceived by the Holy Ghost, born of the Virgin Mary; suffered under Pontius Pilate, was crucified, dead, and buried; he descended into hell, the third day he rose again from the dead; he ascended into heaven, and sitteth at the right hand of God the Father Almighty; from thence he shall come to judge the living and the dead. I believe in the Holy Ghost; the holy Catholic church; the communion of saints; the forgiveness of sins; the resurrection of the body, and life everlasting. Amen.

The Confiteor

I CONFESS to Almighty God, to blessed Mary, ever Virgin, to blessed Michael the Archangel, to blessed

John the Baptist, to the holy Apostles Peter and Paul, and to all the Saints, that I have sinned exceedingly in thought, word, and deed, through my fault, through my fault, through my most grievous fault: therefore I beseech the blessed Mary ever Virgin, blessed Michael the Archangel, blessed John the Baptist, the holy Apostles Peter and Paul, and all the Saints, to pray to the Lord our God for me.

May almighty God have mercy on us, and forgive us our sins, and bring us to life everlasting. Amen.

May the almighty and merciful Lord give us pardon, absolution, and remission of our sins. Amen.

An act of Faith of the presence of God.

O MY God, I firmly believe thou art here and perfectly seest me, and that thou observest all mine actions, all my thoughts, and the most secret motions of my heart. Canst thou suffer in thy holy presence a sinner, who hath so often offended thee? It is thy goodness and liberality which invite and command my poverty to come to thee. Give me grace therefore to pray as I ought.

Come, O Holy Spirit! fill the hearts of thy faithful, and kindle in them the fire of thy love.

V Send forth thy Spirit, and they shall be created.

R. And thou shalt renew the face of the earth.

Let us Pray.

O GOD, who hast taught the hearts of the faithful by the light of the Holy Spirit, grant that we may, by the gift of the same Spirit, be always truly wise, and ever rejoice in his consolations. Through Jesus Christ our Lord. Amen.

An Act of Adoration and Thanksgiving.

O MY God, I adore thee as my Creator and my sovereign Good: and with all possible thanksgiving I acknowledge the many benefits which thou hast conferred upon me, in relation both to body and soul. Thou hast created me out of nothing; redeemed me by the death of thy Son; sanctified me by the grace of thy Holy Spirit; preserved me from an infinity of dangers, and from hell fire, which I deserved by my sins. Thou knowest that I am an unprofitable and an ungrateful servant, nevertheless thou hast all this time had patience with me; thou hast preserved me the night past, and given me this present day, that I may labour with more care and diligence than I have hitherto done, to obtain the crown of immortal glory, which thy goodness hath prepared for me. O my God, how good thou art towards me! What return can I make for such innumerable benefits? I will bless thy holy name, and serve thee all the days of my life.

Here let us renew our sorrow for the sins of our past lives, and make resolutions against the temptations and dangerous occasions we may perhaps meet with during the day.

An Act of Contrition with good Resolutions.

O MY God, how ill have I hitherto lived! How little have I done for thee! I am heartily sorry I have spent and lost that time in offending thee, which thine infinite goodness gave me to be employed in thy service, in advancing the good of my soul, and in purchasing everlasting life. I detest all the sins which I have committed against thy divine Majesty. I am sorry that I have offended thee, because thou art infinitely good, and sin is infinitely displeasing to thee. I love thee with my whole heart and soul, and I firmly purpose, by the help of thy grace, to serve thee more faithfully for the future. Receive, I beseech thee, the remainder of my life: I renew my promises made in baptism; I renounce the devil, his works, and all his pomps; I now begin and will endeavour to spend this day according to thy holy will, both as to the nature and circumstances of mine actions, performing them so as they may be pleasing to thee. I will take particular care to avoid the failings to which I am subject, and to exercise the virtues which are most agreeable to my state and employment.

An Oblation.

I OFFER to thee, O my God, the life and death of thine only Son; and with them these mine affections and resolutions, my thoughts, words, deeds, and sufferings of this day, and of all my life, in honour of thine adorable Majesty, in thanksgiving for all thy benefits, in satisfaction for my sins, and to obtain the assistance of thy grace; that, persevering to the end in doing thy holy will, I may love and enjoy thee for ever in thy glory.

A Petition.

THOU knowest, O God, how weak and unable I am to do good. Leave me not to myself, but take me into thy protection, and give me grace faithfully to comply with these holy resolutions. Enlighten mine understanding with a lively faith, raise up my will to a firm hope, and inflame it with an ardent charity.

Strengthen my weakness, and cure the corruption of my heart; grant that overcoming mine enemies, both visible and invisible, I may make good use of thy grace, and vouchsafe to add to these blessings the inestimable gift of final perseverance.

V. To thee, O Lord, I have lifted up my voice.

R. And early in the morning my prayer shall come before thee.

V. Let my mouth be ever filled with thy praises.

R. That I may publish thy glory, and all the day thy greatness.

V. Turn away thy face, O Lord, from my sins.

R. And blot out all mine iniquities.

V. Create in me a clean heart, O God.

R. And renew a right spirit within me.

V. Cast me not out of thy sight.

R. And take not thy Holy Spirit from me.

V. Restore to me the joy of thy saving mercy.

R. And strengthen me with a perfect Spirit.

V. Our help is in the name of our Lord.

R. Who made heaven and earth.

V. Vouchsafe, O Lord, this day,

R. To keep us from all sin.

V. Have mercy on us, O Lord.

R. Have mercy on us.

V. Let thy mercy, O Lord, be poured upon us.

R. According to the hopes we have placed in thee.

V. O Lord, hear my prayer.

R. Let my supplication come to thee.

Let us Pray.

ALMIGHTY Lord and God, who has brought us to the beginning of this day, let thy powerful grace so conduct us through it, that we may not fall into any sins, but that all our thoughts, words, and actions may be regulated according to the rules of thy heavenly justice, and tend to the observance of thy holy law: Through the merits of Jesus Christ our Lord. Amen.

Let us Pray.

LORD God, and King of heaven and earth, vouchsafe this day to rule and sanctify, to direct and govern our souls and bodies, our senses, words, and actions in a conformity to thy law, and a strict obedience to thy commands; that by the help of thy grace, O Saviour of the world, we may be fenced and freed from all evils, both now and for ever Amen.

Let us Pray.

O GOD, who out of thy unspeakable providence, art pleased to appoint the holy angels for our guardians, give ear to the supplications which we make for a continuance of their protection, and that we may be added to their joyful number for all eternity. Amen.

O blessed Virgin Mary, unspotted Mother of my God and Saviour Jesus Christ, be thou a mother to me, since thy adorable Son has been pleased to call us all his brethren, and to recommend us all to thee, in the person of his beloved disciple, *John*, xix. 26. Take me and mine under thy holy protection, and continually represent to the eternal Father in our behalf the merits of the death and passion of thy Son.

O all you glorious angels and saints, and you in particular, my holy patrons N. and N., happy citizens of the heavenly Sion, pray for us poor children of Eve to our common Lord, by the merits of our common Mediator, that we may ever love him and serve him here, till we come with you to love, praise, and enjoy him for all eternity.

O angel of God, who, by divine appointment, art my Guardian, to watch over me in all my ways, be pleased this day to illuminate, preserve, rule, and govern me, whom the goodness of our God has committed to thy charge, and to defend me from all the powers of darkness.

May our Lord bless us, and preserve us from all evils, and bring us to life everlasting; and may the souls of the faithful, through the mercy of God, rest in peace.

The Angelus Domini.

In Catholic countries, and in some parts again of England (after being discontinued for three hundred years) the church-bell is solemnly rung three times every day, morning, noon, and night, and each time, in memory of our Saviour's becoming Man for our salvation, is said,—

1. THE angel of the Lord declared unto Mary, and she conceived of the Holy Ghost. *Hail Mary, &c.* 2. Behold the handmaid of the Lord, may it be done unto me according to thy word. *Hail Mary, &c.* 3. And

the Word was made flesh, and dwelt among us. *Hail Mary, &c.*

Let us Pray.

POUR forth, we beseech thee, O Lord, thy grace into our hearts, that we, to whom the incarnation of Christ thy Son was made known by the message of an angel, may, by his passion and cross, be brought to the glory of his resurrection, through the same Christ our Lord. Amen.

GRACE BEFORE MEALS.

BLESS us, O Lord, and these thy gifts, which we are about to receive of thy bounty. Through Jesus Christ our Lord. Amen.

GRACE AFTER MEALS.

WE give thee thanks, Almighty God, for all thy benefits, who livest and reignest world without end. Amen.

OCCASIONAL PRAYERS.

FOR THE HOLY CATHOLIC CHURCH.

DEFEND, O Lord, thy servants, we beseech thee, from all dangers both of body and soul; and, by the intercession of the blessed and glorious Virgin Mary, Mother of God, of the blessed Apostles Peter and Paul, of blessed N., and of all thy saints, mercifully grant us the blessings of peace and safety; that all adversities and errors being removed, thy Church may freely and securely serve thee. Through our Lord, &c.

FOR THE POPE.

O GOD, the Pastor and Governor of all the faithful, mercifully look upon thy servant N., whom thou hast been pleased to appoint the pastor of thy Church; grant, we beseech thee, that both by word and example he may edify those over whom he is set; and, together with the flock committed to his care, may attain everlasting life. Through, &c.

FOR THE TEMPTED AND AFFLICTED.

O GOD, who justifiest the ungodly that repent, and wouldst not the death of a sinner; we humbly entreat thy majesty to protect thy servants with thy heavenly assistance, who trust in thy mercy, and preserve them by thy continual protection; that they may constantly serve thee, and by no temptation be separated from thee; through, &c.

FOR PERSEVERANCE IN GOODNESS.

GRANT, O my Lord Jesus Christ, that I may persevere in good purposes, and in thy holy service, to my death; and that I may this day perfectly begin, for all I have hitherto done is nothing. Amen.

A SHORT RECOMMENDATION TO GOD.

INTO the hands of thy unspeakable mercy, O Lord, I commend my soul and body; my senses, my words, my thoughts, and all my actions, with all the necessities of my body and soul; my going forth and coming in; my faith and conversation; the course and end of my life; the day and hour of my death; my rest and resurrection with the saints and elect. Amen.

INSTRUCTIONS AND DEVOTIONS

for

Hearing Mass.

INSTRUCTIONS.

Man has at all times been required to dedicate one day in seven in an especial manner to the worship of his Maker. Under the Jewish dispensation this was the Sabbath or seventh day of the week; but under the New Law the obligation has been transferred from the Sabbath to the Sunday. The Church of God has also, by virtue of the power given to her by Jesus Christ, appointed certain other days in the year to be kept holy; and, to the end that we may duly comply with these obligations, she earnestly exhorts all the faithful to assist at the whole of the public service, and *commands* their attendance at the adorable sacrifice of the altar, on all Sundays and Holydays. The Christian, who reflects that the object of these sacred ordinances is the attainment of eternal salvation, will need no other motive to attend to the short instructions contained in the three following sections; in the *first of* which he will be taught *what the Mass is, and for what ends it is offered:* in the *second* he will be instructed in the *public ceremonies* of the Church, chiefly as they relate to the holy sacrifice: and in the *third* he will find *devotions at Mass.*

SECT. I.

What the Mass is, and for what ends it is to be offered.

1. From the beginning of the world the servants of God were always accustomed to offer *sacrifice* to him, by way of acknowledging his sovereignty, and paying their homage to him: and in all ancient religions, true or false, this worship of *sacrifice* was always looked upon as a most solemn act of religion, due to the deity that they worshipped.

2. In the law of nature, and in the law of Moses, there was a great variety of sacrifices: some bloody, in which the victim was slain, others unbloody: some were called *holocausts* or *whole burnt-offerings,* in which the whole host or victim was consumed in fire upon God's altar, for his *honour* and *glory;* others were called *sin-offerings,* which were offered for *sins;* others were offerings of *thanksgiving;* others, in fine, were *pacific* or *peace-offerings,* which were offered for obtaining favours of God; the word *peace,* in the scripture style, signifying all manner of good and prosperity.

3. All these sacrifices of the law of nature, and of the law of *Moses,* were of themselves but

weak and needy elements, and only figures of a sacrifice to come, *viz.* that of *Jesus Christ;* in consideration of which sacrifice only, and of the *faith* of the offerers, by which they believed in the Redeemer to come, those ancient sacrifices were then accepted by the divine Majesty, when they were accompanied with the inward sacrifice of the heart: but not for any intrinsic worth or dignity of the things offered; for no other blood but the blood of *Christ* could wash away our sins.—Hence in the 39th *Psalm* spoken in the person of *Christ* to his Father, we read, *Sacrifice and oblation thou didst not desire, but a body thou hast fitted to me.*—(So St. Paul reads it, *Heb*. x. 5.) *Burnt-offering and sin-offering thou didst not require: then said I, Behold I come:* to give us to understand, that by reason of the insufficiency of the sacrifices of the old law, *Christ* himself would come to be our sacrifice, and would offer up his own body and blood for us.

4. Accordingly our Saviour *Jesus Christ*, at the time appointed by his Father, having taken flesh for us, was pleased to offer himself a sacrifice for us all, dying upon the cross for the sins of the whole world. By this *one* offering we were completely redeemed, inasmuch as our ransom was paid, and all mercy, grace, and salvation were purchased for us. Neither can there now be any need of his dying any more, or purchasing any other graces for us than those for which he has already paid the price of his blood.

5. Nevertheless, for the daily *application* of this one eternal redemption to our soul, and that the mercy, grace, and salvation, which he

has purchased for us, may be actually communicated to us, he not only continually appears in our behalf in the sanctuary of heaven, there representing and offering to his Father his death and passion for us; but he also instituted the *blessed Eucharist*, the night before his passion, in which he has bequeathed us his body and blood under the sacramental veils, not only to be received by us as a *sacrament*, for the food and nourishment of our souls; but also to be offered and presented by his ministers to his Father (mystically broken and shed) as a sacrifice: not by way of a new death, but by way of a standing *memorial* of his death; a daily celebration and representation of his death to God, and an application to our souls of the fruits of it.

6. This Eucharistic sacrifice of the body and blood of *Christ*, daily offered under the forms of *bread* and *wine*, in remembrance of his passion, is what we call the *Mass*. This is the solemn liturgy of the Catholic Church. This is that *pure offering* which is made to God *in every place* among the Gentiles according to the prophecy of *Malachy*, i. 10, 11. By this *Christ* is a priest for ever according to the order of *Melchisedec*, Ps. cix. whose sacrifice was bread and wine, *Gen.* xv.

7. This sacrifice of the mass is the same in substance with that which *Christ* offered for us upon the cross; because both the *Victim offered*, and the priest, or *principal Offerer*, is the same *Jesus Christ*. The difference is only in the manner of the offering; because, upon the cross, our Saviour offered himself in such a manner, as really to shed his blood and die for

us; whereas now he does not really shed his blood, or die any more. And therefore this is called an *unbloody sacrifice;* and that of the cross a *bloody sacrifice.*

8. By reason of this near alliance which this sacrifice of the mass has with the sacrifice of the cross, it completely answers all the different ends of sacrifice, and that in a manner infinitely more perfect than any of the ancient sacrifices. *Christ* is here both Priest and Victim, representing in Person, and offering up his death and passion to his Father: First, for the *adoration,* praise, honour, and glory of the Divine Majesty. Secondly, in *thanksgiving* for all his benefits. Thirdly, for obtaining pardon for our sins. Fourthly, for obtaining *grace* and salvation for us, by the merits of that same death and passion. And therefore this sacrifice, in order to all these ends, must be infinitely beyond all the *holocausts, thank-offerings, sin-offerings,* and *peace-offerings* of the ancient law.

9. This sacrifice of the mass, then, is offered up to God, in the Catholic Church, *First,* as a daily *remembrance* of the passion of *Christ: Do this for a commemoration of me, St. Luke,* xxii. *Secondly,* As a most solemn *worship* of the Divine Majesty. *Thirdly,* As a most acceptable *thanksgiving* to God, from whence it has the name of *Eucharist. Fourthly,* As a most powerful means to move God to show mercy to us in the *forgiveness of our sins;* for which reason we call it *propitiatory.* And, *lastly,* As a most effectual way to *obtain* of God all that we want, coming to him (as we here do) with *Christ* and through *Christ.*

10. For these ends both priest and people

ought to offer up the sacrifice of the mass: the priest, as *Christ's* minister, and in his person; and the people by the hands of the priest; and both the one and the other by the hands of the great High Priest *Jesus Christ*. And with this offering of *Christ's*, both the one and the other ought to make a total offering of themselves also by his hands, and in union with him.

11. Hence the best devotion for hearing mass, is that which has for its object the passion of *Christ*, and which tends to unite the soul to *Christ*, and through him to his Father; and which most perfectly answers all the other ends of this sacrifice, *viz.* the adoration of God, thanksgiving for all his benefits, the obtaining of pardon for all our sins, and grace in all our necessities.

SECT. II.

The Public Ceremonies of the Church.

Although the homage, which man owes to his Creator, so essentially consists in the interior dispositions of the soul, that without these all outward worship is unprofitable and vain, yet the constitution of our nature is such as to require external signs and ceremonies, which may operate through the medium of the bodily senses upon our souls, and elevate them to God. To this end, then, are directed all the ceremonies of the Church, and it is the Christian's duty to learn to use them accordingly. Hence,

1. The custom of placing a vessel containing *blessed* or HOLY WATER at the entrance of the Church has been handed down to us from the

Apostolic age. Into this the faithful dip the fingers of the right hand, and form upon themselves the sign of the cross, repeating at the same time the invocation of the ever-blessed Trinity. As *water* denotes purity and innocence, by using it on entering the place of worship, we are admonished with what cleanliness of heart and hand we should appear in the presence of our Maker.

2. The SIGN OF THE CROSS, which we make upon ourselves in using holy water as well as on many other occasions, is a sign or ceremony in which with St. Paul [Gal. vi. 14.] we should place our greatest happiness and glory, as being a striking memorial of the sufferings and death of our Redeemer, that mystery whence are derived all our hopes for mercy, grace, and salvation. By the words that accompany this ceremony we are no less forcibly reminded that the God whom we serve, although *one* in nature, exists in *three persons* really distinct from each other.

3. The first object that arrests the Christian's notice on entering the Church, is the *altar* with its *tabernacle* and *crucifix*. The ALTAR is the place of sacrifice—as it were another *Calvary*, whereon is celebrated, as Christ ordained, the memorial of his passion and death by the clean and unbloody sacrifice of his body and blood. Upon the altar we always have a CRUCIFIX, or image of our Saviour upon the cross, that, as the Mass is said in remembrance of Christ's passion and death, both priest and people may have before their eyes, during this sacrifice, the image which puts them in mind of his passion and death.—The TABERNACLE contains certain

particles of the consecrated species. It is to Jesus Christ, therefore, truly present within the tabernacle that we *bend the knee* in homage and adoration, when we enter or depart from the Church.

4. With regard to the VESTMENTS in which the priest says mass, we must observe, that, as the mass represents the passion of *Christ*, and the priest there officiates in *his* person, so these vestments in which he officiates, represent those with which *Christ* was ignominiously clothed at the time of his passion. Thus the *Amice* represents the cloth or rag, with which the *Jews* muffled our Saviour's face, when at every blow they bid him prophesy who it was that struck him. St. Luke, xxii. 64. The *Alb* represents the white garment with which he was vested by *Herod*. The *Girdle*, *Maniple*, and *Stole*, represent the cords and bands with which he was bound in the different stages of his passion. The *Chasuble*, or outward vestment, represents the purple garment with which he was clothed as a mock King: upon the back of which there is a cross, to represent that which *Christ* bore on his sacred shoulders: Lastly, the priest's *Tonsure* or crown, is to represent the crown of thorns which our Saviour wore.

Moreover, as in the old law, the priests, that were wont to officiate in the sacred functions, had, by the appointment of God, *vestments* assigned for that purpose, as well for the greater decency and solemnity of the divine worship, as to signify and represent the virtues which God required of his ministers: so it was proper, that, in the church of the *New Testament*, *Christ's* ministers should in their sacred functions be distinguished, in like manner, from the laity by their sacred vestments: which might also represent the virtues which God requires in them. Thus the *Amice,* which is first put upon the head, represents divine *hope,* which the apostle calls the *helmet of salvation;* the *Alb, innocence of life;* the *Girdle,* (with which the loins are begirt,) *purity and chastity;* the *Maniple,* (which is put on the left arm) *patient suffering* of the labours of this mortal life; the *Stole,* the sweet *yoke* of *Christ,* to be borne in this life, in order to a happy immortality; in fine, the *Chasuble,* which is uppermost, and covers all the rest, represents the virtue of *charity.*

In these vestments the Church makes use of five colours, *viz.* the *white* on the feasts of our Lord, of the B. Virgin, of the angels, and of the saints that were not martyrs; the *red* on the feasts of Pentecost, of the finding and the exaltation of the cross, and of the apostles and martyrs; the *purple,* which is the penitential colour, in the penitential times of *Advent* and *Lent,* and upon *Vigils* and *Ember-days;* the *green* on most of the other *Sundays* and *Ferias* throughout the year; and the *black* on *Good-Friday,* and in the masses for the dead.

5. There are always LIGHTED CANDLES upon the altar during mass, as well to honour the victory and triumph of our Great King by these lights, which are tokens of our joy and of his glory, as to denote the light of faith with which we are to approach to him.

6. A small BELL is rung occasionally during mass. This serves to give notice to such as cannot see the altar, of certain more solemn

parts of the sacrifice, to recall the wandering mind from distraction, and to excite all to greater fervour of devotion.

7. *Incense*, which is used in solemn or high masses, is symbolical of prayer, according to that of holy David; *Let my prayer, O Lord, be directed as incense in thy sight.*

SECT. III.

The Manner of hearing Mass.

When you are going to hear mass, let your first care be to endeavour to recollect yourself, as well as you can, by calling home your wandering thoughts, and taking them off from all other business and concerns. Imagine that you hear within you the sweet voice of your Saviour, inviting you to come to his sacrifice, and to unite yourself to him.

In your way to the church or chapel, put yourself in spirit in the company of the blessed Virgin, and the other pious women going to mount *Calvary*, to be present at the passion and death of our Lord. Represent your Saviour as carrying his cross before you, to be immolated thereon for your sins, and bewail these sins of yours, as the causes of all his sufferings.

When you enter the church or chapel, humble yourself profoundly in the presence of God, whose house you come into; and if the blessed sacrament be kept there, adore your Saviour upon your bended knees. At taking of holy water, make the sign of the cross upon yourself, beg pardon for your sins, and humbly crave that you may be washed and cleansed from them by the blood of the Lamb.

Choose, as much as you can, a place to kneel in, where you may be most recollected, and least disturbed. There represent to yourself, by a lively faith, the majesty of God, and humbly beg his mercy and grace, that you may assist at this tremendous sacrifice in the manner you ought.

PRAYERS BEFORE MASS.*

IN the name of the Father, and of the Son, and of the Holy Ghost. *Amen.*

Come, O Holy Spirit, fill the hearts of thy faithful, and kindle in them the fire of thy love.

Send forth thy Spirit, and our hearts will be regenerated.

And thou wilt renew the face of the earth.

Let us Pray.

O ALMIGHTY and eternal God, who hast appointed us six days in which we may labour, and hast consecrated the seventh to thyself; grant, we beseech thee, that according as thou hast commanded, we may sanctify this day, by devoting it entirely to thy love and service. Mercifully forgive us all our past neglect in this kind; pardon the

* Some of these prayers are also said at the afternoon or evening service occasionally.

sins we have been guilty of during the course of the week; and give us grace to avoid them for the future. Through Jesus Christ our Lord. Amen.

O Lord, open thou our lips,
And our mouth shall declare thy praise.
Let us adore the Lord of glory.
Let us adore the God of our salvation.

The King of heaven inviteth us and graciously calleth us into his sacred presence; to Him we owe all the days of our lives; let us give this day at least to his service.

Let us adore the Lord of glory.

The angels are always assembled in their choirs above; the Saints join their hymns; behold now the Church also prepareth her solemn offices, and summoneth all her children to bring in their tribute of prayer and praise.

Let us adore the God of our Salvation.

Come, let us rejoice before the Lord; let us sing joyfully to God our Saviour: let us make haste to approach his presence, and proclaim his praises; for the Lord is a great God, and a great King above all gods: in his hands are all the ends of the earth.

Let us adore the God that made us.

Let us adore and fall down before the Lord, who created us; for he is the Lord our God, and we are his people, and the sheep of his pasture.

Let us adore and fall down before him.

To-day, If ye shall hear his voice, harden not your hearts, but listen awfully to his word, and bend your knees before his holy altar.

We will adore the Lord of glory; we will worship the God of our Salvation.

Glory be to the Father, &c.

As it was in the beginning, &c.

Our Father, who art in heaven, hallowed be thy name. Thy kingdom come. Thy will be done on earth as it is in heaven.

Give us this day our daily bread. And forgive us our trespasses, as we forgive them that trespass against us. And lead us not into temptation, but deliver us from evil. Amen.

Let us Pray.

O ALMIGHTY and eternal God, grant to us the increase of Faith, Hope, and Charity; and that we may deserve to obtain what thou promisest, make us to love what thou commandest. Through Christ our Lord. *Amen.*

An Act of Faith.

WE firmly believe there is one God, and that in this one God there are three persons, the Father, the Son, and the Holy Ghost; that the Son took to himself the nature of man from the Virgin Mary's womb, by the operation of the power of the Holy Ghost, and that in this our human nature, he was crucified and died for us; that afterwards he rose again, and ascended up into heaven, from whence he shall come to repay the just everlasting glory, and the wicked everlasting punishment. Moreover, we believe whatsoever else the Catholic Church proposeth to be believed, and this because God, who is the Sovereign Truth, which can neither deceive nor be deceived, hath revealed all these things to this his church.

O God, we believe, do thou strengthen our Faith.

An Act of Hope.

O GOD, relying on thine almighty power, and thine infinite mercy and goodness, and because thou art faithful to thy promises, we trust in thee that thou wilt grant us forgiveness of our sins, through the merits of Jesus Christ thy Son; and that thou wilt give us the assistance of thy grace, with which we may labour to continue to the end in the diligent exercise of all good works, and may deserve to obtain the glory which thou hast promised in heaven.

We hope in thee, O Lord; let us never be confounded.

An Act of Charity.

O LORD, our God, we love thee with our whole hearts, and above all things, because thou, O God, art the sovereign good, and for thine own infinite perfections, art most worthy of all love; and for thy sake, we also love our neighbours as ourselves.

We love thee, O God, with our whole hearts, and for thy sake we love our neighbours as ourselves.

An Act of Contrition.

O GOD, for the sake of thy sovereign goodness and infinite perfections, which we love above all things, we are exceedingly sorry from the bottom of our hearts, and are grieved for having offended, by our sins, this thine infinite goodness; and we firmly resolve, by the assistance of thy grace, never more to offend thee for the time to come, and carefully to avoid the occasions of sin.

We are sorry, O Lord, for our sins, we resolve never more to offend thee.

Let us offer up our prayers in behalf of those who are visited with sickness, and of those especially who are members of this congregation.

Heal thy servants, O Lord, that are sick, and put their trust in thee.

Send them help, O Lord, and comfort from thy holy place.

Let us pray.

O ALMIGHTY and everlasting God, the eternal salvation of those who believe in thee, hear us in behalf of thy servants that are sick, for whom we humbly crave the help of thy mercy; that their health, if thou seest good, being restored to them, they may render thanks to thee in thy church; through Jesus Christ our Lord. *Amen.*

Let us pray for his or her Majesty, N. and all the Royal Family.

V. O Lord, save the king, (or queen.) R. And hear us in the day that we shall call upon thee.

Prayer.

O GOD, by whom kings reign, and the princes of the earth exercise their power; O God, who art the strength and support of those kingdoms that serve thee; mercifully hear our prayers, and defend thy servant N. our queen from all dangers: and grant that her safety may conduce to the peace and welfare of thy people. Through, &c.

Let us offer up our prayers for the repose of the souls of the faithful departed, particularly for those of our deceased parents, relations, and friends, and for those who have been members of this congregation.

Psalm cxxix. De profundis.

OUT of the depths I have cried to thee, O Lord. Lord, hear my voice.

Let thine ears be attentive to the voice of my supplication.

If thou, O Lord, wilt mark iniquities, Lord, who shall stand it?

For with thee there is merciful forgiveness: and by reason of thy law I waited for thee, O Lord.

My soul hath relied on his word; my soul hath hoped in the Lord.

From the morning watch even until night, let Israel hope in the Lord.

Because with the Lord there is mercy, and with him plentiful redemption.

And he shall redeem Israel from all his iniquities.

Eternal rest, &c.

Let us pray.

O GOD, the Creator and Redeemer of all the faithful, grant to the souls of thy servants departed the remission of all their sins, that through pious supplications they may obtain that pardon which they have always desired; who livest and reignest with God the Father, in the unity of the Holy Ghost, God, world without end. *Amen.*

An Oblation.

AND now, O Almighty Father, behold we thy people presume to appear before thee this day to offer up to thee by the hands of thy Minister, and by the hands of our great High Priest, Jesus Christ thy Son, the unbloody sacrifice of his body and blood, as a perpetual commemoration of his death and passion. United therefore with this our great Mediator, and with his whole Church of Heaven and Earth, we offer to thee, O Holy Lord, Almighty Father, and Eternal God, this pure sacrifice and spotless victim.

First—For thine own honour, praise, adoration, and glory. Prostrate before thee, sensible of our own unworthiness, and conscious of our absolute dependence on thee, we hereby acknowledge thee as the great arbiter of life and death: we adore thee as the supreme Ruler of us and of all things.

Secondly—Calling to mind with the greatest gratitude the innumerable benefits we have received from thy bounty in our creation, redemption, and preservation, we here offer thee in return this pure oblation, as a sacrifice of thanksgiving for all thy mercies and blessings bestowed upon us and upon all thy creatures.

Thirdly—O God, the consciousness of our manifold crimes forces us to confess our unworthiness to appear before thee. But is not Jesus the propitiation not only for our sins, but for those of the whole world? Him then we offer to thee, who hath cancelled the hand writing that was against us, and whose blood is sufficient to wash away the sins of a thousand worlds, that through him we may obtain mercy, pardon, and full remission of all our crimes.

Fourthly—Acknowledging that nothing is granted by thee to man, but through the merits of the passion and death of thy Son; we here offer thee this same victim of our redemption, for obtaining all those graces and blessings of which we stand so much in need.

For these ends, O eternal Father, graciously accept of the offering which we are preparing to make unto thee. Oh, be thou pleased to assist us in such a manner by thy grace, that we may conduct ourselves this day as we ought to do in thy divine presence, and that we may so commemorate the death and passion of thy divine Son, as to partake most plentifully of the fruits of this holy sacrifice. Through our Lord Jesus Christ thy Son, who, with thee and the Holy Ghost, liveth and reigneth world without end. *Amen.*

Here the Epistle and Gospel may be read in English, and the sermon or lecture made.

A Prayer before the Instructions.

O INCOMPREHENSIBLE Creator, the true fountain of light, and only author of all knowledge, vouchsafe, we beseech thee, to enlighten our understandings, and to remove from us all darkness of sin and ignorance. Thou, who makest eloquent the tongues of those that want utterance, direct our tongues and pour on our lips the grace of thy blessing. Give us a diligent and obedient spirit, quickness of apprehension, capacity of retaining, and the powerful assistance of thy holy grace: that what we hear we may apply to thy honour and the eternal salvation of our own souls, through Jesus Christ our Lord. Amen.

A Prayer after the Instructions.

STRENGTHEN our minds, we beseech thee, O Lord, with the power of thy grace; that as we have now heard what our duty is, we may be enabled to accomplish it, through Christ our Lord. Amen.

A Prayer to be said by the Priest immediately before Mass.

AND now, O God, calling to mind, with the greatest gratitude, the blessed passion of thy Son Christ our Lord, as also his resurrection from the dead, and his glorious ascension into heaven; we prepare to offer to thy divine Majesty a pure, holy, and spotless victim; for so thou hast ordained it; the holy bread of eternal life and the cup of our salvation. Look down therefore upon them, O Lord, with a propitious and serene countenance, and accept them, as thou wast pleased to accept the offerings of thy righteous servant Abel, and the sacrifice of our father Abraham, and that which thy high priest Melchisedech offered to thee, a holy sacrifice and a spotless victim. Amen.

A SHORT EXPLANATION.

From the Catechism.

What is the Mass?—It is the unbloody sacrifice of the Body and Blood of Christ.

What are the ends for which this sacrifice is offered?—1st, For God's honour and glory; 2nd, As a thanksgiving for all His benefits; 3rd, For obtaining pardon of our sins; and 4th, For obtaining all graces and blessings through Jesus Christ.

Is it not also a memorial of the Passion and Death of our Lord?—Yes; for Christ, at His last Supper, commanded it to be offered in remembrance of Him.

How should we hear Mass?—With great attention and devotion.

ON ENTERING A CHURCH,

Take holy water, bless yourself, and say,

CLEANSE me, O Lord, from my sins; in the name of the Father, ✠ and of the Son, and of the Holy Ghost. Amen.

THE ASPERGES.

BEFORE HIGH MASS ON SUNDAYS.

Ant. Asperges me, Domine, hyssopo, et mundabor: lavabis me, et super nivem dealbabor.

Ps. Miserere mei Deus, secundum magnam misericordiam tuam.

V. Gloria, &c.

Ant. Asperges me, &c.

Ant. Thou shalt sprinkle me with hyssop, O Lord, and I shall be cleansed; thou shalt wash me, and I shall be made whiter than snow.

Ps. Have mercy on me, O God, according to thy great mercy.

V. Glory, &c.

Ant. Thou shalt sprinkle me, &c.

The Priest returning to the foot of the Altar, says:

V. Ostende nobis, Domine, misericordiam tuam.

R. Et salutare tuum da nobis.

V. Domine, exaudi orationem meam.

R. Et clamor meus ad te veniat.

V. Dominus vobiscum.

V. Shew us, O Lord, thy mercy

R. And grant us thy salvation.

V. O Lord, hear my prayer.

R. And let my cry come unto thee.

V. The Lord be with you.

THE ASPERGES.

R. Et cum spiritu tuo.

R. And with thy spirit.

Oremus.

Let us Pray.

Exaudi nos, Domine sancte, Pater omnipotens, æterne Deus: et mittere digneris sanctum angelum tuum de cœlis, qui custodiat, foveat, protegat, visitet atque defendat omnes habitantes in hoc habitaculo. Per Christum Dominum nostrum.

Graciously hear us, O holy Lord, Father Almighty, Eternal God: and vouchsafe to send thy holy angel from heaven, who may keep, cherish, protect, visit and defend all who dwell in this habitation. Through Christ our Lord.

R. Amen.

R. Amen.

From Easter to Whitsunday inclusively, instead of the foregoing Anthem, *the following is sung, and* Alleluia *is added to the* V. (Ostende nobis), *and also to its* R. (Et Salutare.)

Ant. Vidi aquam egredientem de templo, a latere dextro, Alleluia: et omnes ad quos pervenit aqua ista, salvi facti sunt, et dicent: Alleluia.

Ant. I saw water coming forth from the temple, on the right side, Alleluia: and all those to whom this water came, were saved, and shall say, Alleluia.

Ps. Confitemini Domino, quoniam bonus: quoniam in sæculum misericordia ejus.

Ps. Give praise to the Lord, for he is good: for his mercy endureth for ever.

V. Gloria, &c.

V. Glory, &c.

Ant. Vidi aquam.

Ant. I saw water.

DEVOTIONS FOR MASS.

In the name of the Father, and of the Son, and of the Holy Ghost. Amen.

✠

Prayer at the beginning of Mass.

O ALMIGHTY Lord of heaven and earth, behold I, a wretched sinner, presume to appear before thee this day, to offer up to thee by the hands of our High Priest, Jesus Christ, thy Son, the sacrifice of his body and the sacrifice which he offered to thee upon the cross: first, for thine own honour, praise, adoration, and glory; secondly, in remembrance of his death and passion; thirdly, in thanksgiving for all thy blessings bestowed on him and on his whole church, whether triumphant in heaven or militant on earth, and especially for those bestowed on me, the most unworthy of all;

fourthly, for obtaining pardon and remission of all my sins, and of those of all others, whether living or dead, for whom I ought to pray; and lastly, for obtaining all graces and blessings both for myself and for thy whole church. Oh! be thou pleased to assist me in such manner by thy grace, that I may behave myself this day as I ought to do in thy divine presence, and that I may so commemorate the death and passion of thy Son, as to partake most plentifully of the fruits of it. Through the same Jesus Christ our Lord.

At the Confiteor.

O BLESSED Trinity, one God, Father, Son, and Holy Ghost, prostrate in spirit before thee, I here confess, in the sight of the whole court of heaven, and of all thy faithful, mine innumerable treasons against thy divine Majesty. I have sinned, O Lord, I have sinned: I have grievously offended thee through the whole course of my life, in thought, word, and deed; and therefore am most unworthy to lift mine eyes to heaven, or so much as to name thy sacred name: how much more am I unworthy to appear here in thy sanctuary, and to assist among thine angels at these heavenly mysteries, which require so much purity; because Jesus Christ himself is here in person both Priest and Victim! But, O my God! thy mercies are above all thy works, and thou wilt not despise a contrite and humble heart: and therefore I here venture to come into thy temple, and with the poor publican, and, as I hope, with the same penitential spirit, I strike my breast and say, O God, be merciful to me a sinner, O God, be merciful to me a sinner, O God, be merciful to me a sinner. And I humbly hope to find this mercy which I crave, through that passion and death which is here celebrated. O fountain of mercy, grant this mercy to me and to all poor sinners. Amen.

When the Priest goes up to the Altar.

TAKE away from us, we beseech thee, O Lord, our iniquities, that we may be worthy to enter with pure minds into the holy of holies, through Christ our Lord. Amen.

At the Introit.

GRANT, O Lord, that we may be truly prepared for offering this great Sacrifice to thee this day: and because our sins alone can render us displeasing to thee, therefore we cry aloud to thee for mercy. Glory be to the Father, &c.

DEVOTIONS FOR MASS.

At the Kyrie Eleison.

Have mercy on me, O Lord, and forgive me all my sins.

Have mercy on me, O Lord, have mercy on me.

GLORIA IN EXCELSIS.

GLORIA in excelsis Deo, et in terrâ pax hominibus bonæ voluntatis. Laudamus te, benedicimus te, adoramus te, glorificamus te. Gratias agimus tibi propter magnam gloriam tuam. Domine

GLORY be to God on high, and on earth peace to men of good will. We praise thee, we bless thee, we adore thee, we glorify thee. We give thee thanks for thy great glory, O Lord God, heavenly King, God

Deus, Rex cœlestis, Deus Pater omnipotens. Domine Fili unigenite Jesu Christe. Domine Deus, Agnus Dei, Filius Patris, qui tollis peccata mundi, miserere nobis. Qui tollis peccata mundi, suscipe deprecationem nostram. Qui sedes ad dexteram Patris, miserere nobis. Quoniam Tu solus sanctus, Tu solus Dominus, Tu solus altissimus, Jesu Christe, cum Sancto Spiritu, in

the Father Almighty. O Lord Jesus Christ, the only-begotten Son, O Lord God, Lamb of God, Son of the Father, who takest away the sins of the world, have mercy on us. Who takest away the sins of the world, receive our prayers. Who sittest at the right hand of the Father, have mercy on us. For Thou only art holy, Thou only art the Lord, Thou only, O Jesus Christ,

gloriâ Dei Patris. Amen.

together with the Holy Ghost, art most high in the glory of God the Father. Amen.

[The *Gloria in Excelsis* is omitted in Masses for the Dead.]

At the Collects.

O Almighty and eternal God, we humbly beseech thee mercifully to give ear to the prayers here offered thee, by thy servant in the name of thy whole church, and in behalf of us thy people. Accept them to the honour of thy name, and the good of our souls; and grant to us all mercy, grace, and salvation. Thro' our Lord Jesus Christ. Amen.

On the Festival of a Saint.

Grant, we beseech thee, Almighty God, that the examples of thy Saints may effectually move us to reform our lives, that while we celebrate their festivals, we may also imitate their actions. Through our Lord Jesus Christ. Amen.

At the Epistle.

Thou hast vouchsafed, O Lord, to teach us thy sacred truths by the prophets and apostles. Oh! grant that we may so improve by their doctrine and examples in the love of thy holy name, and of thy holy law, that we may show forth by our lives whose disciples we are; that we may no longer follow the corrupt inclinations of flesh and blood, but master all our passions; that we may be ever directed by thy light, and strengthened by thy grace, to walk in the way of thy commandments, and to serve thee with clean hearts. Through our Lord Jesus Christ.

At the Gradual.

How wonderful, O Lord, is thy name in the whole earth! I will bless thee, O Lord, at all times; thy praise shall ever be in my mouth. Be thou my

God and protector for ever; I will put my whole trust in thee; Oh! let me never be confounded.

During the Gospel.

O Lord Jesus Christ, who camest down from heaven to instruct us in all truth, and continuest daily to teach us by thy holy gospel, and the preachers of thy word; grant me grace that I may not be wanting in any care necessary for being instructed in thy saving truths: let me be as industrious for my soul, as I am for my body; that while I take pains in the affairs of this world, I may not, through stupidity or neglect, let my soul starve and perish everlastingly. Let the rules of the gospel be the direction of my life, that I may not only know thy will, but likewise do it; that I may observe thy commandments, and that, resisting all the inclinations of corrupt nature, I may ever follow thee, who art the Way, the Truth, and the Life; for thus only can I be thy true disciple; and thus only, O Jesus, canst thou be my master.

THE NICENE CREED.

CREDO in unum Deum, Patrem omnipotentem, factorem cœli et terræ, visibilium omnium et invisibilium.

Et in unum Dominum Jesum

I BELIEVE in one God, the Father Almighty, Maker of heaven and earth, and of all things visible and invisible.

And in one Lord Jesus Christ,

Dei unigenitum, et ex Patre natum ante omnia sæcula; Deum de Deo, lumen de lumine, Deum verum de Deo vero; genitum non factum, consubstantialem Patri, per quem omnia facta sunt. Qui propter nos homines, et propter nostram salutem, descendit de cœlis; et incarnatus est de Spiritu Sancto, ex Mariâ Virgine; ET HOMO FACTUS EST.* Cru-

Son of God, and born of the Father before all ages; God of God, light of light, true God of true God; begotten not made; consubstantial to the Father, by whom all things were made. Who for us men and for our salvation, came down from heaven; and became incarnate by the Holy Ghost, of the Virgin Mary; AND WAS MADE MAN.* He was crucified

* Kneel in reverence of Christ's Incarnation.

cifixus etiam pro nobis, sub Pontio Pilato passus, et sepultus est. Et resurrexit tertiâ die, secundum scripturas; et ascendit in cœlum; sedet ad dexteram Patris; et iterum venturus est cum gloriâ, judicare vivos et mortuos; cujus regni non erit finis.

Et in Spiritum Sanctum, Dominum et vivifican-

also for us, suffered under Pontius Pilate, and was buried. And the third day he rose again according to the scriptures; and ascended into heaven, sitteth at the right hand of the Father; and he is to come again with glory to judge both the living and the dead; of whose kingdom there shall be no end.

And in the Holy Ghost, the Lord and giver of

tem, qui ex Patre Filioque procedit; qui cum Patre et Filio simul adoratur, et conglorificatur; qui locutus est per Prophetas. Et unam sanctam Catholicam et Apostolicam Ecclesiam. Confiteor unum Baptisma in remissionem peccatorum. Et expecto resurrectionem mortuorum, et vitam venturi sæculi. Amen.

life, who proceedeth from the Father and the Son, who together with the Father and the Son, is adored and glorified; who spoke by the prophets. And one holy Catholic and Apostolic Church. I confess one Baptism for the remission of sins. And I expect the resurrection of the dead, and the life of the world to come. Amen.

At the Offertory.

ACCEPT, O eternal Father, this offering which is here made to thee by thy minister, in the name of us all here present, and of thy whole church. It is as yet only bread and wine, but by a miracle of thy power and grace, will shortly become the body and blood of thy beloved Son. He is our High Priest, and he is our Victim. With him and through him we desire to approach to thee this day, and by his hands to offer thee this sacrifice for thine own honour, praise, and glory; in thanksgiving for all thy benefits; in satisfaction for all our sins, and for obtaining conversion for all unbelievers, and mercy, grace, and salvation for all thy faithful. And with this offering of thine only-begotten Son, we offer ourselves to thee, begging that by virtue of this sacrifice we may be happily united to thee. and that nothing in life or death may ever separate us any more from thee. Through Jesus Christ our Lord. Amen.

After the Offering of the Chalice.

In a contrite heart and humble spirit let us be accepted by thee, O Lord; and so let our sacrifice be made in thy sight this day, that it may please thee, O Lord God.

Come, O Almighty and eternal God, the sanctifier, and bless this sacrifice prepared for thy holy name.

At the Lavabo, or washing the fingers.

Oh! what cleanness and purity of heart ought we to bring with us to this great sacrifice! but, alas! I am a poor unclean sinner. Oh! wash me, dear Lord, from all the stains of sin in the blood of the Lamb, that I may be worthy to be present at these heavenly mysteries. Glory be to the Father. &c.

When the Priest stands bowing down at the middle of the Altar.

O Most holy and adorable Trinity, vouchsafe to receive this our sacrifice in remembrance of our Saviour's passion, resurrection, and glorious ascension: and grant that we may die with him to our sins, rise with him to a new life, and ascend with him to thee. Let those saints, whose memory we celebrate on earth, remember us before thy throne in heaven, and obtain mercy for us, through the same Jesus Christ our Lord. Amen.

At the Orate, Fratres.

MAY the Lord receive the sacrifice from thy hands, to the praise and glory of his own name, for our benefit, and that of all his holy church.

At the Secreta.

MERCIFULLY hear our prayers, O Lord, and graciously accept this oblation which we thy servants make to thee.

and as we offer it to the honour of thy name, so may it be to us a means of obtaining thy grace here, and life everlasting hereafter. Through our Lord Jesus Christ. Amen.

On the Festival of a Saint.

SANCTIFY, O Lord, we beseech thee, these gifts which we offer thee in this solemnity of thy holy servant N. and so strengthen us by thy grace, that both in prosperity and adversity, our ways may be ever directed to thy honour. Thro' our Lord Jesus Christ.

THE PREFACE.

It is truly meet and just, right and salutary, that we always, and in all places, should give thanks to thee, O holy Lord, almighty Father, eternal God; who with thine only-begotten Son, and the Holy Ghost, art one God, one Lord; not in the singularity of one person, but in the Trinity of one substance. For what we believe of thy glory, as thou hast revealed it, that we believe of thy Son, that of the Holy Ghost, without any difference. That in the confession of the true and eternal Deity, propriety in persons, unity in essence, and equality in majesty may be adored. Which the angels praise, and the archangels, the cherubim also and the seraphim;

who cease not to cry out daily, saying with one voice, Holy, holy, holy, Lord God of Sabaoth. The heavens and earth are full of thy glory, Hosanna in the highest. Blessed is he that cometh in the name of the Lord, Hosanna in the highest.

A Prayer at the beginning of the Canon.

O ETERNAL and most merciful Father, behold we come to offer thee our homage this day; we desire to adore, praise, and glorify thee, and to give thee thanks for thy great glory, joining our hearts and voices with all thy blessed in heaven, and with thy whole church upon earth. But acknowledging our great unworthiness and innumerable sins, for which we are heartily sorry, and humbly beg thy pardon, we dare not venture to approach thee otherwise than in company of thy Son, our Advocate and Mediator, Jesus Christ, whom thou hast given us to be both our High Priest and Sacrifice.—With him, therefore, and through him, we venture to offer thee this sacrifice: to his most sacred intentions we desire to unite ours; and with this offering which he makes of himself, we desire to make an offering of our whole being to thee. With him, and through him, we beseech thee to exalt thy holy Catholic Church throughout the whole world; to maintain her in peace, unity, holiness, and truth; to have mercy on thy servant N. our chief bishop, N. our prelate, N. our Queen, and on all that truly fear thee; on our pastor, [parents, children,] friends and benefactors, &c., on all those whom we have in any way scandalized, injured, or offended, or for whom we are in any way bound to pray; on all that are in their agony, or under violent temptations, or other necessities, corporal or spiritual; on all our enemies; and, in a word, on all poor sinners; that we may be all converted to thee, and find mercy, through Jesus Christ, thy Son; through whom we hope one day to be admitted into the company of all thy saints and elect, whose memory we here celebrate, whose prayers we desire, and with whom we communicate in these holy mysteries.

When the Priest extends his hands over the Oblation.

We present to thee, O Lord, this bread and wine, which being composed of many, reduced into one, are symbols of concord and unity; that by thine all-powerful blessing they may be made for us the precious body and blood of thy beloved Son; and that through him, and through his death and passion, applied to our souls by these sacred mysteries, we may obtain mercy, grace, and peace, in this life, and eternal happiness in the next.

At the Elevation of the Host.

HAIL eternally, most sacred flesh of Christ, to me before all, and above all, sweetness supreme! The Body of our Lord Jesus Christ be to me, a sinner, the way and the life! Amen.

At the Elevation of the Chalice.

HAIL eternally, heavenly drink, to me before all, and above all, sweetness supreme! The Body and Blood of our Lord Jesus Christ profit me, a sinner, as an eternal remedy, unto life everlasting. Amen.

A Prayer after the Elevation.

LOOK down now, O Lord, we beseech thee, upon this sacred victim which was once offered to thee upon the cross, and is now daily offered to thee. Remember that thine only begotten Son, for us poor sinners, was conceived and born into this world; that he suffered a bitter agony and sweat of blood; for us he was betrayed into the hands of sinners, buffeted, spit upon, and in many ways abused; for us he was scourged at a pillar, crowned with thorns, and nailed to a cross; for us he died, and for us he triumphed over death by his resurrection, and he opened heaven for us by his ascension. We desire gratefully to commemorate all these mysteries this day, in the oblation of this pure and holy sacrifice. Oh! look not on our sins, but on the infinite ransom paid for them. And whilst we offer it here below upon our altars, do thou receive it upon thine altar above, from the hands of the Angel of the great Council, the eternal Priest; and from thence send down thy blessing upon all us, who here below assist at thy divine mysteries. Through the same Christ our Lord. Amen.

At the Memento.

REMEMBER also, O Lord, thy servants N. and N. who are gone before us with the sign of faith, and repose in the sleep of peace.

Here particular mention is silently made of such of the Dead as are to be prayed for.

To these, O Lord, and to all that rest in Christ, grant, we beseech thee, a place of refreshment, light, and peace. Through the same Christ our Lord. Amen.

At the Nob·is quoque peccatoribus.

WE humbly implore thy mercy, O Lord, for ourselves also: we beg pardon for all our sins; we desire to detest them, and to renounce them for ever. All our hope is in the multitude of thy tender mercies, from which we confidently expect forgiveness, through Jesus Christ; and to be one day, through him, admitted into the company of the blessed apostles and martyrs, in thy heavenly paradise. In the meantime we desire to offer thee daily, thro' him, all honour and glory.

Here the Priest says in a loud voice,

V. Per omnia sæcula sæculorum. Amen.

V. For ever and ever. R. Amen.

THE PATER NOSTER.

Oremus. | *Let us pray.*

PRÆCEPTIS salutaribus moniti, et divinâ institutione formati, audemus dicere:

Pater noster, qui es in cœlis, sanctificetur nomen tuum; adveniat regnum tuum; fiat voluntas tua sicut in cœlo, et in terra; panem nostrum quotidianum da nobis hodiè; et dimitte nobis debita nostra, sicut et nos dimittimus debitoribus nostris; et ne nos inducas in

INSTRUCTED by thy saving precepts, and following thy divine directions, we presume to say,

Our Father, who art in heaven, hallowed be thy name; thy kingdom come; thy will be done on earth, as it is in heaven; give us this day our daily bread; and forgive us our trespasses, as we forgive them that trespass against us: and lead us not into temptation. R.,

tentationem. R. Sed libera nos à malo. P. Amen.

But deliver us from evil. P. Amen.

Deliver us from those evils which we labour under at present; from past evils, which can be nothing but our manifold sins; and from the evils to come, which will be the just chastisement of our offences, if our prayers, and those more powerful ones of thy saints, who intercede for us, intercept not thy justice, or excite not thy bounty.

At the breaking of the Host.

THY body was broken, and thy blood was shed for us, grant that the commemoration of this holy mystery may obtain for us peace; and that those who receive it may find everlasting rest.

THE AGNUS DEI.

Bowing, and striking his breast, the priest says,

AGNUS Dei, qui tollis peccata mundi,* miserere nobis.

LAMB of God, who takest away the sins of the world,* have mercy on us.

Agnus Dei, qui

Lamb of God,

tollis peccata mundi,* miserere nobis.

Agnus Dei, qui tollis peccata mundi,* dona nobis pacem.

who takest away the sins of the world,* have mercy on us.

Lamb of God, who takest away the sins of the world,* give us peace.

In Masses for the Dead, he says twice, * Give them rest, *and lastly,* * Give them eternal rest.

After the Agnus Dei.

IN saying to thine apostles, My peace I leave you, my peace I give you, thou hast promised, O Lord, to all thy Church, that peace which the world cannot give—peace with thee, and peace with ourselves.

LET nothing, O Lord, ever interrupt this holy peace: let nothing separate us from thee, to whom we heartily desire to be united, through this blessed sacrament of peace and reconciliation. Let this food of angels strengthen us in every Christian duty, so as never more to yield under temptations, or fall into our common weaknesses.

At the Domine, non sum dignus, say thrice,

LORD, I am not worthy that thou shouldst enter under my roof; but only say the word, and my soul shall be healed.

[Here the bell is rung thrice, and Communion is given. If you are not going to receive Holy Communion,* make a Spiritual Communion, say,]

O MY sweet Saviour Jesus Christ, thou art my Sovereign Good,

* Devotions for Communion, page 227, and following pages to page 300.

the Fountain of all Good, my God and my All. I most firmly believe, that for us sinners, and for our salvation, thou wast pleased to come down from heaven, to take upon thee, by the mystery of thine incarnation, our human nature, and to become one of us, that so thou mightest be our High Priest and our Victim. I most firmly believe, that thou offeredst thyself upon the cross a sacrifice for us all, after having suffered many cruel torments for us; and that, by thy glorious resurrection and admirable ascension, thou hast opened the gates of heaven for us. I most firmly believe, that in these sacred mysteries thou art truly and really present, and that thy sacred body and blood are here offered up in sacrifice, and verily and indeed received by the faithful in remembrance of thy death. Oh! how happy are those souls, who worthily receive thee in this divine sacrament. Oh! what graces, what sanctity do they receive from this fountain of all sanctity! Oh! that I were so happy as to approach this day to thy heavenly banquet, and to feed on the food of life, the bread of angels! But alas! I am the most wretched of all sinners, who, from my first coming to the use of reason, till this hour, have in innumerable ways offended thee, my God. My soul is overspread with an universal leprosy, covered on all sides with ulcers, and unclean and filthy beyond measure, and therefore, infinitely unworthy to approach to the Lord of all purity and sanctity. In this lamentable state that I am, I dare not so much as look up to thine altar, much less approach to it; but with eyes and heart cast down, and with a deep sense of my manifold treasons and great unworthiness, I humbly beg pardon of thee for all my sins, and implore thy mercy. O merciful Saviour, have compassion on me, and suffer me at least to sigh after thee; and though I am unworthy of thine embraces, permit me, like the penitent Magdalen, to present myself at least before thy feet, and wash them in spirit with my tears! Oh! may thy sacred blood, which thou hast shed for all sinners, cleanse my poor soul this day from all its filth! Oh! come to me, dear Lord, in spirit, and take possession of all the powers of my soul! Recollect my memory in thee, enlighten mine understanding, and inflame my will with thy love. Oh! let me be thine, and thou mine, from henceforth, and for ever: and grant that nothing, in life or death, may ever separate me from thee any more! In this one prayer, hear me, O Lord, and in all things else, do with me what thou wilt.

Prayer after the Communion.

I RETURN thee now most hearty thanks, O my God, through Jesus Christ thy Son, that thou hast been pleased to deliver him up to death for us, and to give us his body and blood both as a sacrament and a sacrifice, in these holy mysteries; at which thou hast permitted me, a most unworthy sinner, to assist this day. May all heaven and earth bless and praise thee for ever, for all thy mercies. Oh! pardon me, dear Lord, all my distractions, and the manifold negligences which I have been guilty of this day in thy sight; and let me not depart without thy benediction. Behold, I desire from this moment to give up myself, and all that belongs to me, into thy hands; and I beg that all mine undertakings, all my thoughts, words, and actions, may henceforward tend to thy glory, through the same Jesus Christ our Lord. Amen.

The beginning of the Gospel of St. John.

IN the beginning was the Word, and the Word

was with God, and the Word was God. The same was in the beginning with God. All things were made by him; and without him was made nothing that was made. In him was life, and the life was the light of men; and the light shineth in darkness, and the darkness did not comprehend it. There was a man sent from God, whose name was John. This man came for a witness, to give testimony of the light, that all men might believe through him. He was not the light, but was to give testimony of the light. That was the true light, which enlighteneth every man that cometh into this world. He was in the world, and the world was made by him, and the world knew him not. He came unto his own, and his own received him not. But as many as received him, he gave them power to be made the sons of God; to them that believe in his name, who are born, not of blood, nor of the will of the flesh, nor of the will of man, but of God. And *the Word was made flesh,* and dwelt among us, (and we saw his glory, the glory, as it were, of the only begotten of the Father,) full of grace and truth.

ON SUNDAYS, AFTER HIGH MASS,

THE FOLLOWING V., R., AND PRAYER, ARE SUNG FOR THE QUEEN.

P. Domine, salvam fac Reginam nostram N.

R. Et exaudi nos in die qua invocaverimus te. Gloria Patri, &c.

Oremus.

QUÆSUMUS, omnipotens Deus, ut famula tua N. Regina nostra, quæ tuâ miseratione suscepit regni gubernacula, virtutum etiam omnium percipiat incrementum; quibus decenter ornata, vitiorum monstra devitare, (hostes

P. O Lord, save N. our Queen.

R. And hear us in the day when we shall call upon thee. Glory, &c.

Let us pray.

WE beseech thee, O almighty God, that thy servant N. our Queen, who through thy mercy hath undertaken the government of these realms, may also receive an increase of all virtues, wherewith being adorned she may avoid the enor-

superare,*) et ad te, qui via, veritas, et vita es, cum prole regiâ, gratiosa valeat pervenire. Per Christum Dominum nostrum. Amen.

mity of sin, (vanquish her enemies;)* and being rendered acceptable in thy sight, may, with the Royal Family, come at length to thee, who art the way, the truth, and the life. Through Christ our Lord. Amen.

PRAYERS AFTER MASS.
Let us pray.

WE give thee thanks, almighty and gracious Father, that thou hast permitted us this day to offer our homage to thy divine Majesty, and especially that thou hast allowed us to be present at the most holy sacrifice of the body and blood of thy beloved Son. If we have been wanting in attention and devotion, pardon us, we

* In time of war.

beseech thee, in pity to our weakness. For the sake of him, whose sufferings and death we have commemorated, grant the petitions which we have made in his name, and send down upon us thy blessing, which may remain with us for ever, through the same Jesus Christ our Lord. Amen.

In Lent and Advent, the Miserere, *(to be found at page 216,) is said, with the following prayer:*

O GOD, who by sin art offended, and by penance pacified, mercifully regard the prayers of thy people, who make supplication to thee, and turn away the scourges of thine anger, which we deserve for our sins. Spare, O Lord, spare thy people, that having been justly punished for our sins, we may find comfort in thy mercy. Through our Lord Jesus Christ, &c.

Prayer for Advent.

RAISE up our hearts, O Lord, we beseech thee, to prepare the ways of thine only Son; that, by his coming, being reconciled to thee, we may serve thee in holiness all the days of our lives; who livest, &c.

Conclude with this Prayer.

ACCEPT, O most gracious God, this our service; whatever, by thy grace, we may have performed with diligence, in thy clemency regard; and what we have done with negligence, mercifully pardon, through Jesus Christ our Lord. Amen.

May the blessing of Almighty God, Father, Son, and Holy Ghost, descend upon us now, and remain with us for ever. Amen.

Litany of the Holy Mass.

To prepare ourselves to assist worthily at Mass, let us raise up our minds to the dignity and efficacy of this great sacrifice of the New Law, and direct our intention to the Four great ends for which it was instituted.

LORD, have mercy on us. *Lord, have, &c.*
Christ, have mercy on us. *Christ, &c.*
Lord, have mercy on us. *Lord, &c.*
Christ, hear us. *Christ, graciously hear us.*

O God the Father, Creator of the world,
O God the Son, Redeemer of mankind,
O God the Holy Ghost, perfecter of the elect,
O adorable Trinity, in three persons, one God,
Jesus, who being from all eternity in the form of God, didst, at thine incarnation, take upon thee the form of a servant, and become like unto man, *Phil.* ii. 7.
Jesus, who for our sakes didst become obedient unto death, even the death of the cross, *Phil.* ii. 8.
Jesus, who ascending to thy Father, wouldst not leave us orphans, but wouldst still continue with us under the sacramental veils, *John*, xiv. 18.
Jesus, the Tree of Life, of which whosoever eateth, shall live for ever, *Gen.* iii. 22.
Jesus, the Paschal Lamb, by whose blood we are saved from the sword of the destroying angel, *Exod.* xii. 13.
Jesus, the bread from heaven, con-

taining in thyself all sweetness, *Wisd.* xvi. 20.

Jesus, the Priest for ever, according to the order of Melchisedech, *Ps.* cix.

Jesus, who having offered us this sacrifice on Mount Calvary, by the effusion of thy blood continuest to offer up the same in an unbloody manner upon our altars until the end of the world,

Have mercy on us.

Have mercy on us, O Jesus. *And pardon our sins.*

Have mercy on us, O Jesus. *And hear our prayers.*

From opposing the uncertain testimony of our senses to the infallible truth of thy word, *O Jesus, deliver us.*

From a loathing of this heavenly manna, and from receiving it to our own condemnation,

From slighting this adorable sacrifice, and from assisting at it with irreverence and distraction,

Through thine irresistible power, which changeth the course of nature as thou pleasest,

Through thine infinite goodness, for which no miracles are too great to testify thy love for us,

O Jesus, deliver us.

Through all the mysteries of thy life and passion, and especially through the sacrifice of thyself on the cross, *O Jesus, deliver us.*

We sinners, *Beseech thee to hear us.*

I. That thou, O eternal Father of our Lord Jesus Christ, wouldst accept of this *Holocaust* of himself, which he here offers thee, in testimony of thy being the Master of life and death, the Lord of us and all things, *We beseech thee hear us.*

II. That thou wouldst accept of this *Eucharistic* sacrifice in thanksgiving for thy creating, preserving, and sanctifying us; for making us members of thy holy Catholic Church, and for every other favour thou hast bestowed upon us,

That thou wouldst receive it in commemoration of the incarnation, birth, *(manifestation—transfiguration—passion)* life, and death, as also of the resurrection and ascension of our Saviour Jesus Christ, and of his institution of this adorable sacrament and sacrifice,

That thou wouldst receive it in thanksgiving for thy graces and glory conferred on the B. V. Mary *(whose conception—birth—annunciation—assumption—festival we celebrate this day,)* and on all the holy angels and saints in heaven, *(particularly of the holy Apostle—Martyr—Confessor—Virgin—Widow—St. N., whose festival we celebrate this day,)*

III. That thou wouldst accept of this *Propitiatory* sacrifice as a sin-offering, to atone for our many grievous sins, and our abuse of thy divine graces, and to avert thy heavy judgments which we have thereby provoked,

That thou wouldst accept of it in reparation for all the sacrileges, blasphemies, and other sins committed throughout the world, and especially for those perpetrated against these adorable mysteries,

That thou wouldst receive it in satisfaction for the sufferings due to thy justice by the faithful departed, especially our deceased parents, relations, and benefactors, that they may be released from

We beseech thee hear us.

their torments, and admitted to the blissful sight of thee,

IV. That through this *Impetratory* sacrifice thou wouldst protect and exalt the holy Catholic Church, enlighten the hearts of infidels, heretics, and schismatics, and reclaim all sinners, especially of this congregation, from the ways of death in which they are walking,

That through it thou wouldst pour down thy special graces on the Catholics of this land; so that leading lives worthy of their faith, they may be a light to direct others into the road that leadeth to thee,

That by means of it thou wouldst fill us with thy blessings for soul and body, enabling us to repress the vices to which we are most subject, and to acquire the virtues of which we stand most in need,

That thou wouldst impart the efficacy of this most acceptable oblation, accordingly as they stand in need of it, to our relations, benefactors, friends, and enemies; to our supreme Pastor, N., to our

We beseech thee hear us.

Bishop, N., and all his clergy, to their Majesties, N., the royal family, and the nation in general, *We beseech thee hear us.*

Son of God, *We beseech thee to hear us.*

O Lamb of God, who takest away the sins of the world, *Spare us, O Lord.*

O Lamb of God, who takest away the sins of the world, *Hear us, O Lord.*

O Lamb of God, who takest away the sins of the world, *Have mercy on us.*

Christ, hear us, *Christ, graciously hear us.*

Let us Pray.

O MOST wise and bountiful Lord, who in this great sacrifice of the New Law hast accumulated thy former mercies, and hast caused it to answer the ends of all the ancient sacrifices; graciously hear the manifold petitions which, through the same, we now present to thee. Look not upon us, O Lord, but upon the divine Victim that is presented to thee, even thy beloved Son, in whom thou art always well pleased, and, for his sake, grant us whatever we ask of thee, who, with the same Son and Holy Ghost, livest and reignest, &c. *Amen*

Eternal God, who, by a succession of illustrious types and ceremonies, didst, from the beginning of the world, prefigure this adorable sacrifice, in order to raise in us a suitable idea of its importance, and who didst require so great a preparation and such legal expiations from those who offered up sheep and oxen, to signify the purity and sanctity we ought to bring with us to this oblation of thy divine Son; grant us, we beseech thee, the necessary dispositions for assisting at Mass worthily. Cleanse our consciences from the filth of sin, and clothe them with the robe of charity, that we may not deserve to be cast out from this heavenly feast. Dispel every shadow of infidelity or diffidence from our minds, that no objection of our weak understandings may rise up against thine all-powerful word. Banish all distractions from our imagination, that no concern of the world may draw our attention from the great action performed on this altar, at which the angels assist with awe. Drive away all tepidity from our hearts, that thy condescension in this wonderful sacrifice may not cause us to look upon it with less veneration, nor thy facility in admitting us so frequently to it, make us assist at it with less devotion. And oh, that we were all of us worthy to partake of this divine Victim, by actually receiving him into our breasts! Grant, at least, that we may all spiritually receive him by the communication of his graces; through the same Christ our Lord. *Amen.*

O spotless Virgin, whose divine Son is at the same time the Victim and the Priest in this adorable sacrifice, pray that our unworthiness may not deprive us of the inestimable benefits therein contained. Through our Lord Jesus Christ. *Amen.*

All ye blessed orders of Angelic Spirits, all ye holy Saints, now possessors of the heavenly mansions, once the inhabitants of this our land of exile; ye Patriarchs and Prophets, ye Apostles and Martyrs, ye Confessors and Virgins, pray for us, that we may in such manner adore Jesus Christ under these sacramental veils, that we may hereafter be admitted with you to the clear sight and the possession of him in eternal felicity; who, with the Father and the Holy Ghost, liveth and reigneth one God, world without end. *Amen.*

The Manner of Serving at Mass.

The Clerk or Servitor kneeling at the left hand of the Priest, shall answer him as follows:

Pr. INTROIBO ad altare Dei.
Cl. Ad Deum, qui lætificat juventutem meam.

Pr. Judica me, Deus, et discerne causam meam de gente non sancta: ab homine iniquo et doloso erue me.

Cl. Quia tu es, Deus, fortitudo mea; quare me repulisti, et quare tristis incedo dum affligit me inimicus!

Pr. Emitte lucem tuam et veritatem tuam: ipsa me deduxerunt, et adduxerunt in montem sanctum tuum et in tabernacula tua.

Cl. Et introibo ad altare Dei: ad Deum qui lætificat juventutem meam.

Pr. Confitebor tibi in cithara, Deus, Deus meus: quare tristis es anima mea, et quare conturbas me?

Cl. Spera in Deo, quoniam adhuc confitebor illi; salutare vultus mei, et Deus meus.

Pr. Gloria Patri, et Filio, et Spiritui Sancto.

Cl. Sicut erat in principio, et nunc, et semper, et in sæcula sæculorum. Amen.

Pr. Introibo ad altare Dei.

Cl. Ad Deum, qui lætificat juventutem meam.

Pr. Adjutorium nostrum in nomine Domini.

Cl. Qui fecit cœlum et terram.

Pr. Confiteor Deo, &c.

Cl. Misereatur tui omnipotens Deus, et, dimissis peccatis tuis, perducat te ad vitam æternam.

Pr. Amen.

Cl. Confiteor Deo omnipotenti, beatæ Mariæ semper Virgini, beato Michaeli Archangelo, beato Joanni Baptistæ, sanctis Apostolis Petro et Paulo omnibus sanctis, et tibi, Pater, quia peccavi nimis cogitatione, verbo et opere [*here he strikes his breast thrice*] meâ culpâ, meâ culpâ, meâ maxima culpâ. Ideo precor beatam Mariam semper Virginem, beatum Michaelem Archangelum, beatum Joannem Baptistam, sanctos Apostolos Petrum et Paulum, omnes sanctos, et te, Pater, orare pro me ad Dominum Deum nostrum.

Pr. Misereatur vestri, &c. Cl. Amen.

Pr. Indulgentiam, absolutionem, &c.
Cl. Amen.

When a Bishop says mass, he here takes the maniple, which the clerk must be ready to give him.

Pr. Deus tu conversus, vivificabis nos.
Cl. Et plebs tua lætabitur in te.
Pr. Ostende nobis, Domine, misericordiam tuam.
Cl. Et salutare tuum da nobis.
Pr. Domine, exaudi orationem meam.
Cl. Et clamor meus ad te veniat.
Pr. Dominus vobiscum.
Cl. Et cum spiritu tuo.
Pr. Kyrie eleison. Cl. Kyrie eleison.
Pr. Kyrie eleison. Cl. Christe eleison.
Pr. Christe eleison. Cl. Christe eleison.
Pr. Kyrie eleison. Cl. Kyrie eleison.
Pr. Kyrie eleison.
Pr. Dominus vobiscum, [*A bishop says* Pax vobis] *or* Flectamus genua.
Cl. Et cum spiritu tuo, *or* Levate.
Pr. Per omnia sæcula sæculorum.
Cl. Amen.

At the end of the Epistle say, Deo gratias.

The Epistle, Gradual, and *Alleluia*, or Tract, being read, remove the Mass-book to the right-hand of the altar, making a reverence as you pass before the middle of the altar. Let the clerk ever kneel or stand on the contrary side to the Mass-book.

Pr. Dominus vobiscum.
Cl. Et cum spiritu tuo.
Pr. Sequentia sancti Evangelii secundum &c.

Making the sign of the cross, say,

Cl. Gloria tibi, Domine.

Make a reverence at the beginning and ending of the Gospel, and at the name of JESUS; and at the end say,

Cl. Laus tibi Christe,
Pr. Dominus vobiscum.
Cl. Et cum spiritu tuo.

Here the clerk is to give wine and water, and prepare the basin, water, and towel for the priest. The priest having washed his fingers, let him kneel in his former place, and answer,

Pr. Orate Fratres, &c.
Cl. Suscipiat Dominus sacrificium de manibus tuis ad laudem et gloriam nominis sui, ad utilitatem quoque nostram, totiusque ecclesiæ suæ sanctæ.
Pr. Per omnia sæcula sæculorum.
Cl. Amen.
Pr. Dominus vobiscum.
Cl. Et cum spiritu tuo.

Pr. Sursum corda.
Cl. Habemus ad Dominum.
Pr. Gratias agamus Domino Deo nostro.
Cl. Dignum et justum est.

At Sanctus, Sanctus, Sanctus, &c. *ring the little bell where this is customary.*

And again, when you see the priest spread his hands over the chalice, give warning by the bell, of the consecration which is about to be made. Then holding up the vestment with your left hand, and having the bell in your right, ring during the elevation of the Host; which being ended, you must kiss the vestment, and presently do the same at the elevation of the chalice. As often as you pass by the blessed Sacrament, adore on your knees.

Pr. Per omnia sæcula sæculorum.
Cl. Amen.
Pr. Et ne nos inducas in tentationem.
Cl. Sed libera nos a malo.
Pr. Per omnia sæcula sæculorum.
Cl. Amen.
Pr. Pax Domini sit semper vobiscum.
Cl. Et cum spiritu tuo.

The priest's communion being ended, be ready to give him first wine and then wine and water. But if there be communicants, first provide them with a towel, and say the *Confiteor*. Then remove the book to the left-hand of the altar, take away the towel from the communicants if there were any, and return to your former place. A Bishop here again washes his hands, as at the Offertory.

Pr. Dominus vobiscum.
Cl. Et cum spiritu tuo.
Pr. Per omnia sæcula sæculorum.
Cl. Amen.
Pr. Ite, Missa est, *or* Benedicamus Domino.
Cl. Deo gratias.

In Masses for the Dead.

Pr. Requiescant in pace.   Cl. Amen.

Remove the book, if it be left open; kneel and receive the priest's blessing.

At a Bishop's Mass.

B. Sit nomen Domini benedictum.
Cl. Ex hoc nunc et usque in sæculum.
B. Adjutorium nostrum in nomine Domini.
Cl. Qui fecit cœlum et terram.
Pr. Pater, et Filius, et Spiritus Sanctus.
Cl. Amen.

At the beginning of the last Gospel.

Pr. Dominus vobiscum.

Cl. Et cum spiritu tuo.

Pr. Initium, *or* Sequentia sancti Evangelii, &c.

Cl. Gloria tibi, Domine.

At the end say, Deo gratias.

Put out the candles, and lay all up carefully.

Other Devotions for Sundays and Holydays.

The Benedicite, or Canticle of the three Children. Daniel iii.

ALL ye works of the Lord, bless the Lord, praise and exalt him above all for ever.

O ye angels of the Lord, bless the Lord: O ye heavens, bless the Lord.

O all ye waters that are above the heavens, bless the Lord: O all ye powers of the Lord, bless the Lord.

O ye sun and moon, bless the Lord; O ye stars of heaven, bless the Lord.

O every shower and dew, bless ye the Lord; O all ye spirits of God, bless the Lord.

O ye fire and heat, bless the Lord; O ye cold and heat, bless the Lord.

O ye dews and hoar frosts, bless the Lord; O ye frost and cold, bless the Lord.

O ye ice and snow, bless the Lord; O ye nights and days, bless the Lord.

O ye light and darkness, bless the Lord; O ye lightnings and clouds, bless the Lord.

O let the earth bless the Lord: let it praise and exalt him above all for ever.

O ye mountains and hills, bless the Lord; O all ye things that spring up in the earth, bless the Lord.

O ye fountains, bless the Lord; O ye seas and rivers, bless the Lord.

O ye whales, and all that move in the waters, bless the Lord; O all ye fowls of the air, bless the Lord.

O all ye beasts and cattle, bless the Lord; O ye sons of men, bless the Lord.

O let Israel bless the Lord; let them praise and exalt him above all for ever.

O ye priests of the Lord, bless the Lord; O ye servants of the Lord, bless the Lord.

O ye spirits and souls of the just, bless the Lord; O ye holy and humble of heart, bless the Lord.

O Ananias, Azarias, and Misael, bless

ye the Lord; praise and exalt him above all for ever.

Let us bless the Father, and the Son, with the Holy Ghost; let us praise him and magnify him for ever.

Blessed art thou, O Lord, in the firmament of heaven; and worthy of praise, and glorious, and magnified for ever.

Psalms of Adoration, Praise, and Thanksgiving.

Psalm xciv.

COME, let us praise the Lord with joy; let us joyfully sing to God our Saviour.

Let us come before his presence with thanksgiving, and make a joyful noise to him with psalms.

For the Lord is a great God, and a great King above all gods.

For in his hand are all the ends of the earth, and the heights of the mountains are his.

For the sea is his, and he made it; and his hands formed the dry land.

Come, let us adore and fall down: and weep before the Lord that made us.

For he is the Lord our God: and we are the people of his pasture, and the sheep of his hand.

To-day, if you shall hear his voice, harden not your hearts:

As in the provocation, according to the day of temptation in the wilderness: where your fathers tempted me, they proved me and saw my works.

Forty years long was I offended with that generation; and I said, These always err in heart.

And these men have not known my ways; so I swore in my wrath, that they shall not enter into my rest.

Glory be to the Father, and to the Son, and to the Holy Ghost. As it was in the beginning, is now, and ever shall be world without end. Amen.

Psalm xcix.

SING joyfully to God, all the earth; serve ye the Lord with gladness.

Come in before his presence with exceeding great joy.

Know ye that the Lord he is God; he made us, and not we ourselves.

We are his people, and the sheep of his pasture. Go ye into his gates with praise, into his courts with hymns, and give glory to him.

Praise ye his name, for the Lord is sweet; his mercy endureth for ever, and his truth to generation and generation. Glory, &c.

Psalm cii.

BLESS the Lord, O my soul, and let all that is within me bless his holy name.

Bless the Lord, O my soul, and never forget all that he hath done for thee.

Who forgiveth all thine iniquities; who healeth all thy diseases.

Who redeemeth thy life from destruction: who crowneth thee with mercy and compassion.

Who satisfieth thy desire with good things; thy youth shall be renewed like the eagle's.

The Lord doth mercies and judgment for all that suffer wrong.

He hath made his ways known to Moses; his wills to the children of Israel.

The Lord is compassionate and merciful; long suffering, and plenteous in mercy.

He will not always be angry; nor will he threaten for ever.

He hath not dealt with us according to our sins, nor rewarded us according to our iniquities.

For according to the height of the heaven above the earth, he hath strengthened his mercy towards them that fear him.

As far as the east is from the west, so far hath he removed our iniquities from us.

As a father hath compassion on his children, so hath the Lord compassion on them that fear him.

For he knoweth our frame; he remembereth that we are dust.

Man's days are as grass, as the flower of the field, so shall he flourish.

For the spirit shall pass in him, and he shall not be; and he shall know his place no more.

But the mercy of the Lord is from eternity, and unto eternity, upon them that fear him.

And his justice unto children's children, to such as keep his covenant,

And are mindful of his commandments to do them.

The Lord hath prepared his throne in heaven: and his kingdom shall rule over all.

Bless the Lord, all ye his angels; you that are mighty in strength, and execute his word, hearkening to the voice of his orders.

Bless the Lord, all ye his hosts; you ministers of his that do his will.

Bless the Lord, all his works, in every place of his dominion; O my soul, bless thou the Lord. Glory be to the Father, &c.

Psalm cxvi.

O PRAISE the Lord, all ye nations: praise him, all ye people.

For his mercy is confirmed upon us; and the truth of the Lord remaineth for ever. Glory, &c.

Psalm cxxxvii.

I WILL praise thee, O Lord, with my whole heart; for thou hast heard the words of my mouth.

I will sing praise to thee in the sight of the angels; I will worship towards thy holy temple, and I will give glory to thy name.

For thy mercy and for thy truth; for thou hast magnified thy holy name above all.

In what day soever I shall call upon thee, hear me, thou shalt multiply strength in my soul.

May all the kings of the earth give glory to thee, O Lord; for they have heard all the words of thy mouth.

And let them sing in the ways of the Lord; for great is the glory of the Lord.

For the Lord is high and looketh on the low; and the high he knoweth afar off.

If I shall walk in the midst of tribulation, thou wilt quicken me: and thou hast stretched forth thy hand against the wrath of mine enemies; and thy right hand hath saved me.

The Lord will repay for me. Thy mercy, O Lord, endureth for ever: O despise not the works of thy hands. Glory, &c.

Psalm cxlviii. *Alleluia*

PRAISE ye the Lord from the heavens: praise ye him in the high places.

Praise ye him, all his angels: praise ye him, all his hosts.

Praise ye him, O sun and moon: praise him, all ye stars and light.

Praise him, ye heavens of heavens: and let all the waters that are above the heavens praise the name of the Lord.

For he spoke, and they were made: he commanded, and they were created.

He hath established them for ever and for ages of ages: he hath made a decree, and it shall not pass away.

Praise the Lord from the earth, ye dragons and all ye deeps.

Fire, hail, snow, ice, stormy winds, which fulfil his word.

Mountains and all hills; fruitful trees and all cedars.

Beasts and all cattle; serpents and feathered fowls.

Kings of the earth, and all people; princes and all judges of the earth.

Young men and maidens: let the old with the younger praise the name of the Lord; for his name alone is exalted.

The praise of him is above heaven and earth; and he hath exalted the horn of his people.

A hymn to all his saints: to the

children of Israel, a people approaching to him. Glory, &c.

Psalm cl.

PRAISE ye the Lord in his holy places; praise ye him in the firmament of his power.

Praise ye him for his mighty acts; praise ye him according to the multitude of his greatness.

Praise him with sound of trumpet; praise him with psaltery and harp.

Praise him with timbrel and choir; praise him with strings and organs.

Praise him on high sounding cymbals; praise him on cymbals of joy: let every spirit praise the Lord. Glory, &c.

The Benedictus, or Canticle of Zachary
Luke i.

BLESSED be the Lord God of Israel, because he hath visited and wrought the redemption of his people;

And hath raised up a horn of salvation to us in the house of David his servant;

As he spoke by the mouth of his holy prophets, who are from the beginning;

Salvation from our enemies, and from the hand of all that hate us.

To perform mercy to our fathers, and to remember his holy testament.

The oath which he swore to Abraham our father, that he would grant to us,

That being delivered from the hand of our enemies, we may serve him without fear

In holiness and justice before him all our days.

And thou, child, shalt be called the prophet of the Highest; for thou shalt go before the face of the Lord to prepare his ways.

To give knowledge of salvation to his people, unto the remission of their sins;

Through the bowels of the mercy of our God, in which the Orient from on high hath visited us.

To enlighten them that sit in darkness and in the shadow of death; to direct our feet into the way of peace. Glory, &c.

Ejaculatory Prayer
TO THE HOLY FAMILY.

[Indulgence: 300 days each time.]

JESUS, Mary, and Joseph, I give you my heart and my soul.

Jesus, Mary, and Joseph, assist me in my last agony.

Jesus, Mary, and Joseph, may I die in peace in your blessed company.

An Universal Prayer,
FOR ALL THINGS NECESSARY TO SALVATION.

O MY God, I believe in thee; do thou strengthen my faith. All my hopes are in thee; do thou secure them. I love thee with my whole heart; teach me to love thee daily more and more. I am sorry that I have offended thee; do thou increase my sorrow.

I adore thee as my first beginning; I aspire after thee as my last end. I give thee thanks as my constant Benefactor: I call upon thee as my sovereign Protector.

Vouchsafe, O my God, to conduct me by thy wisdom, to restrain me by thy justice, to comfort me by thy mercy, to defend me by thy power.

To thee I desire to consecrate all my thoughts, words, actions, and sufferings; that henceforward I may think of thee, speak of thee, willingly refer all my actions to thy greater glory, and suffer willingly whatever thou shalt appoint.

Lord, I desire that in all things thy will may be done, because it is thy will, and in the manner thou willest.

I beg of thee to enlighten my understanding, to inflame my will, to purify my body, and to sanctify my soul.

Give me strength, O my God, to expiate my offences, to overcome my temptations, to subdue my passions, and to acquire the virtues proper for my state.

Fill my heart with a tender affection for thy goodness, a hatred for my faults, a love for my neighbour, and a contempt of the world.

Let me always remember to be submissive to my superiors, condescending to my inferiors, faithful to my friends, and charitable to my enemies.

Assist me to overcome sensuality by mortification, avarice by alms-deeds, anger by meekness, and tepidity by devotion. O my God, make me prudent in my undertakings, courageous in dangers, patient in afflictions, and humble in prosperity.

Grant that I may be ever attentive at my prayers, temperate at my meals, diligent in my employments, and constant in my good resolutions.

Let my conscience be ever upright and pure, my exterior modest, my conversation edifying, and my comportment regular.

Assist me, that I may continually labour to overcome nature, to correspond with thy grace, to keep thy commandments, and to work out my salvation.

Discover to me, O my God, the nothingness of this world, the greatness of heaven, the shortness of time, and the length of eternity.

Grant that I may prepare for death, that I may fear thy judgments, that I may escape hell, and in the end obtain heaven, through the merits of our Lord Jesus Christ. Amen.

Vespers for Sundays.

The Our Father and Hail Mary being said in silence, the Priest sings aloud,

V. Deus in adjutorium meum intende.
R. Domine ad adjuvandum me festina.
Gloria Patri, et Filio, * et Spiritui Sancto.

Sicut erat in principio, et nunc, et semper,* et in sæcula sæculorum. Amen. Alleluia.

V. O God, come to my assistance.
R. O Lord, make haste to help me.
Glory be to the Father, and to the Son, and to the Holy Ghost.

As it was in the beginning, is now, and ever shall be, world without end. Amen. Allelui.

Before each of the Psalms an Antiphon, which varies according to the Festivals, is recited.

Ant. Dixit Dominus. *Anth.* The Lord said.

In Paschal time the only Anthem to all the Psalms is Alleluia.

Psalm cix.

DIXIT Dominus Domino meo : * Sede à dextris meis.

2 Donec ponam inimicos tuos : * scabellum pedum tuorum.

3 Virgam virtutis tuæ emitte Dominus ex Sion : * dominare in medio inimicorum tuorum.

THE Lord said to my Lord : Sit thou at my right hand : 2 Until I make thine enemies thy footstool. 3 The Lord will send forth the sceptre of thy power out of Sion : rule thou in the midst of thine enemies. 4 With thee is the principality in the

4 Tecum principium in die virtutis tuæ, in splendoribus sanctorum : * ex utero ante luciferum genui te.

5 Juravit Dominus, et non pœnitebit eum : * tu es Sacerdos in æternum secundum ordinem Melchisedech.

6 Dominus à dextris tuis : * confregit in die iræ suæ reges.

7 Judicabit in nationibus, implebit ruinas : * conquassabit capita in terra multorum.

8 De torrente in via bibet : * propterea exaltabit caput. Gloria Patri, &c.

day of thy strength, in the brightness of the saints : from the womb, before the day star, I begot thee. 5 The Lord hath sworn, and he will not repent : Thou art a priest for ever according to the order of Melchisedech. 6 The Lord, at thy right hand, hath broken kings in the day of his wrath. 7 He shall judge among nations, he shall fill ruins : he shall crush the heads in the land of many. 8 He shall drink of the torrent in the way : therefore shall he lift up the head. Glory be to the Father, &c.

Gloria Patri, &c. *is said at the end of every Psalm.*

Ant. Dixit Dominus Domino meo, Sede à dextris meis.
Ant. Fidelia.

Anth. The Lord said to my Lord, Sit thou at my right-hand.
Anth. True.

Psalm cx.

CONFITEBOR tibi Domine in toto corde meo : * in consilio justorum, et congregatione.

I WILL praise thee, O Lord, with my whole heart : in the council of the just, and in the congregation. 2 Great

2 Magna opera Domini : * exquisita in omnes voluntates ejus.

3 Confessio et magnificentia opus ejus : * et justitia ejus manet in sæculum sæculi.

4 Memoriam fecit mirabilium suorum, misericors et miserator Dominus : * escam dedit timentibus se.

5 Memor erit in sæculum testamenti sui : * virtutem operum suorum annuntiabit populo suo.

6 Ut det illis hæreditatem Gentium : * opera manuum ejus, veritas et judicium.

7 Fidelia omnia mandata ejus, confirmata in sæculum sæculi : * facta in veritate et æquitate.

8 Redemptionem misit populo suo : * mandavit in æternum testamentum suum.

9 Sanctum et terribile nomen ejus : * initium sapientiæ timor Domini.

10 Intellectus bonus omnibus facientibus

are the works of the Lord : sought out according to all his wills.

3 His work is praise and magnificence : and his justice continueth for ever and ever. 4 He hath made a remembrance of his wonderful works, being a merciful and gracious Lord : he hath given food to them that fear him. 5 He will be mindful for ever of his covenant : he will show forth to his people the power of his works. 6 That he may give them the inheritance of the Gentiles : the works of his hands are truth and judgment. 7 All his commandments are faithful, confirmed for ever and ever : made in truth and equity. 8 He hath sent redemption to his people : he hath commanded his covenant for ever. 9 Holy and terrible is his name : the fear of the Lord is the beginning of wisdom. 10 A good understanding to all that do it : his praise con-

eum : * laudatio ejus manet in sæculum sæculi.

Ant. Fidelia omnia mandata ejus ; confirmata in sæculum sæculi.

Ant. In mandatis.

tinueth for ever and ever.

Anth. True are all his ordinances; confirmed for ever and ever.

Anth. In his commandments.

Psalm cxi.

BEATUS vir qui timet Dominum: * in mandatis ejus volet nimis.

2 Potens in terra erit semen ejus: * generatio rectorum benedicetur.

3 Gloria et divitiæ in domo ejus : * et justitia ejus manet in sæculum sæculi.

4 Exortum est in tenebris lumen rectis : * misericors, et miserator et justus.

5 Jucundus homo qui miseretur et commodat, disponet sermones suos in judicio : * quia in æternum non commovebitur.

6 In memoria æterna erit justus : * ab auditione mala non timebit.

7 Paratum cor ejus sperare in Domino, con-

BLESSED is the man that feareth the Lord : he shall delight exceedingly in his commandments. 2 His seed shall be mighty upon the earth : the generation of the righteous shall be blessed. 3 Glory and wealth shall be in his house : and his justice remaineth for ever and ever. 4 To the righteous a light is risen up in darkness : he is merciful, and compassionate, and just. 5 Acceptable is the man that showeth mercy and lendeth : he shall order his words with judgment, because he shall not be moved for ever. 6 The just shall be in everlasting remem-

firmatum est cor ejus: * non commovebitur donec despiciat inimicos suos.

8 Dispersit, dedit puperibus, justitia ejus manet in sæculum sæculi: * cornu ejus exaltabitur in gloria.

9 Peccator videbit et irascetur, dentibus suis fremet et tabescet: * desiderium peccatorum peribit.

brance: he shall not fear the evil hearing. 7 His heart is ready to hope in the Lord, his heart is strengthened: he shall not be moved, until he look over his enemies. 8 He hath distributed, he hath given to the poor, his justice remaineth for ever and ever: his horn shall be exalted in glory. 9 The wicked shall see and shall be angry; he shall gnash with his teeth and pine away: the desire of the wicked shall perish.

Ant. In mandatis ejus cupit nimis.

Anth. In his commandments he shall take great delight.

Ant. Sit nomen Domini.

Anth. Let the name of the Lord.

Psalm cxii.

LAUDATE pueri Dominum: * laudate nomen Domini.

2 Sit nomen Domini benedictum: * ex hoc nunc, et usque in sæculum.

3 A solis ortu usque ad occasum: * laudabile nomen Domini.

4 Excelsus super om-

PRAISE the Lord, ye children: praise ye the name of the Lord.

2 Blessed be the name of the Lord: from henceforth now and for ever.

3 From the rising of the sun, unto the going down of the same, the name of the Lord is worthy of praise. 4

nes gentes Dominus: * et super cœlos gloria ejus.

5 Quis sicut Dominus Deus noster, qui in altis habitat: * et humilia respicit in cœlo et in terra?

6 Suscitans à terra inopem: * et de stercore erigens pauperem.

7 Ut collocet eum cum principibus: * cum principibuis populi sui.

8 Qui habitare facit sterilem in domo: * matrem filiorum lætantem.

Ant. Sit nomen Domini benedictum in sæcula.

Ant. Nos qui vivimus.

The Lord is high above all nations: and his glory above the heavens. 5 Who is as the Lord our God, who dwelleth on high: and looketh down on the low things in heaven and in earth? 6 Raising up the needy from the earth, and lifting up the poor out of the dunghill: 7 That he may place him with princes, with the princes of his people. 8 Who maketh a barren woman to dwell in a house, the joyful mother of children.

Anth. Let the name of the Lord be blessed for evermore.

Anth. We who are alive.

Psalm cxiii.

IN exitu Israel de Ægypto: * domus Jacob de populo barbaro.

2 Facta est Judæa sanctificatio ejus: * Israel potestas ejus.

3 Mare vidit et fugit: * Jordanis conversus est retrorsum.

WHEN Israel went out of Egypt, the house of Jacob from a barbarous people: 2 Judea was made his sanctuary, Israel his dominion. 3 The sea saw and fled: Jordan was turned back. 4

4 Montes exultaverunt ut arietes: * et colles sicut agni ovium.

5 Quid est tibi mare, quod fugisti? * et tu Jordanis, quia conversus es retrorsum?

6 Montes exultastis sicut arietes? * et colles sicut agni ovium.

7 A facie Domini mota est terra: * à facie Dei Jacob.

8 Qui convertit petram in stagna aquarum: * et rupem in fontes aquarum.

9 Non nobis Domine, non nobis: * sed nomini tua da gloriam.

10 Super misericordia tua, et veritate tua: * nequando dicant Gentes, ubi est Deus eorum?

11 Deus autem noster in cœlo: * omnia quæcumque voluit, fecit.

12 Simulacra Gentium argentum et aurum: * opera manuum hominum.

13 Os habent, et non loquentur: * oculos habent, et non videbunt.

The mountains skipped like rams, and the hills like the lambs of the flock. 5 What ailed thee, O thou sea, that thou didst flee: and thou, O Jordan, that thou wast turned back? 6 Ye mountains, that ye skip like rams, and ye hills, like the lambs of the flock. 7 At the presence of the Lord the earth was moved, at the presence of the God of Jacob. 8 Who turned the rock into pools of water, and the stony hill into fountains of water. 9 Not to us, O Lord, not to us; but to thy name give glory. 10 For thy mercy, and for thy truth's sake: lest the Gentiles should say, Where is their God? 11 But our God is in heaven: he hath done all things whatsoever he would. 12 The idols of the Gentiles are silver and gold, the works of the hands of men. 13 They have mouths and speak not: they have eyes and see not. 14

14 Aures habent, et non audient: * nares habent, et non odorabunt.

15 Manus habent et non palpabunt; pedes habent et non ambulabunt: * non clamabunt in gutture suo.

16 Similes illis fiant qui faciunt ea: * et omnes qui confidunt in eis.

17 Domus Israel speravit in Domino: * adjutor eorum, et protector eorum est.

18 Domus Aaron speravit in Domino: *adjutor eorum, et protector eorum est.

19 Qui timent Dominum speraverunt in Domino: * adjutor eorum, et protector eorum est.

20 Dominus memor fuit nostri: * et benedixit nobis.

21 Benedixit domui Israel: * benedixit domui Aaron.

22 Benedixit omnibus qui timent Dominum: * pusillis cum majoribus.

23 Adjiciat Dominus

They have ears and hear not: they have noses and smell not: 15 They have hands and feel not: they have feet and walk not: neither shall they cry out through their throat. 16 Let them that make them become like unto them; and all such as trust in them. 17 The house of Israel hath hoped in the Lord: he is their helper and their protector. 18 The house of Aaron hath hoped in the Lord: he is their helper and their protector. 19 They that fear the Lord have hoped in the Lord: he is their helper and their protector. 20 The Lord has been mindful of us, and hath blessed us. 21 He hath blessed the house of Israel: he hath blessed the house of Aaron. 22 He hath blessed all that fear the Lord, both little and great. 23 May the Lord add blessings upon you: upon you and upon your chil-

super vos: * supervos et super filios vestros.
24 Benedicti vos à Domino: * qui fecit cœlum et terram.
25 Cœlum cœli Domino: * terram autem dedit filiis hominum.
26 Non mortui laudabunt te Domine: * neque omnes qui descendunt in infernum.
27 Sed nos qui vivimus, benedicimus Domino: * ex hoc nunc et usque in sæculum.

Ant. Nos qui vivimus benedicimus Domino.

Ant. Tempore Pascali, *Alleluia, Allel. Allel.*

dren. 24 Blessed be you of the Lord, who made heaven and earth.
25 The heaven of heavens is the Lord's: but the earth he hath given to the children of men.
26 The dead shall not praise thee, O Lord: nor any of them that go down to hell. 27 But we that live bless the Lord: from this time now and for ever.

Anth. We who are alive, bless the Lord.

Anth. In Paschal time, *Alleluia.*

This Psalm is frequently sung instead of the *In Exitu Israel.*

Psalm cxvi.

LAUDATE Dominum omnes gentes: * laudate eum omnes populi.
2 Quoniam confirmata est super nos misericordia ejus: * et veritas Domini manet in æternum. Gloria Patri, &c.

O PRAISE the Lord, all ye nations: praise him, all ye people.
2 For his mercy is confirmed upon us: and the truth of the Lord remaineth for ever.
Glory be to the Father, &c.

The Little Chapter. 2 Cor. i.

BENEDICTUS Deus, et Pater Domini

BLESSED be the God and Father of our

nostri Jesu Christi, Pater misericordiarum, et Deus totius consolationis, qui consolatur nos in omni tribulatione nostra.

R. Deo gratias.

Lord Jesus Christ, the Father of mercies, and the God of all comfort, who comforteth us in all our tribulation.

R. Thanks be to God.

Hymn.

1 LUCIS Creator optime,
Lucem dierum proferens,
Primordiis lucis novæ,
Mundi parans originem.

1 O GREAT Creator of the light,
Who, from the darksome womb of night,
Brought'st forth new light at nature's birth,
To shine upon the face of earth.

2 Qui mane junctum vesperi
Diem vocari præcipis;
Illabitur tetrum chaos,
Audi preces cum fletibus.

2 Who, by the morn and ev'ning ray,
Hast measur'd time, and called it day;
Vouchsafe to hear our prayers and tears,
Whilst sable night involves the spheres.

3 Ne mens gravata crimine,
Vitæ sit exul munere,
Dum nil perenne cogitat,
Seseque culpis illigat.

3 Lest our frail mind, with sins defil'd,
From gift of life should be exil'd,
And whilst this passing world beguiles,
She sinks a prey to Satan's wiles.

4 Cœleste pulset ostium:
Vitale tollat præmium:
Vitemus omne noxium:
Purgemus omne pessimum.

4 O may she soar to heaven above,
The happy seat of life and love!
O may she grieve for every sin,
And all her faults to shun begin!

5 Præsta, pater piissime,
Patrique compar unice,
Cum Spiritu-Paraclito,
Regnans per omne sæculum. Amen.

5 This prayer, most gracious Father, hear,
Thine equal Son incline his ear;
Who with the holy Ghost and thee,
Doth live and reign eternally. Amen.

V. Dirigatur Domine, oratio mea,
R. Sicut incensem in conspectu tuo.

V. Let my prayer ascend, O Lord,
R. Like incense in thy sight.

Then is said or sung the Anthem at Magnificat.

Song of the B. V. Mary. Luke i. 46.

MAGNIFICAT * anima mea Dominum.
2 Et exultavit spiritus meus: * in Deo salutari meo.
3 Quia respexit humilitatem ancillæ suæ:* ecce enim ex hoc, beatam me dicent omnes generationes.
4 Quai fecit mihi

MY soul doth magnify the Lord. 2 And my spirit hath rejoiced in God my Saviour. 3 Because he hath regarded the humility of his handmaid: for behold from henceforth all generations shall call me blessed. 4 Because he that is mighty hath

magna qui potens est : * et sanctum nomen ejus.

5 Et misericordia ejus à progenie in progenies, * timentibus eum.

6 Fecit potentiam in brachio suo : * dispersit superbos mente cordis sui.

7 Deposuit potentes de sede : * et exaltavit humiles.

8 Esurientes implevit bonis : * et divites dimisit inanes.

9 Suscepit Israel puerum suum : * recordatus misericordiæ suæ.

10 Sicut locutus est ad patres nostros : * Abraham, et semini ejus in sæcula. Gloria Patri, &c.

done great things to me: and holy is his name. 5 And his mercy is from generation unto generation, to them that fear him. 6 He hath showed might in his arm : he hath scattered the proud in the conceit of their heart. 7 He hath put down the mighty ones from their seat : and hath exalted the humble. 8 He hath filled the hungry with good things : and the rich he hath sent empty away. 9 He hath received Israel, his servant : being mindful of his mercy. 10 As he spoke to our fathers : to Abraham and to his seed for ever. Glory, &c.

The Anthem at Magnificat is here repeated, after which the Prayer proper for the day is sung by the Priest.

Oremus.   *Let us Pray.*

EXCITA, quæsumus Domine, potentiam tuam, et veni: ut ab imminentibus peccatorum nostrorum periculis te mereamur protegente eripi, te liberante salvari. Qui vivis et regnas,

EXERT, we beseech thee, O Lord, thy power, and come, that through thy protection we may be freed from the imminent danger of our sins, and be saved by thy deliverance.

in sæcula sælorum. Amen.

V. Dominus vobiscum.
R. Et cum spiritu tuo.
V. Benedicamus Domino.
R. Deo gratias.
V. Fidelium animæ per misericordiam Dei requiescant in pace.

R. Amen.
Pater noster *(in silence.)*
V. Dominus det nobis suam pacem.
R. Et vitam æternam. Amen.

Who livest and reignest world without end. Amen.

V. The Lord be with you.
R. And with thy spirit.
V. Let us bless the Lord.
R. Thanks be to God.
V. May the souls of the faithful departed, through the mercy of God, rest in peace.
R. Amen.
Our Father *(in secret.)*
V. The Lord give us his peace.
R. And eternal life. Amen.

Here one of the Anthems is sung, to be found after Complin.

The Complin.

THE READER BEGINS,

JUBE Domine benedicere.

Benedictio.
Noctem quietam, et finem perfectum conce-

PRAY, Father, give me your blessing.

The Blessing.
May the Lord Almighty grant us a qui-

dat nobis Dominus omnipotens.
R. *Amen.*

et night, and a perfect end.
R. *Amen.*

The Short Lesson. 1 Peter, v.

FRATRES, sobrii estote et vigilate; quia adversarius vester diabolus tanquam leo rugiens circuit, quærens quem devoret: cui resistite fortes in fide.— Tu autem Domine, misere nobis.

BRETHREN, be sober, and watch: because your adversary the devil, as a roaring lion, goeth about seeking whom he may devour; whom resist ye strong in faith. But thou, O Lord, have mercy on us.

R. Deo gratias.

R. Thanks be to God.

V. Adjutorium nostrum in nomine Domini.
R. Qui fecit cœlum et terram. Pater noster, &c.

V. Our help is in the name of the Lord.
R. Who made heaven and earth. Our Father, &c.

Then the Priest makes the Confession.

Confiteor Deo omnipotenti, &c.

I confess to Almighty God, &c.

The Choir answers,

Misereatur tui omnipotens Deus, et dimissis peccatis tuis, perducat te ad vitam æternam.
R. *Amen.*

May Almighty God have mercy on thee, forgive thee thy sins, and bring thee to life everlasting.
R. *Amen.*

THE COMPLIN.

Then the Choir repeats the Confession.

Confiteor Deo omnipotenti, beatæ Mariæ semper virgini, beato Michaeli Archangelo, beato Joanni Baptistæ, sanctis Apostolis Petro et Paulo, omnibus sanctis, et tibi Pater, quia peccavi nimis cogitatione, verbo et opere: *mea culpa, mea culpa, mea maxima culpa.* Ideo precor beatam Mariam semper Virginem, beatum Michaelum Archangelum, beatum Joannem Baptistam, sanctos Apostolos Petrum et Paulum, omnes sanctos, et te Pater, orare pro me ad Dominum Deum nostrum.

I confess to Almighty God, to B. Mary, ever a virgin, to B. Michael the Archangel, to B. John Baptist, to the holy apostles Peter and Paul, to all the saints, and to you, Father, that I have grievously sinned in thought, in word, and in deed: *thro' my fault, thro' my fault, thro' my exceeding great fault.* Therefore I beseech the B. Mary ever a Virgin, B. Michael the Archangel, B. John Baptist, the holy Apostles Peter and Paul, all the saints, and you, Father, to pray to the Lord our God for me.

Then the Priest says,

Misereatur vestri omnipotens Deus, et dimissis peccatis vestris, perducat vos ad vitam æternam.
R. *Amen.*
Indulgentiam, absolutionem, et remissionem peccatorum nos-

May Almighty God have mercy on you, and forgiving your sins bring you to life everlasting.
R. *Amen.*
May the Almighty and merciful Lord grant us pardon, abso-

trorum, tribuat nobis omnipotens et misericors Dominus.

R. *Amen.*

V. Converte nos Deus salutaris noster.

R. Et averte iram tuam a nobis.

V. Deus in adjutorium meum intende.

R. Domine ad adjuvandum me festina.

Gloria Patri, &c.

Ant. Miserere.

lution, and remission of our sins.

R. *Amen.*

V. Convert us, O God our Saviour. R. And turn off thine anger from us. V. O God, come to my assistance. R. O Lord, make haste to help me. Glory be to the Father, &c. As it was in the beginning, &c.

Ant. Have mercy.

In Paschal Time, Anth. *Alleluia.*

Psalm iv.

CUM invocarem exaudivit me Deus justitiæ meæ: * in tribulatione dilatasti mihi.

2 Miserere mei: * et exaudi orationem meam.

3 Filii hominum usquequo gravi corde? * Ut quid diligitis vanitatem, et quæritis mendacium?

4 Et scitote quoniam mirificavit Dominus sanctum suum: * Dominus exaudiet me, cum clamavero ad eum.

WHEN I called upon him the God of my justice heard me; when I was in distress, thou hast enlarged me. 2 Have mercy on me, and hear my prayer. 3 O ye sons of men, how long will you be dull of heart? Why do you love vanity and seek after lying? 4 Know ye also that the Lord hath made his holy One wonderful: the Lord will hear me when I shall cry unto him. 5 Be ye

5 Irascimini, et nolite peccare: * quæ dicitis in cordibus vestris, in cubilibus vestris, compungimini.

6 Sacrificate sacrificium justitiæ, et sperate in Domino: * Multi dicunt, quis ostendit nobis bona?

7 Signatum est super nos lumen vultus tui Domine: * dedisti lætitiam in corde meo.

8 A fructu frumenti vini et olei sui, * multiplicati sunt.

9 In pace in'idipsum * dormiam, et requiescam.

10 Quoniam tu Domine singulariter in spe * constituisti me.

Gloria Patri, &c.

angry, and sin not: the things you say in your hearts, be sorry for them upon your beds. 6 Offer up the sacrifice of justice, and trust in the Lord: many say, Who showeth us good things? 7 The light of thy countenance, O Lord, is signed upon us: thou hast given gladness in my heart. 8 By the fruit of their corn, their wine, and oil, they are multiplied. 9 In peace in the self same, I will sleep, and I will rest. 10 For thou, O Lord, singularly hast settled me in hope.

Glory be to the Father, &c.

Psalm xxx.

IN te Domine speravi, non confundar in æternum: * in justitia tua libera me.

2 Inclina ad me aurem tuam: * accelera ut eruas me.

3 Esto mihi in Deum protectorem, et in do-

IN thee, O Lord, have I hoped, let me never be confounded: deliver me in thy justice. 2 Bow down thine ear to me, make haste to deliver me. 3 Be thou unto me a God, a protector: and a house of

mum refugii: * ut salvum me facias.

4 Quoniam fortitudo mea, et refugium meum es tu: * et propter nomen tuum deduces me, et enutries me.

5 Educes me de laqueo hoc, quem absconderunt mihi: * quoniam tu es protector meus.

6 In manus tuas commendo spiritu meum: * redimisti me Domine, Deus veritatis.

Gloria Patri, &c

refuge: to save me. 4 For thou art my strength and my refuge: and for thy name's sake thou wilt lead me and nourish me. 5 Thou wilt bring me out of this snare, which they have hidden for me, for thou art my protector. 6 Into thy hands I commend my spirit: thou hast redeemed me, O Lord the God of truth. Glory be to the Father. &c.

Psalm xc.

QUI habitat in adjutorio Altissimi, * in protectione Dei cœli commorabitur.

2 Dicet Domino susceptor meus es tu, et refugium meum: * Deus meus sperabo in eum.

3 Quoniam ipse liberavit me de laqueo venantium, * et a verbo aspero.

4 Scapulis suis obumbrabit tibi: * et sub pennis ejus: sperabis.

5 Scuto circumdabit te veritas ejus: * non

HE that dwelleth in the aid of the Most High, shall abide under the protection of the God of heaven. 2 He shall say to the Lord: thou art my protector and my refuge: my God, in him will I trust. 3 For he hath delivered me from the snare of the hunters, and from the sharp word. 4 He will overshadow thee with his shoulders, and under his wings thou shalt trust.

timebis a timore nocturno.

6 A sagitta volante in die, a negotio perambulante in tenebris, * ab incursu, et dæmonio meridiano.

7 Cadent a latere tuo mille, et decem millia a dextris tuis : * ad te autem non appropinquabit.

8 Verumtamen oculis tuis considerabis ; * et retributionem peccatorum videbis.

9 Quoniam tu es Domine spes mea : * altissimum posuisti refugium tuum.

10 Non accedet ad te malum : * et flagellum non appropinquabit tabernaculo tuo.

11 Quoniam angelis suis mandavit de te : * ut custodiant te in omnibus viis tuis.

12 In manibus portabunt te : * ne forte offendas ad lapidem pedem tuum.

13 Super aspidem et basiliscum ambulabis ; * et conculcabis leonem et draconem.

5 His truth shall compass thee with a shield : thou shalt not be afraid of the terror of the night : 6 Or the arrow that flieth in the day : of the business that walketh about in the dark : of invasion, or of the noon-day devil. 7 A thousand shall fall at thy side, and ten thousand at thy right hand : but it shall not come nigh thee. 8 But thou shalt consider with thine eyes, and shalt see the reward of sinners. 9 Because thou, O Lord, art my hope : thou hast made the Most High thy refuge. 10 There shall no evil come to thee : nor shall the scourge come near thy dwelling. 11 For he hath given his angels charge over thee : to keep thee in all thy ways. 12 In their hands they shall bear thee up : lest thou dash thy foot against a stone. 13 Thou shalt walk upon the asp and the basilisk ; and thou shalt

11—P

14 Quoniam in me speravit liberabo eum; * protegam eum, quoniam cognovit nomen meum.

15 Clamabit ad me, et ego exaudiam eum; * cum ipso sum in tribulatione: eripiam eum, et glorificabo eum.

16 Longitudine dierum replebo eum: * et ostendam illi salutare meum. Gloria Patri, &c.

14 Because he hoped in me, I will deliver him: I will protect him, because he hath known my name. 15 He shall cry to me and I will hear him: I am with him in tribulation: I will deliver him, and I will glorify him. 16 I will fill him with length of days: and I will show him my salvation. Glory be to the Father, &c.

Psalm cxxxiii.

ECCE nunc benedicite Dominum, * omnes servi Domini.

2 Qui statis in domo Domini: * in atriis domus Dei nostri.

3 In noctibus extollite manus vestras in sancta, * et benedicite Dominum.

4 Benedicat te Dominus ex Sion, * qui fecit coelum et terram.

Gloria Patri, &c.

Ant. Miserere mihi Domine, et exaudi orationem meam.

BEHOLD now, bless ye the Lord, all ye servants of the Lord. 2 Who stand in the house of the Lord, in the courts of the house of our God. 3 In the nights lift up your hands to the holy places, and bless ye the Lord. 4 May the Lord out of Sion bless thee, he that made heaven and earth. Glory, &c.

Ant. Have mercy on me, O Lord, and hear my prayer.

In Paschal time, Anth. *Alleluia, Alleluia, Alleluia.*

The Hymn.

TE lucis ante terminum,	BEFORE the closing of the day,
Rerum Creator poscimus,	Creator, we thee humbly pray,
Ut pro tua clementia,	That for thy wonted mercy's sake,
Sis præsul et custodia.	Thou us into protection take.
2 Procul recedant somnia,	2 May nothing in our minds excite,
Et noctium phantasmata:	Vain dreams and phantoms of the night;
Hostemque nostrum comprime,	Our enemies repress, that so
Ne polluantur corpora.	Our bodies no uncleanness know.
3 Præsta, Pater piissime,	3 In this, most gracious Father, hear,
Patrique compar unice,	With Christ thine equal Son, our prayer,
Cum Spiritu Paraclito,	Who, with the Holy Ghost and thee,
Regnans per omne sæculum. *Amen.*	Doth live and reign eternally. *Amen.*

The Little Chapter. Jeremias xiv.

TU autem in nobis es Domine, et nomen sanctum tuum invoca- | BUT thou, O Lord, art among us; and thy holy name is called upon tum est super nos; ne derelinquas nos, Domine Deus noster.

R. Deo gratias.

Resp. In manus tuas Domine, commendo spiritum meum.

R. In manus, &c.

V. Redemisti nos Domine Deus, veritatis. Commendo spiritum meum. Gloria Patri, &c.

R. In manus, &c.

V. Custodi nos Domine ut pupillam oculi.

R. Sub umbra alarum tuarum protege nos.

Ant. Salva nos.

us; forsake us not, O Lord our God.

R. Thanks be to God.

Res. Into thy hands, O Lord, I commend my spirit. R. Into thy hands, O Lord, &c. V. Thou hast redeemed us, O Lord, the God of truth: R. I commend my spirit. V. Glory be to the Father, and to the Son, and to the Holy Ghost. R. Into thy hands, O Lord, I commend my spirit. V. Keep us, O Lord, as the apple of thine eye. R. Protect us under the shadow of thy wings.

Ant. Save us.

The Song of Simeon. Luke ii.

NUNC dimittis servum tuum, Domine, * secundum verbum tuum, in pace.

2 Quia viderunt oculi mei; * salutare tuum.

3 Quod parasti, * ante faciem omnium populorum.

4 Lumen ad revelationem Gentium; * et

NOW thou dost dismiss thy servant, O Lord, according to thy word, in peace.

2 Because mine eyes have seen thy salvation.

3 Which thou hast prepared before the face of all peoples.

4 A light to the revelation of the Gentiles,

gloriam plebis tuæ Israel. Gloria Patri, &c.

Ant. Salva nos Domina vigilantes, custodi nos dormientes; ut vigilemus cum Christo, et requiescamus in pace.

Kyrie eleison. Christe eleison. Kyrie eleison. Pater noster, *(secreto.)*

V. Et ne nos inducas intentationem.

R. Sed libera nos a malo. Credo in Deum, *(secreto.)*

V. Carnis resurrectionem.

R. Et vitam æternam. *Amen.*

V. Benedictus es Domine, Deus patrum nostrorum.

R. Et Laudabilis et gloriosus in sæcula.

V. Benedicamus Patrem et Filium cum Sancto Spiritu.

R. Laudemus, et super exaltemus eum in sæcula.

V. Benedictus es Domine in firmamento cœli.

R. Et laudabilis, et gloriosus, et super exaltatus in sæcula.

and the glory of thy people Israel. Glory, &c.

Ant. Save us, O Lord, waking, and keep us sleeping, that we may watch with Christ, and rest in peace.

Lord, have mercy on us. Christ, have mercy on us. Lord, have mercy on us. Our Father, &c.

V. Lead us not into temptation. R. But deliver us from evil. I believe in God, &c. V. The resurrection of the body. R. And life everlasting. Amen. V. Blessed art thou, O Lord, the God of our fathers.

R. And worthy of praise, and glorious for ever. V. Let us bless the Father, and the Son, with the Holy Ghost. R. Let us praise him and magnify him for ever. V. Thou art blessed, O Lord, in the firmament of heaven. R. And worthy of praise, and glorious, and magnified for ever. V. May the almighty and merciful Lord bless us and

V. Benedicat et custodiat nos omnipotens et misericors Dominus.

R. *Amen.*

V. Dignare Domine nocte ista.

R. Sine peccato nos custodire.

V. Miserere nostri Domine.

R. Miserere nostri.

V. Fiat misericordia tua Domine super nos.

R. Quemadmodum speravimus in te.

V. Domine exaudi orationem meam.

R. Et clamor meus ad te veniat.

V. Dominus vobiscum.

R. Et cum spiritu tuo.

keep us. R. Amen.
V. Vouchsafe, O Lord, this night. R. To keep us without sin. V. Have mercy on us, O Lord. R. Have mercy on us. V. Let thy mercy, O Lord, be upon us. R. As we have hoped in thee. V. O Lord, hear my prayer. R. And let my cry come to thee. V. The Lord be with you. R. And with thy spirit.

Oremus.

VISITA, quæsumus Domine, habitationem istam, et omnes insidias inimici ab ea longe repelle; angeli tui sancti habitent in ea, qui nos in pace custodiant; et benedictio tua sit super nos semper. Per Dominum.

Let us Pray.

VISIT, we beseech thee, O Lord, this habitation, and drive far from it all snares of the enemy; let thy holy angels dwell herein, who may keep us in peace; and let thy blessing be always upon us. Through our Lord Jesus Christ. Amen.

ANTHEMS.

V. Dominus vobiscum.
R. Et cum spiritu tuo.
V. Benedicamus Domino.
R. Deo gratias. *(Benedictio:)* Benedicat et custodiat nos omnipotens et misericors Dominus, Pater, et Filius, et Spiritus Sanctus. R. Amen.

V. The Lord be with you. R. And with thy spirit. V. Let us bless the Lord. R. Thanks be to God. May the almighty and merciful Lord, Father, Son, and Holy Ghost, bless us, and keep us. Amen.

Then is said one of the following anthems and a prayer in commemoration of the Blessed Virgin.

Anthems

FOR PARTICULAR PERIODS OF THE YEAR.

Anthem from First Sunday of Advent till the Purification.

ALMA Redemptoris mater, quæ pervia cœli,
Porta manes, et stella maris, succurre cadenti Surgere qui curat populo; tu quæ genuisti, Natura mirante, tuum sanctum genitorem.
Virgo priùs ac posteriùs, Gabrielis ab ore

MOTHER of Jesus, heaven's open gate,
Star of the sea, support the falling state
Of mortals; thou, whose womb thy Maker bore,
And yet (strange thing!) a Virgin as before.
Who didst from Gabriel's "Hail!" the news receive,

Sumens illud Ave, peccatorum miserere.

V. Angelus Domini nuntiavit Mariæ.

R. Et concepit de Spiritu Sancto.

Oremus.

GRATIAM tuam, quæsumus Domine, mentibus nostris infunde: ut qui angelo nuntiante Christi Filii tui incarnationem cognovimus, per passionem ejus et crucem ad resurectionis gloriam perducamur. Per eundem Christum Dominum nostrum.—Amen.

Repenting sinners by thy prayers relieve.

V. The angel of the Lord declared unto Mary.

R. And she conceived by the Holy Ghost.

Let us Pray.

POUR forth, we beseech thee, O Lord, thy grace into our hearts; that we, to whom the incarnation of Christ thy Son was made known by the message of an angel, may, by his passion and cross, be brought to the glory of his resurrection, through the same Christ our Lord. Amen.

From the first Vespers of Christmas-day is said,

V. Post partum virgo inviolata permansisti.

R. Dei genitrix intercede pro nobis.

V. After child-birth, thou didst remain a pure virgin.

R. O Mother of God, intercede for us.

Oremus.

DEUS, qui salutis æternæ, beatæ Mariæ virginitate fœcun-

Let us Pray.

O GOD, who by the fruitful virginity of blessed Mary, hast

da, humano generi præ-
mia præstitisti : tribue
quæsumus, ut ipsam pro
nobis intercedere sen-
tiamus, per quam mer-
uimus auctorem vitæ
suscipere Dominum nos-
trum Jesum Christum,
Filium tuum. Amen.

given to mankind the
rewards of eternal sal-
vation: grant, we be-
seech thee, that we may
experience her inter-
cession, by whom we
received the Author of
Life, our Lord Jesus
Christ thy Son. R.
Amen.

Anthem from the Purification till Maunday Thursday.

AVE regina cœlorum,
Ave domina angel-
orum,

Salve radix, salve porta,

Ex qua mundo lux est
orta.
Gaude virgo gloriosa,

Super omnes speciosa;

Vale o valde, decora,

Et pro nobis Christum
exora.

V. Dignare me, lua-
dare te, virgo sacrata.

R. Da mihi virtutem
contra hostes tuos.

HAIL, Mary, queen
of heavenly spheres!
Hail, whom the angelic
host reveres!
Hail, fruitful root!
Hail, sacred gate,
Whence the world's
light derives its date!
O glorious maid, with
beauty blest!
May joys eternal fill
thy breast!
Thus crowned with
beauty and with joy,
Thy prayers for us with
Christ employ.

V. Vouchsafe, O sa-
cred Virgin, to accept
my praises.

R. Give me strength
against thine enemies.

Oremus.

CONCEDE, misericors Deus fragilitati nostræ præsidium: ut qui sanctæ Dei Genitricis memoriam agimus, intercessionis ejus auxilio, à nostris iniquitatibus resurgamus. Per eundem Christum Dominum nostrum. Amen.

Let us Pray.

GRANT us, O merciful God, strength against our enemies; that we who celebrate the memory of the holy Mother of God, may be enabled to rise again from our iniquities. Through the same Christ our Lord. Amen.

Anthem from Holy Saturday till Trinity-Eve.

REGINA cœli lætare, Alleluia.
Quia quem meruisti portare, Alleluia.
Resurrexit sicut dixit, Alleluia.
Ora pro nobis Deum, Alleluia.

TRIUMPH, O Queen of heaven, to see
The sacred infant born of thee,
Return in glory from the tomb,
And with thy prayers prevent our doom.

V. Gaude et lætare, Virgo Maria. Alleluia.

R. Quia surrexit Dominus vere. Alleluia,

V. Rejoice, and be glad, O Virgin Mary. Alleluia.

R. For the Lord is truly risen. Alleluia.

Oremus.

DEUS, qui per resurrectionem Filii tui Domini nostri Jesu Christi mundum lætificare dignatus es; præ-

Let us Pray.

O GOD, who hast designed, by the resurrection of thy Son our Lord Jesus Christ, to fill the world with joy;

sta quæsumus, ut per ejus genitricem, virginem Mariam perpetuæ capiamus gaudia vitæ. Per eundem Christum Dominum nostrum. Amen.

grant, we beseech thee, that through the V. M. his Mother, we may receive the joys of eternal life. Through, &c. Amen.

Anthem from Trinity-Eve till Advent.

SALVE Regina, mater misericordiæ!— vita, dulcedo, et spes nostra, salve!

Ad te clamamus exules Filii Hevæ,
Ad te suspiramus gementes et flentes in hac lacrymarum valle.

Eia ergo advocata nostra, illos tuos misericordes oculos ad nos converte.
Et Jesum, benedictum fructum ventris tui, nobis post hoc exilium ostende.
O clemens, O pia, O dulcis virgo Maria.

V. Ora pro nobis sancta Dei genitrix.
R. Ut digni efficiamur promissionibus Christi.

HAIL, happy Queen, thou mercy's parent, hail.
Life, hope, and comfort of this earthly vale.

To thee we, Eva's wretched children, cry,
In sighs and tears, to thee we suppliants fly.

Rise, glorious advocate, exert thy love,
And let our vows those eyes of pity move.
O sweet, O pious maid! for us obtain,
For us who long have in our exile lain,
To see thy infant Jesus, and with him to reign.

V. Pray for us, O holy Mother of God.
R. That we may be made worthy of the promises of Christ.

Oremus.   *Let us Pray.*

OMNIPOTENS sempiterne Deus, qui gloriosæ Virginis Matris Mariæ corpus et animam, ut dignum Filii tui habitaculum effici mereretur, Spiritu Sancto co-operante, præparasti: da, ut cujus commemoratione lætamur, ejus pia intercessione ab instantibus malis et a morte perpetua liberemur. Per eundem Christum Dominum nostrum. Amen.

ALMIGHTY and eternal God, who, by the co-operation of the Holy Ghost, didst prepare the body and soul of the glorious Virgin Mother Mary, that she might become a worthy habitation for thy Son; grant that, as with joy we celebrate her memory, so by her pious intercession we may be delivered from present evils, and eternal death. Through, &c. R. Amen.

V. Divinum auxilium maneat semper nobiscum. Amen. Pater. Ave. Credo. *(in silence.)*

V. May the divine assistance remain always with us. Our Father. Hail Mary. I believe. *(in silence.)*

Ejaculations to Jesus in the B. Sacrament.

I adore thee every moment, O Living Bread of Heaven, great Sacrament!

Jesus, Heart of Mary, I pray thee send thy blessing on my soul.

Holiest Jesu! loving Saviour! I give thee my heart.

[Indulgence, 200 days each time.]

BENEDICTION.

PRAYER AT BENEDICTION,
OR AT THE BEGINNING OF EACH VISIT TO THE BLESSED SACRAMENT.

MY Lord Jesus Christ, who for the love which thou bearest to men, dost remain day and night in this Sacrament, full of mercy and of love, inviting, expecting, receiving all them who come to visit thee, I believe that thou art present in the blessed Sacrament of the altar. I adore thee, confessing my own misery and nothingness, and I thank thee for all the mercies which thou hast bestowed upon me, especially for having given me thyself in this Sacrament, for having given me thy most holy Mother Mary for my advocate, and for having called me to visit thee at this time. I salute thy most loving heart, and I desire to do so for three ends: first, in thanksgiving for this great gift; secondly, to atone for all the injuries thou hast received from thine enemies in this Sacrament; thirdly, to adore thee in all places in which thou art least honoured and most neglected in the holy Sacrament. O my Jesus, I love thee with all my heart; I am sorry for having hitherto displeased thy infinite goodness; I resolve, with the assistance of thy grace, never more to offend thee; and at this moment, miserable as I am, I desire to consecrate my whole being to thee. I give thee my will, my affections, my desires, and all that I have. From this day forward do with me, and whatever belongs to me, what thou pleasest; I ask and desire only thy love, the gift of final perseverance, and the perfect accomplishment of thy holy will. I recommend to thee the souls in purgatory, particularly those who were most devout to the Blessed Sacrament and to holy Mary; and I recommend to thee all poor sinners. Finally, my dear Saviour, I unite all my affections with those of thy most loving Heart; and thus united, I offer them to thy Eternal Father and I beseech him, in thy name, and for thy sake, to accept them. Amen.

Benediction of the Blessed Sacrament.

When the priest opens the Tabernacle, and incenses the Blessed Sacrament, is sung the hymn,

O SALUTARIS Hostia,
Quæ cœli pandis ostium:

Bella premunt hostilia,

Da robur, fer auxilium.

O VICTIM of salvation's cause,
Who Heaven's gates hast open laid,

While overwhelmed with hostile wars,

Afford us strength and grant us aid

Uni trinoque Domino,	To great JEHOVAH, one and three,
Sit sempiterna gloria,	Be everlasting glory given:
Qui vitam sine termino	A life of endless bliss may He
Nobis donet in patria. Amen.	Award us in the realms of heaven. Amen.

Then follows the Litany of the Blessed Virgin, *page* 184, *or some Psalm or Hymn appropriate to the Feast.*

Then the Hymn Tantum ergo Sacramentum, *all present making a profound inclination at the words* Veneremur cernui.

TANTUM ERGO.

TANTUM ergo Sacramentum *Veneremur cernui;*	TO the sacred Host inclining, In adoring awe we bend;

Et antiquum documentum	Ancient forms. their place resigning
Novo cedat ritui:	Unto rites of nobler end:
Præstet fides supplementum	Faith the senses dark refining,
Sensuum defectui.	Mysteries to comprehend.
Genitori, Genitoque,	Sire and Son all power possessing,
Laus et jubilatio,	God, to Thee all glory be,
Salus, honor, virtus quoque	Might, salvation, honour, blessing,
Sit et benedictio:	Unto all eternity;
Procedenti ab utroque	Holy Ghost from both proceeding,
Compar sit laudatio. Amen.	Equal glory be to Thee. Amen.

BENEDICTION.

V. Panem de cœlo præstitisti eis. [*Alleluia.*]

R. Omne delectamentum in se habentem. [*Alleluia.*]

Oremus.

DEUS qui nobis, sub sacramento mirabili, passionis tuæ memoriam reliquisti: tribue, quæsumus, ita nos corporis et sanguinis tui, sacra mysteria venerari, ut redemptionis tuæ fructum in nobis jugiter sentiamus. Qui vivis et regnas

V. Thou hast given them bread from heaven. [*Alleluia.*]

R. Replenished with whatever is delicious. [*Alleluia.*]

Let us pray.

O GOD, who in this wonderful sacrament hast left us a memorial of thy passion: grant us, we beseech thee, so to reverence the sacred mysteries of thy body and blood, as in our souls to be always sensible of the redemption thou hast purchased for us. Who livest and

in sæcula sæculorum. Amen.

reignest for ever and ever. Amen.

AFTER BENEDICTION.

Adoremus in æternum Sanctissimum Sacramentum.

Let us adore for ever the most Holy Sacrament.

Psalm 116. *Laudate.*

Laudate Dominum omnes gentes :* laudate eum omnes populi.

Praise the Lord all ye nations: praise him all ye people.

Quoniam confirmata est super nos misericordia ejus :* et veritas Domini manet in æternum.

Because his mercy is confirmed upon us: and the truth of the Lord remaineth for ever.

Gloria Patri, &c.

Glory be, &c.

Adoremus, &c.

Let us adore, &c.

HYMN TO THE BLESSED SACRAMENT.

JESUS! my Lord, my God, my all!
    How can I love thee as I ought?
And how revere this wondrous gift,
    So far surpassing hope or thought?
        Sweet Sacrament! we thee adore!
        Oh, make us love thee more and more!

Had I but Mary's sinless heart
    To love thee with, my dearest King,
Oh, with what bursts of fervent praise
    Thy goodness, Jesus, would I sing.
        Sweet Sacrament! we thee adore!
        Oh, make us love thee more and more!

Oh, see: within a creature's hand
    The vast Creator deigns to be,
Reposing infant-like, as though
    On Joseph's arm, or Mary's knee.
        Sweet Sacrament! we thee adore!
        Oh, make us love thee more and more!

Thy Body, Soul, and Godhead all!
    Oh, mystery of love divine!
I cannot compass all I have;
    For all thou hast and art are mine!
        Sweet Sacrament! we thee adore!
        Oh, make us love thee more and more!

O Sacrament most holy! O Sacrament divine!
All praise and all thanksgiving be every moment thine.

One hundred days indulgence each time. Plenary once a month if said daily.

Spiritual Communion, and Visits to the Blessed Sacrament.

You make a *Spiritual Communion* when you tell Jesus that you believe He is present in the Blessed Sacrament, and desire that He would give Himself to you, for which you may say this prayer:

I BELIEVE in thee, O my Jesus, present in the most holy Sacrament of the Altar: I love thee above all things; and I desire to receive thee into my soul. Since I cannot now receive thee sacramentally, come at least spiritually into my heart. I embrace thee and I unite myself to thee, as if thou wast already there. Oh, permit me not ever to be separated from thee.—*St. Liguori.*

Say this prayer when you go into a church *to visit the Blessed Sacrament*, also at home, at work, or anywhere.

DIVINE PRAISES.

Pius VII. granted an Indulgence of one year to all who recite the following.

Blessed be God.
Blessed be His Holy Name.
Blessed be Jesus Christ, true God and true Man.
Blessed be the Name of Jesus.
Blessed be Jesus in the most holy Sacrament of the Altar.

Blessed be the great Mother of God, Mary most holy.
Blessed be her holy and Immaculate Conception.
Blessed be the name of Mary, Virgin and Mother.
Blessed be God in His Angels and in His Saints. Amen.

THE QUARANT' ORE,
OR,
Forty Hours Devotion to the Blessed Sacrament,

Was commenced at Milan in 1534, and was introduced into Rome by St. Philip Neri in 1548. It was sanctioned by Pope Clement VIII., and to encourage this devotion Pope Clement XIII. granted a Plenary Indulgence to the faithful who, on confessing their sins and receiving the Blessed Eucharist, should visit any church or chapel where this devotion was being carried on.

The Indulgence may be gained, 1st, by visiting the Blessed Sacrament once each day during the three days of exposition; 2nd, to receive the Holy Communion on one of the three days; but not necessarily in the same church or chapel where the Blessed Sacrament is exposed.

Pope Paul V. also granted an Indulgence of ten years and ten *quadragenæ* for every visit made to the Blessed Sacrament while thus exposed.

Suitable prayers will be found at page 182.

ACTS OF ADORATION
To Jesus in the Blessed Sacrament.

[For every recital, an Indulgence of 300 days, applicable to the souls in purgatory.]

I. I adore thee profoundly, my Jesus, in the Blessed Sacrament; I acknowledge thee true God and true Man. By this my act of adoration I intend to make thee reparation for the coldness of so many of thy people, who pass before thy churches, nay, before thy very tabernacle, where hour after hour thou dost deign to dwell in loving impatience to communicate thyself to thy faithful; yet do not even bow the knee before thee, but, like the Israelites in the wilderness, seem by their indifference to loathe this heavenly manna. I offer thee thine own most Precious Blood which thou didst shed from the wound in thy left foot, in reparation for this hateful coldness, and, entering therein, I say, and will never cease to say:

    Blessed and praised every moment
   Be the most holy and divine Sacrament.
Our Father. Hail Mary. Glory, &c.

II. I adore thee profoundly, my Jesus; I acknowledge thee present in the most holy Sacrament. By this act of adoration, I would make amends for the forgetfulness of so many Christian people, who, when they see thee go to the poor sick, to be their strength in their great journey give thee even one outward sign of homage. I offer thee, in reparation for this coldness, that most Precious Blood which thou didst shed from the wound in thy right foot, and, entering therein, I say, and will never cease to say,

> Blessed and praised every moment
> Be the most holy and divine Sacrament.

Our Father. Hail Mary. Glory, &c.

III. I adore thee profoundly, my Jesus, true bread of life eternal; and by this my act of adoration I would make thee compensation for all the wounds with which thy Sacred Heart bleeds daily to see the profanation of those churches wherein thou dost vouchsafe to abide beneath the sacramental species, to receive the love and adoration of thy people. I offer thee, in reparation for all those irreverences, that most Precious Blood which thou didst shed from the wound in thy left hand, and entering therein, I say every moment,

> Blessed and praised every moment
> Be the most holy and divine Sacrament!

Our Father. Hail Mary. Glory, &c.

IV. I adore thee profoundly, my Jesus, the living bread which has come down from heaven; and by this act of adoration I would make amends for all the acts of irreverence which thy people day by day commit whilst they assist at holy Mass, in which bloodless sacrifice thou dost renew the very sacrifice which once thou didst consummate on Calvary for our salvation. I offer thee, in reparation for all this ingratitude, that most Precious Blood which thou didst shed from the wound in thy right hand; and entering therein, I unite my voice with the voices of the holy angels who adore around thy throne, saying with them:

Blessed and praised every moment
Be the most holy and divine Sacrament!
Our Father. Hail Mary. Glory, &c.

V. I adore thee profoundly, my Jesus, true victim of expiation for our sins; and I offer thee this act of adoration in compensation for the sacrilegious outrages thou dost receive from so many of thy ungrateful people, who dare to draw nigh to thee and receive thee in communion with mortal sin upon their souls. In reparation for these hateful sacrileges, I offer thee those last drops of thy most Precious Blood which thou didst shed from the wound in thy side; and entering therein, I approach thee with acts of adoration, love, and thanksgiving, and with all holy souls who are devout to thee in the most holy Sacrament, I say:

Blessed and praised every moment
Be the most holy and divine Sacrament!
Our Father. Hail Mary. Glory, &c.
Tantum ergo Sacramentum, page 175.
V. Panem de cœlo, &c., page 177.
Deus qui nobis, &c.

LITANY OF THE B. VIRGIN.

WE fly to thy patronage, O holy Mother of God, despise not our petitions in our necessities, but deliver us from all dangers, O ever glorious and blessed Virgin.

SUB tuum præsidium confugimus, sancta Dei genitrix, nostras deprecationes ne despicias in necessitatibus nostris, sed a periculis cunctis libera nos, semper Virgo gloriosa et

LITANY OF THE BLESSED VIRGIN.

Lord, have mercy on us.	Kyrie eleison.
Lord, have mercy on us.	*Kyrie eleison.*
Christ, have mercy on us.	Christe eleison.
Christ, have mercy on us.	*Christe eleison.*
Lord, have mercy on us.	Kyrie eleison.
Lord, have mercy on us.	*Kyrie eleison.*
Christ, hear us.	Christe audi nos.
Christ, graciously hear us.	*Christe exaudi nos.*
God, the Father heaven,	Pater de cœlis Deus,
God the Son, Redeemer of the world,	Fili Redemptor mundi Deus,
God the Holy Ghost,	Spiritus Sancte Deus,
Holy Trinity, one God,	Sancta Trinitas, unus Deus,
Holy Mary, *Pray for us.*	Sancta Maria, *Ora pro nobis.*
Holy Mother of God,	Sancta Dei genitrix,
Holy Virgin of virgins,	Sancta Virgo virginum,

Have mercy on us. — *Miserere nobis.*

Pray for us. — *Ora pro nobis.*

LITANY OF THE BLESSED VIRGIN

Mother of Christ,	Mater Christi,
Mother of divine grace,	Mater divinæ gratiæ,
Mother most pure,	Mater purissima,
Mother most chaste,	Mater castissima,
Mother inviolate,	Mater inviolata,
Mother undefiled,	Mater intemerata,
Mother most amiable,	Mater amabilis,
Mother most admirable,	Mater admirabilis,
Mother of our Creator,	Mater Creatoris,
Mother of our Redeemer,	Mater Salvatoris,
Virgin most prudent,	Virgo prudentissima,
Virgin most venerable,	Virgo veneranda,
Virgin most renowned,	Virgo prædicanda,
Virgin most powerful,	Virgo potens,
Virgin most merciful,	Virgo clemens,
Virgin most faithful,	Virgo fidelis,
Mirror of justice,	Speculum justitiæ,
Seat of Wisdom,	Sedes Sapientiæ,

Pray for us. — *Ora pro nobis.*

LITANY OF THE BLESSED VIRGIN.

Cause of our joy	Causa nostræ lætitiæ,
Spiritual Vessel,	Vas spirituale,
Vessel of honour,	Vas honorabile,
Vessel of singular devotion,	Vas insigne devotionis,
Mystical Rose,	Rosa Mystica,
Tower of David,	Turris Davidica,
Tower of ivory,	Turris eburnea,
House of gold,	Domus aurea,
Ark of the covenant,	Fœderis arca,
Gate of heaven,	Janua cœli,
Morning Star,	Stella matutina,
Health of the weak,	Salus infirmorum,
Refuge of sinners,	Refugium peccatorum,
Comforter of the afflicted,	Consolatrix afflictorum,
Help of Christians,	Auxilium Christianorum,
Queen of angels,	Regina angelorum,
Queen of patriarchs,	Regina patriarcharum,
Queen of prophets,	Regina prophetarum,
Queen of apostles,	Regina apostolorum,
Queen of martyrs,	Regina martyrum,

Pray for us. *Ora pro nobis.*

188 LITANY OF THE BLESSED VIRGIN.

Queen of confessors, — Regina confessorum,
Queen of virgins, — Regina Virginum,
Queen of all saints, — Regina sanctorum omnium,
Queen conceived without original sin, — Regina sine labe originali concepta,

Pray for us. — *Ora pro nobis.*

Lamb of God, who takest away the sins of the world, *Spare us, O Lord.* — Agnus Dei, qui tollis peccata mundi, *Parce nobis Domine.*

Lamb of God, who takest away the sins of the world, *Graciously hear us, O Lord.* — Agnus Dei, qui tollis peccata mundi, *Exaudi nos, Domine.*

Lamb of God, who takest away the sins of the world, *Have mercy on us.* — Agnus Dei, qui tollis peccata mundi, *Miserere nobis.*

Christ hear us. — Christe audi nos.
Christ graciously hear us. — *Christe exaudi nos.*

V. Pray for us, O holy Mother of God. — V. Ora pro nobis, sancta Dei Genetrix.

LITANY OF THE BLESSED VIRGIN.

R. That we may be made worthy of the promises of Christ.

R. Ut digni efficiamur promissionibus Christi.

LET US PRAY.

POUR forth we beseech thee, O Lord, thy grace into our hearts; that we, to whom the incarnation of Christ thy Son was made known, by the message of an angel, may, by his passion and cross, be brought to the glory of his resurrection; thro' the same Christ our Lord. *Amen.*

OREMUS.

GRATIAM tuam quæsumus Domine, mentibus nostris infunde, ut qui Angelo nuntiante, Christi Filii tui Incarnationem cognovimus, per passionem ejus et crucem ad Resurrectionis gloriam perducamur. Per eundem Christum Dominum nostrum. *Amen*

Indulgences: i. 300 days each time it is recited.
ii. To all who recite it daily, a Plenary Indulgence on the Feasts of the Immaculate Conception, the Nativity, the Annunciation, the Purification, and the Assumption, if, after Confession and Communion, they visit a public church and pray for the intention of the Pope.

INDULGENCES.

"To those who seek God's love and the glory of heaven, Indulgences are a rich treasure, and may be compared to so many precious gems."— *St. Ignatius of Loyola.*

What is an Indulgence? An Indulgence is a remission of the *temporal punishment* which often remains due to sin, after its guilt has been forgiven.

There are two sorts of Indulgences: 1, those that are *plenary* or general; and 2, those that are *partial* or limited.

1. A plenary Indulgence is so called, because it remits the whole of the temporal punishment due to sins already forgiven. Accordingly, a person who may have been fortunate enough to gain such an indulgence, and receive its full application, would be like a newly-baptized adult—free from sin and its penalty; so that if he were to die in this happy state, he would go up directly to heaven, without passing through the fire of purgatory.

2. A partial Indulgence is one that remits only a portion of the penalty due to sin. Such, for instance, is an Indulgence of 40 or 100 days; 7 weeks; or a year, &c. But in thus granting an Indulgence of a certain defined number of days, weeks, or years, the Holy See does not thereby intend a corresponding abridgment of the pains of purgatory. Such phraseology has reference merely to the penance enjoined by the ancient rules or canons of the Church. Wherefore, an Indulgence of 100 days, or a year, for example is the remission of as much temporal punishment

as would have been formerly atoned for, before God, by a canonical penance of 100 days or a year.

What are the dispositions necessary for gaining Indulgences?

They are three in number. 1. The *intention*, by which a person proposes to himself to gain an Indulgence. A *virtual* intention is sufficient. St. Leonard of Port Maurice used to advise the faithful to form each day, at morning prayer, an intention of gaining all the indulgences annexed to the various practices of piety and good works which they might perform in the course of the day.

2. *The state of grace.* To gain an Indulgence for himself a person should be in a state of grace. Hence a single mortal sin on the soul would be an obstacle to a person gaining the smallest Indulgence for himself.

3. *The faithful accomplishment of the works or conditions prescribed.* Hence, a person wishing to gain an Indulgence should take care to fulfil all the conditions laid down for that purpose.

N.B. Try to gain an Indulgence every day, or every week, either for yourself or for the souls in purgatory.

PLENARY INDULGENCES GRANTED TO THE FAITHFUL IN ENGLAND.

I. Christmas day, and the 12 days following, to the day of the Epiphany, inclusively.

II. The first week of Lent, beginning with the first Sunday, and ending with the second Sunday, inclusively.

III. Easter, *i.e.* from Palm Sunday, inclusively, to Low Sunday, inclusively,

IV. From Whit-Sunday, inclusively, to the end of the Octave of Corpus Christi.

V. On the feast of St. Peter and St. Paul, and during the Octave.

VI. From the Sunday preceding the feast of the Assumption of the Blessed Virgin Mary till the 22nd day of August inclusively. If the festival fall on a Sunday, the indulgence begins on that day.

VII. From the Sunday preceding the feast of St. Michael till the Sunday following inclusively. If the festival fall on a Sunday, the indulgence begins on that day.

VIII. From the Sunday preceding the feast of All Saints till the 8th day of November inclusively. If the festival fall on a Sunday, the indulgence begins on that day.

These are the Seasons of the Plenary Indulgences granted to the Catholics of England, and assigned in the year 1810, by the Right Rev. Vicars Apostolic to the following conditions:

For Christmas, Easter, Assumption, and Michaelmas.

1. To confess their sins with a sincere repentance to a priest approved of by the bishop.
2. Devoutly and worthily to receive the Holy Communion.
3. To visit some chapel or oratory where mass is celebrated, and there offer up their prayers for the peace and welfare of God's Church.
4. That they be in a disposition, if their circumstances will allow it, to assist the poor with alms in proportion to their abilities; or to frequent catechism and sermons; or to visit and

comfort the sick, and such as are near their end, if they have the opportunity.

It is not required, for the gaining of these four indulgences, that these works of mercy, corporal or spiritual, or the assisting at catechism or sermons, be done on the same day with the Communion; but only that persons be then in a disposition or readiness of mind to do these things, or some of them at least, when opportunity shall offer.

For Lent, Whitsuntide, and All Saints.

1. To confess their sins with a sincere repentance to a priest approved of by the bishop.
2. Devoutly and worthily to receive the Holy Communion.
3. If their condition will allow it, to give some alms to the poor either on the eve or the day of their Communion.
4. On the day of their Communion to offer up some prayers to God for the whole state of the Catholic Church throughout the world, for the bringing in of all straying souls to the fold of Christendom, and for the blessing of God upon this nation.

For St. Peter and St. Paul.

1. To confess their sins with a sincere repentance to a priest approved of by the bishop.
2. Devoutly and worthily to receive the Holy Communion.
3. For some space of time, on the day of their Communion, to pray to God, with a sin-

cere heart, for the conversion of heretics, and for the free propagation of the holy faith.

To gain the Indulgences *it is sufficient* to say with devotion 5 Our Fathers and 5 Hail Marys.

INDULGENCED PRAYERS,

ALL APPLICABLE TO THE SOULS IN PURGATORY.

"All that we give in charity to the faithful departed is changed into grace for us, and, after our death, we shall find its merit doubled a hundred-fold."—St. Ambrose.

1. Indulgence of 50 days for making the sign of the Cross, saying the words at the same time.

2. *Acts of Faith, Hope, and Charity.*

Indulgence of 7 years and 7 quarantines each time. Plenary once a month for those who recite them frequently. *Any form* may be used.

3.—Merciful Jesus, Lover of souls, I pray thee, by the agony of thy most Sacred Heart, and by the woes of thy Immaculate Mother, wash in thy blood the sinners of the whole world, who are now in their agony and to die this day. Amen. Heart of Jesus, once in agony, pity the dying.

Indulgence 100 days each time. Plenary once a month if said daily 3 times at distant intervals.

4.—Eternal Father! I offer thee the Precious Blood of Jesus in satisfaction for my sins, and for the wants of thy holy Church.

Indulgence: 100 days each time it is said.

5. *Offering before a picture of the Sacred Heart.*

My loving Jesus, I (N. N.) give thee my heart; and I consecrate myself wholly to thee out of the grateful love I bear thee, and as a reparation for all my unfaithfulness to grace, and with thine aid I purpose never to sin again.

One hundred days indulgence once a day. Plenary once a month if said daily.

6. *Consecration to the Blessed Virgin.*
To be said after the Hail Mary.

My Queen and my Mother! to thee I offer myself without any reserve; and to give thee a mark of my devotion, I consecrate to thee during this day, my eyes, my ears, my mouth, my heart, and my whole person. Since I belong to thee, O my good mother! preserve and defend me as thy property and possession.

One hundred days indulgence once a day for reciting it morning and evening. Plenary once a month if said daily.

7. *Blue Scapular of the Immaculate Conception.*

Those who wear it can, by reciting six Paters six Aves, and six Glorias in honour of the Blessed

Trinity, of the Immaculate Conception, and for the intentions of the Church, gain each time, without confession, all the Indulgences of the Seven Basilicas of Rome, of Portiuncula, of St. James of Compostella, and of the Holy Land. Twenty years for each visit to the sick; 60 years for half an hour's daily meditation, &c. Plenary first Sunday of every month.

8.—O angel of God, whom God hath appointed to be my guardian, enlighten and protect, direct and govern me.

Indulgence, 100 days each time it is said. Plenary once a month if said daily.

9.—May the Sacred Heart of Jesus be everywhere loved.

100 days each time.

10. For every Ave (Hail Mary) or other prayer said for the conversion of England, 300 days indulgence each time.

Indulgences attached to other prayers in this book will be found in their proper places

---

DEVOTIONS FOR THE TIME OF JUBILEES,
OR OTHER INDULGENCES.

The following prayer was first published upon occasion of the Jubilee in 1751; and may be proper for any other time of indulgence. It may be said on the day of communion, as it is directed for the usual intentions for which the faithful ought to offer up their prayers in order to gain the indulgence.

A PRAYER

For the whole state of Christ's Church *upon Earth, and all the intentions of the Indulgence.*

O ETERNAL Father of our Lord Jesus Christ, Creator of all things, visible and invisible, Source of all our good; infinitely good in thyself, and infinitely gracious, bountiful, and good to us; behold we, thy poor servants, the work of thy hands, redeemed by the blood of thine only Son, come in answer to his summons by his vicegerent, to present ourselves as humble petitioners before the throne of thy mercy. We come in communion with all thy church in heaven, hoping to be assisted by their prayers and merits; and with Jesus Christ at our head, our High-Priest and Mediator, in whose precious blood we put all our trust.

We prostrate ourselves here before thee, and most humbly beseech thee to sanctify thine own most holy name, by sanctifying and exalting thy holy Catholic Church throughout the whole world. O eternal King, who hast sent thine only

Son down from thy throne above into this earth of ours, to establish a kingdom here amongst us, from whence we might hereafter be translated to thine eternal kingdom; look down, we beseech thee, upon this kingdom of thy Son, and propagate it through all nations, and through all hearts. Sanctify it in all truth; maintain it in peace, unity, and holiness. Give to it saints for its rulers, its chief pastor, and all its other prelates; enlighten them with all heavenly wisdom, make them all men according to thine own heart. Give thy grace and blessing to all the clergy; and send amongst them that heavenly fire, which thy Son came to cast on the earth, and which he so earnestly desired should be enkindled. Assist and protect all apostolic Missionaries, that they may zealously and effectually promote thy glory, and the salvation of souls redeemed by the blood of thy Son. Sanctify all religious men and women of all orders; give them the grace to serve thee with all perfection, according to the spirit of their institute, and to shine like lights to the rest of the faithful.

Have mercy on all Christian princes; grant them those lights and graces that are necessary for the perfect discharge of their duty to thee, and to their subjects; that they may be true servants to thee, the King of kings, true fathers to their people, and nursing fathers to thy Church. Have mercy on all magistrates and men in power; that they may all fear thee, love thee, and serve thee; and ever remember that they are thy deputies, and ministers of thy justice. Have mercy on all thy people throughout the world, and give thy blessing to thine inheritance; remember thy congregation, which thou hast possessed from the beginning; and give that grace to all thy children here upon earth, that they may do thy holy will in all things, even as the blessed do in heaven.

Extend thy mercy also to all poor infidels, who sit in darkness and in the shadow of death: to all those nations that know not thee, and that have not yet received the faith and law of thy Son their Saviour; to all Pagans, Mahometans, and Jews. Remember, O Lord, that all these poor souls are made after thine own image and likeness, and redeemed by the blood of thy Son. Oh! let not Satan any longer exercise his tyranny over these thy creatures, to the great dishonour of thy name. Let not the precious blood of thy Son be shed for them in vain. Send among them zealous preachers and apostolic labourers, endued with the like graces and gifts as thine apostles were, and bless them with the like success, for the glory of thy name: that all these poor souls may be brought to know thee, love thee, and serve thee, here in thy church, and bless thee hereafter for all eternity.

Look down also with an eye of pity and compassion on all those deluded souls, who under the name of Christians, have gone away from the paths of truth and unity, and from the one fold of the one Shepherd, thine only Son Jesus Christ, into the by-paths of error and schism. Oh! bring them back to thee and to thy church. Dispel their darkness by thy heavenly light, take off the veil from before their eyes, with which the common enemy hath blindfolded them: let them see how they have been misled by misapprehensions and misrepresentations. Remove the prejudices of their education; take away from them the spirit of obstinacy, pride, and self-conceit. Give them an humble and a docile heart. Give them a strong desire of finding out thy truth, and a strong grace to enable them to embrace it, in spite of all the opposition of the world, the flesh, and the devil. For why should these poor souls perish, for which Christ died? Why should Satan any longer possess these souls, which by their baptism were dedicated to thee, to be thine eternal temple.

O Father of lights, and God of all truth, purge the whole world from all errors, abuses, corruptions, and vices. Beat down the standard of Satan, and set up everywhere the standard of Christ. Abolish the reign of sin, and establish the kingdom of grace in all hearts. Let humility triumph over pride and ambition; charity over hatred, envy, and malice; purity and temperance over lust and excess; meekness over passion; and disinterestedness and poverty of spirit over covetousness and love of this perishable world. Let the gospel of Jesus Christ, both in its belief and practice, prevail throughout all the universe.

Grant to us thy peace, O Lord, in the days of our mortality, even that peace which thy Son bequeathed as a legacy to his disciples: a perpetual peace with thee, a perpetual peace with one another, and a perpetual peace within themselves. Grant that all Christian princes and states may love, cherish, and maintain an inviolable peace among themselves. Give them a right sense of the dreadful evils that attend on wars. Give them an everlasting horror of all that bloodshed, of the devastation and ruin of so many territories, of the innumerable sacrileges, and the eternal loss of so many thousand souls, which are the dismal consequences of war. Turn their hearts to another kind of warfare, teach them to fight for a heavenly kingdom.

Remove, O Lord, thy wrath, which we have reason to apprehend actually hanging over our heads for our sins. Deliver all Christian people from the dreadful evil of mortal sin; make all sinners sensible of their misery; give them the grace of a sincere conversion to thee, and a truly penitential spirit, and discharge them from all their bonds. Preserve all Christendom, and in particular this nation, from all the evils that threaten impenitent sinners, such as plagues, famines, earthquakes, fires, inundations, mortality of cattle, sudden and unprovided death, and thy many other judgments here, and eternal damnation hereafter. Comfort all that are under any affliction, sickness, or violence of pain; support all that are under temptation; reconcile all that are at variance; deliver all that are in slavery or captivity; defend all that are in danger; grant a relief to all in their respective necessities; give a happy passage to all that are in their agony. Grant thy blessing to our friends and benefactors, and to all those for whom we are particularly bound to pray; and have mercy on all our enemies. Give eternal rest to all the faithful departed; and bring us all to everlasting life, through Jesus Christ thy Son. Amen.

O TURN TO JESUS, MOTHER, TURN.

O TURN to Jesus, Mother, turn,
  And call him by his tenderest names;
Pray for the holy souls that burn
  This hour amid the cleansing flames.

Ah, they have fought a gallant fight;
  In death's cold arms they persevered;
And after life's uncheery night
  The harbour of their rest is neared.

Spouses of Christ they are, for he
  Was wedded to them by his blood;
And angels o'er their destiny
  In wondering adoration brood.

They are the children of thy tears;
  Then hasten, Mother, to their aid;
In pity think each hour appears
  An age while glory is delayed.

O Mary, let thy Son no more
  His lingering spouses thus expect;
God's children to their God restore,
  And to the Spirit his elect.

Pray, then, as thou hast ever prayed;
  Angels and souls all look to thee;
God waits thy prayers, for He hath made
  Those prayers his law of charity.

The Seven Penitential Psalms.

Proper to be recited on Fasting Days and other penitential times.

Anthem. Remember not, O Lord, our offences, nor those of our parents, and take not revenge of our sins.

Psalm vi.　*Domine in ne furore.*

O LORD, rebuke me not in thine indignation, nor chastise me in thy wrath.

Have mercy on me, O Lord, for I am weak: heal me, O Lord, for my bones are troubled.

And my soul is troubled exceedingly: but thou, O Lord, how long?

Turn to me, O Lord, and deliver my soul: O save me for thy mercy's sake.

For there is no one in death that is mindful of thee: and who shall confess to thee in hell?

I have laboured in my groanings; every night I will wash my bed, I will water my couch with my tears.

Mine eye is troubled through indignation; I have grown old amongst all mine enemies.

Depart from me, all ye workers of iniquity; for the Lord hath heard the voice of my weeping.

The Lord hath heard my supplication: the Lord hath received my prayer.

Let all mine enemies be ashamed, and be very much troubled: let them be turned back and be ashamed very speedily. Glory, &c.

Psalm xxxi. *Beati quorum.*

BLESSED are they whose iniquities are forgiven, and whose sins are covered.

Blessed is the man, to whom the Lord hath not imputed sin, and in whose spirit there is no guile.

Because I was silent, my bones grew old: whilst I cried out all the day long. For day and night thy hand was heavy upon me: I am turned in mine anguish, whilst the thorn is fastened.

I have acknowledged my sin to thee: and mine injustice I have not concealed.

I said, I will confess against myself, mine injustice to the Lord: and thou hast forgiven the wickedness of my sin.

For this shall every one that is holy pray to thee, in a seasonable time.

And yet in a flood of many waters, they shall not come nigh unto him.

Thou art my refuge from the trouble which hath encompassed me; my joy, deliver me from them that surround me.

I will give thee understanding, and I will instruct thee in this way in which thou shalt go: I will fix mine eyes upon thee.

Do not become like the horse and the mule, which have no understanding.

With bit and bridle bind fast their jaws, who come not near unto thee.

Many are the scourges of the sinner, but mercy shall encompass him that hopeth in the Lord.

Be glad in the Lord, and rejoice, ye just, and glory, all ye right of heart. Glory, &c.

Psalm xxxvii.   *Domine ne in furore.*

REBUKE me not, O Lord, in thine indignation: nor chastise me in thy wrath.

For thine arrows are fastened in me, and thy hand hath been strong upon me.

There is no health in my flesh, because of thy wrath: there is no peace for my bones, because of my sins.

For mine iniquities are gone over my head: and as a heavy burden, are become heavy upon me.

My sores are putrefied and corrupted, because of my foolishness.

I am become miserable, and am bowed down even to the end: I walked sorrowful all the day long.

For my loins are filled with illusions: and there is no health in my flesh.

I am afflicted and humbled exceedingly: I roared with the groaning of my heart.

Lord, all my desire is before thee: and my groaning is not hidden from thee.

My heart is troubled, my strength hath left me: and the light of mine eyes itself is not with me.

My friends and my neighbours have drawn near, and stood against me.

And they that were near me, stood afar off: and they that sought my soul, used violence.

And they that sought evils to me, spoke vain things: and studied deceits all the day long.

But I, as a deaf man, heard not: and *was* as a dumb man, not opening his mouth.

And I became as a man that heareth not: and that hath no reproofs in his mouth.

For in thee, O Lord, have I hoped: thou wilt hear me, O Lord my God.

For I said, lest at any time mine enemies rejoice over me: and whilst my feet are moved, they speak great things against me.

For I am ready for scourges: and my sorrow is continually before me.

For I will declare mine iniquity: and I will think for my sin.

But mine enemies live, and are stronger than I: and they that hate me wrongfully are multiplied.

They that render evil for good, have detracted me, because I followed goodness.

Forsake me not, O Lord my God: do not thou depart from me.

Attend unto my help, O Lord, the God of my salvation. Glory, &c

Psalm l. *Miserere.**

HAVE mercy on me, O God, according to thy great mercy.

And according to the multitude of thy tender mercies, blot out mine iniquity.

Wash me yet more from mine iniquity: and cleanse me from my sin.

For I know mine iniquity, and my sin is always before me.

* Latin words at page 217.

To thee only have I sinned and have done evil before thee: that thou mayest be justified in thy words, and mayest overcome when thou art judged.

For behold I was conceived in iniquities: and in sins did my mother conceive me.

For behold thou hast loved truth. the uncertain and hidden things of thy wisdom thou hast made manifest to me.

Thou shalt sprinkle me with hyssop, and I shall be cleansed: thou shalt wash me, and I shall be made whiter than snow.

To my hearing thou shalt give joy and gladness: and the bones that have been humbled shall rejoice.

Turn away thy face from my sins, and blot out all mine iniquities.

Create a clean heart in me, O God: and renew a right spirit within my bowels.

Cast me me not away from thy face; and take not thy Holy Spirit from me.

Restore unto me the joy of thy salvation, and strengthen me with a perfect spirit.

I will teach the unjust thy ways:

and the wicked shall be converted to thee.

Deliver me from blood, O God, thou God of my salvation, and my tongue shall extol thy justice.

O Lord, thou wilt open my lips; and my mouth shall declare thy praise.

For if thou hadst desired sacrifice, I would indeed have given it; with burnt-offerings thou wilt not be delighted.

A sacrifice to God is an afflicted spirit; a contrite and humbled heart, O God, thou wilt not despise.

Deal favourably, O Lord, in thy good will with Sion, that the walls of Jerusalem may be built up.

Then shalt thou accept the sacrifice of justice, oblations, and whole burnt-offerings; then shall they lay calves upon thine altar. Glory, &c.

Psalm ci. *Domine exaudi.*

HEAR, O Lord, my prayer, and let my cry come to thee.

Turn not away thy face from me; in the day when I am in trouble, incline thine ear to me.

In what day soever I shall call upon thee, hear me speedily.

For my days are vanished like smoke; and my bones are grown dry like fuel for the fire.

I am smitten as grass, and my heart is withered, because I forgot to eat my bread.

Through the voice of my groaning, my bone hath cleaved to my flesh.

I am become like a pelican of the wilderness; I am like a night raven in the house.

I have watched, and am become as a sparrow all alone on the house top.

All the day long mine enemies reproached me; and they that praised me did swear against me.

For I did eat ashes like bread, and mingled my drink with weeping.

Because of thine anger and indignation; for having lifted me up thou hast thrown me down.

My days have declined like a shadow, and I am withered like grass.

But thou, O Lord, endurest for ever; and thy memorial to all generations.

Thou shalt arise and have mercy on Sion; for it is time to have mercy on it, for the time is come.

For the stones thereof have pleased

thy servants, and they shall have pity
on the earth thereof.

And the Gentiles shall fear thy name,
O Lord, and all the kings of the earth
thy glory.

For the Lord hath built up Sion; and
he shall be seen in his glory.

He hath had regard to the prayer of
the humble; and he hath not despised
their petition.

Let these things be written unto another generation; and the people that
shall be created shall praise the Lord.

Because he hath looked forth from
his high sanctuary; from heaven the
Lord hath looked upon the earth.

That he might hear the groans of
them that are in fetters; that he might
release the children of the slain.

That they may declare the name of
the Lord in Sion, and his praise in Jerusalem.

When the people assemble together,
and kings, to serve the Lord.

He answered them in the way of his
strength; Declare unto me the fewness
of my days.

Call me not away in the midst of my

days: thy years are unto generation and generation.

In the beginning, O Lord, thou foundedst the earth: and the heavens are the works of thy hands.

They shall perish, but thou remainest; and all of them shall grow old like a garment.

And as a vesture thou shalt change them, and they shall be changed; but thou art always the self same, and thy years shall not fail.

The children of thy servants shall continue, and their seed shall be directed for ever. Glory, &c.

Psalm cxxix. *De profundis.*

OUT of the depths I have cried to thee, O Lord; Lord, hear my voice.

Let thine ears be attentive to the voice of my supplication.

If thou, O Lord, wilt mark iniquities; Lord, who shall stand it?

For with thee there is merciful forgiveness: and by reason of thy law I have waited for thee, O Lord.

My soul hath relied on his word; my soul hath hoped in the Lord.

From the morning watch even until night, let Israel hope in the Lord.

Because with the Lord there is mercy, and with him plentiful redemption.

And he shall redeem Israel from all his iniquities. Glory, &c.

Psalm cxlii. *Domine exaudi.*

HEAR, O Lord, my prayer; give ear to my supplication in thy truth: hear me in thy justice.

And enter not into judgment with thy servant: for in thy sight no man living shall be justified.

For the enemy hath persecuted my soul, he hath brought down my life to the earth.

He hath made me to dwell in darkness, as those that have been dead of old; and my spirit is in anguish within me, my heart within me is troubled.

I remembered the days of old, I meditated on all thy works; I mused upon the works of thy hands.

I stretched forth my hands to thee; my soul is as earth without water unto thee.

Hear me speedily, O Lord; my spirit hath fainted away.

Turn not away thy face from me, lest I be like unto them that go down into the pit.

Cause me to hear thy mercy in the morning, for in thee have I hoped.

Make the way known to me wherein I should walk; for I have lifted up my soul to thee.

Deliver me from mine enemies, O Lord; to thee have I fled; teach me to do thy will, for thou art my God.

Thy good spirit shall lead me into the right land; for thy name's sake, O Lord, thou wilt quicken me in thy justice.

Thou wilt bring my soul out of trouble: and in thy mercy thou wilt destroy mine enemies.

And thou wilt cut off all them that afflict my soul; for I am thy servant. Glory, &c.

Anthem. Remember not, O Lord, our offences, nor those of our parents; and take not revenge of our sins.

Indulgence: 40 days each time the Seven Penitential Psalms are said devoutly.

MISERERE.

MISERERE mei, Deus : * secúndum magnam misericórdiam tuam.

Et secúndum multitúdinem miseratiónum tuárum : * dele iniquitátem meam.

Amplius lava me ab iniquitáte mea : * et a peccáto meo munda me.

Quóniam, iniquitátem meam ego cognosco : * et peccátum meum contra me est semper.

Tibi soli peccávi, et malum coram te feci : * ut justificéris in sermónibus tuis, et vincas cum judicáris.

Ecce enim in iniquitátibus concéptus sum : * et in peccátis concépit me mater mea.

Ecce enim veritátem dilexísti : * incérta et occúlta sapiéntiæ tuæ manifestásti mihi.

Aspérges me hyssópo, et mundábor : * lavábis me, et super nivem dealbábor.

Audítui meo dabis gaúdium et lætítiam : * et exultábunt ossa humiliáta.

Avérte fáciem tuam a peccátis meis : * et omnes iniquitátes meas dele.

Cor mundum crea in me, Deus : * et spíritum rectum innova in viscéribus meis.

Ne projícias me a fácie tua : * et Spíritum sanctum tuum ne aúferas a me.

Redde mihi lætítiam salutáris tui : et spíritu principáli confírma me.

Docébo iníquos vias tuas : * et ímpii ad te converténtur.

Líbera me de sanguínibus, Deus, Deus salútis meæ : * et exultábit lingua mea justítiam tuam.

Dómine, lábia mea apéries : * et os meum annuntiábit laudem tuam.

Quóniam si voluísses sacrifícium dedíssem útique : * holocaústis non delectáberis.

Sacrifícium Deo spíritus contribulátus : * cor contrítum et humiliátum, Deus, non despícies.

Benigne fac, Dómine, in bona voluntáte tua Sion : * ut ædificéntur muri Jerúsalem.

Tunc acceptábis sacrifícium justítiæ, oblatiónes, et holocaústa : * tunc impónent super altáre tuum vitulos.

Gloria, &c.

THE
LITANY OF THE SAINTS.

REMEMBER not, O Lord, our offences, nor those of our parents, and take not revenge of our sins.

Lord, have mercy on us.
Lord, have mercy on us.
Christ, have mercy on us.
Christ, have mercy on us.
Lord, have mercy on us.
Lord, have mercy on us.
Christ, hear us.
Christ, graciously hear us.
God the Father of heaven, *Have mercy on us.*
God the Son, Redeemer of the world, *Have mercy on us.*
God the Holy Ghost, *Have mercy on us.*
Holy Trinity, one God, *Have mercy on us.*
Holy Mary, *Pray for us.*
Holy Mother of God,
Holy Virgin of Virgins,
St. Michael,
St. Gabriel,
St. Raphael,
All ye holy angels and archangels,

Pray for us.

All ye holy orders of blessed spirits,
St. John Baptist,
St. Joseph,
All ye holy patriarchs and prophets,
St. Peter,
St. Paul,
St. Andrew,
St. James,
St. John,
St. Thomas,
St. James,
St. Philip,
St. Bartholomew,
St. Matthew,
St. Simon,
St. Thaddeus,
St. Matthias,
St. Barnabas,
St. Luke,
St. Mark,
All ye holy apostles and evangelists,
All ye holy disciples of our Lord,
All ye holy innocents,
St. Stephen,
St. Laurence,
St. Vincent,
SS. Fabian and Sebastian,
SS. John and Paul,
SS. Cosmas and Damian,
SS. Gervase and Protase,
All ye holy martyrs,
St. Silvester,
St. Gregory,
St. Ambrose,
St. Augustin,
St. Jerom,
St. Martin,
St. Nicholas,
All ye holy bishops and confessors,
All ye holy doctors,
St. Antony,
St. Benedict,
St. Bernard,
St. Dominic,

Pray for us.

St. Francis,
All ye holy priests and levites,
All ye holy monks and hermits,
St. Mary Magdalen,
St. Agatha,
St. Lucy,
St. Agnes,
St. Cecily,
St. Catharine,
St. Anastasia,
All ye holy virgins and widows,

Pray for us.

All ye men and women, saints of God,
Make intercession for us.
Be merciful to us. *Spare us, O Lord.*
Be merciful to us. *Graciously hear us, O Lord.*

From all evil,
From all sin,
From thy wrath,
From sudden and unprovided death,
From the deceits of the devil,
From anger, hatred, and all ill-will,
From the spirit of fornication,
From lightning and tempest,
From everlasting death,
Through the mystery of thy holy incarnation,
Through thy coming,
Through thy nativity,
Through thy baptism and holy fasting,
Through thy cross and passion,

O Lord, deliver us.

Through thy death and burial,
Through thy holy resurrection,
Through thine admirable ascension,
Through the coming of the Holy Ghost, the Comforter,
In the day of judgment,
We sinners, *do beseech thee hear us.*
That thou spare us,
That thou pardon us,
That thou vouchsafe to bring us to true penance,
That thou vouchsafe to govern and preserve thy holy Church,
That thou vouchsafe to preserve our apostolic prelate, and all ecclesiastical orders in holy religion,
That thou vouchsafe to humble the enemies of thy holy church,
That thou vouchsafe to give peace and true concord to Christian kings and princes,
That thou vouchsafe to give peace and unity to all Christian people,
That thou vouchsafe to confirm and preserve us in thy holy service,
That thou lift up our minds to heavenly desires,
That thou render eternal good things to all our benefactors,

O Lord, deliver us

We beseech thee, hear us.

That thou deliver our souls, and those of our brethren, relations, and benefactors, from eternal damnation,
That thou vouchsafe to give and preserve the fruits of the earth,
That thou vouchsafe to give eternal rest to all the faithful departed,
That thou vouchsafe graciously to hear us,
Son of God,

We beseech thee, hear us.

Lamb of God, who takest away the sins of the world. *Spare us, O Lord.*

Lamb of God, who takest away the sins of the world. *Graciously hear us, O Lord.*

Lamb of God, who takest away the sins of the world. *Have mercy on us.*

Christ, hear us. *Christ, graciously hear us.* Lord, have mercy on us. *Christ, have mercy on us.* Lord, have mercy on us. Our Father, &c.

V. And lead us not into temptation.
R. But deliver us from evil. Amen.

Psalm lxix.

O GOD, come to my assistance: O Lord, make haste to help me.

Let them be confounded and ashamed that seek my soul.

Let them be turned backward, and blush for shame, that desire evils to me.

Let them be presently turned away, blushing for shame, that say to me, 'Tis well, 'tis well.

Let all that seek thee rejoice, and be glad in thee: and let such as love thy salvation say always, The Lord be magnified.

But I am needy and poor: O God, help me.

Thou art my helper and my deliverer: O Lord, make no long delay. Glory be, &c.

V. Save thy servants.

R. Trusting in thee, O my God.

V. Be unto us, O Lord, a tower of strength.

R. Against the face of the enemy.

V. Let not the enemy have advantage over us.

R. Nor the son of iniquity have power to hurt us.

V. O Lord, deal not with us according to our sins.

R. Nor reward us according to our iniquities.

EVENING DEVOTIONS. 225

V. Let us pray for our chief bishop N.

R. The Lord preserve him, and give him life, and make him blessed upon the earth, and deliver him not up to the will of his enemies.

V. Let us pray for our benefactors.

R. Vouchsafe, O Lord, for thy name's sake, to reward with eternal life all them that have done us good.

V. Let us pray for the faithful departed.

R. Eternal rest give to them, O Lord; and let perpetual light shine upon them.

V. May they rest in peace. R. Amen.

V. For our absent brethren.

R. O my God, save thy servants trusting in thee.

R. Send them help, O Lord, from the sanctuary.

R. And defend them out of Sion.

V. O Lord, hear my prayer.

R. And let my cry come to thee.

Let us pray.

O GOD, whose property is always to have mercy, and to spare, receive our petition: that we and all thy servants who are bound by the chain of sins, may, by the compassion of thy goodness, mercifully be absolved.

HEAR, we beseech thee, O Lord, the prayers of the suppliants, and pardon the sins of them that confess to thee; that, in thy bounty, thou mayest give us pardon and peace.

OUT of thy clemency, O Lord, show thine unspeakable mercy to us, that so thou mayest both acquit us of our sins, and deliver us from the punishments which we deserve for them.

O GOD, who by sin art offended, and by penance pacified, mercifully regard the prayers of thy people making supplication to thee, and turn away the scourges of thine anger, which we deserve for our sins.

O ALMIGHTY and eternal God, have mercy on thy servant N. our chief bishop, and direct him according to thy clemency, in the way of everlasting salvation; that, by thy grace, he may desire those things that are agreeable to thee, and perform them with all his strength.

O GOD, from whom are holy desires, right counsels, and just works, give to thy servants that peace which the world cannot give; that both our hearts may be disposed to keep thy commandments, and the fear of enemies being removed, the times, by thy protection, may be peaceable.

INFLAME, O Lord, our reins and heart with the fire of thy holy Spirit, that we may serve thee with a chaste body, and please thee with a clean heart.

O GOD, the Creator and Redeemer of all the faithful, give to the souls of thy servants departed the remission of all their sins; that, through pious supplications, they may obtain the pardon which they have always desired.

PREVENT, we beseech thee, O Lord, our actions by thy holy inspirations, and carry them on by thy gracious assistance; that every prayer and work of ours may begin always from thee, and by thee be happily ended.

O ALMIGHTY and eternal God, who hast dominion over the living and the dead, and art merciful to all, who thou foreknowest shall be thine by faith and good works: we humbly beseech thee, that they, for whom we have determined to offer up our prayers, whether this present world still detain them in the flesh, or the world to come hath already received them out of their bodies, may, by the clemency of thy goodness (all thy saints interceding for them) obtain pardon and remission of all their sins, through our Lord Jesus Christ thy Son, who with thee and the Holy Ghost, liveth and reigneth, God, world without end. Amen.

V. O Lord, hear my prayer.

R. And let my cry come to thee.

V. May the almighty and merciful Lord graciously hear us. R. Amen.

V. And may the souls of the faithful, through the mercy of God, rest in peace.

R. Amen.

EVENING HYMN.

SWEET Saviour! bless us ere we go;
  Thy word into our minds instil;
And make our lukewarm hearts to glow
  With lowly love and fervent will.
Through life's long day and death's dark night
O gentle Jesus! be our light!

The day is done, its hours have run;
  And thou hast taken count of all—
The scanty triumphs grace hath won,
  The broken vow, the frequent fall.
Through life's long day and death's dark night
O gentle Jesus! be our light!

Grant us, dear Lord, from evil ways
  True absolution and release;

And bless us more than in past days
  With purity and inward peace.
Through life's long day and death's dark night
O gentle Jesus! be our light!

Do more than pardon; give us joy,
  Sweet fear and sober liberty,
And simple hearts without alloy,
  That only long to be like thee.
Through life's long day and death's dark night
O gentle Jesus! be our light!

Labour is sweet, for thou hast toiled;
  And care is light, for thou hast cared:
Ah! never let our works be soiled
  With strife, or by deceit ensnared.
Through life's long day and death's dark night
O gentle Jesus! be our light!

Sweet Saviour! bless us; night is come,
  Mary and Joseph near us be;
Good Angels, watch about our home;
  May we each day be nearer thee;
Through life's long day and death's dark night
O gentle Jesus! be our light!

NIGHT PRAYERS.

IN the name of the Father, and of the Son, and of the Holy Ghost. *Amen.*

Blessed be the holy and undivided Trinity, now and for ever. *Amen.*

Our Father, &c. Hail Mary, &c.

I believe in God, &c.

Come, O Holy Spirit, fill the hearts of thy faithful, and kindle in them the fire of thy love.

V. Send forth thy Spirit, and they shall be created.

R. And thou shalt renew the face of the earth.

Let us place ourselves in the presence of God, and give him thanks for all the benefits which we have received from him, particularly this day.

O MY God, I firmly believe that thou art here, and perfectly seest me, and that thou observest all my actions, all my thoughts, and the most secret motions of my heart. Thou watchest over me with an incomparable love, every moment bestowing favours, and preserving me from evil. Blessed be thy holy name, and may all creatures bless thy goodness for the benefits which I have ever received from thee, and particularly this day. May the saints and angels supply my defect in rendering thee due thanks.

Never permit me to be so base and wicked, as to repay thy bounties with ingratitude, and thy blessings with offences and injuries.

Let us ask of our Lord Jesus Christ grace to discover the sins which we have committed this day; and beg of him a true sorrow for them, and a sincere repentance.

O MY Lord Jesus Christ, judge of the living and the dead, before whom I must appear one day to give an exact account of my whole life ; enlighten me, I beseech thee, and give me an humble and contrite heart, that I may see wherein I have offended thine infinite Majesty ; and judge myself now with such a just severity, that then thou mayest judge me with mercy and clemency.

Let us here examine what sins we have committed this day, by thought, word, deed, or omission.

(If nothing occur to your mind, wherein you have offended, renew your sorrow for the sins of your past life.)

Let us conceive a great sorrow for having offended God.

O MY God, I detest these and all other sins, which I have committed against thy divine Majesty. I am extremely sorry that I have offended thee, because thou art infinitely good, and sin displeaseth thee. I love thee with my whole heart, and firmly purpose, by the help of thy grace, never more to offend thee. I resolve to avoid the occasions of sin ; I will confess my sins, and will endeavour to make satisfaction for them. Have mercy on me, O God, have mercy, and pardon me, a wretched sinner. In the name of thy beloved Son, Jesus, I humbly beg of thee so to wash me with his precious blood, that my sins may be entirely remitted.

Let us endeavour, as much as possible, to put ourselves in the dispositions in which we desire to be found at the hour of death.

O MY God, I accept of death as a homage and adoration which I owe to thy divine Majesty, and as a punishment justly due to my sins; in union with the death of my dear Redeemer, and as the only means of coming to thee, my beginning and last end.

I firmly believe all the sacred truth which the Catholic church believeth and teacheth, because thou hast revealed them. And by the assistance of thy holy grace, I am resolved to live and die in the communion of this thy church.

Relying upon thy goodness, power, and promises, I hope to obtain pardon of my sins, and life everlasting, through the merits of thy Son, Jesus Christ, my only Redeemer, and by the intercession of his blessed mother, and all the saints.

I love thee with all my heart and soul, and desire to love thee as the blessed do in heaven. I adore all the designs of thy divine Providence, resigning myself entirely to thy will.

I also love my neighbour for thy sake, as I love myself; I sincerely forgive all who have injured me, and ask pardon of all whom I have injured.

I renounce the devil with all his works; the world, with all its pomps; the flesh, with all its temptations.

I desire to be dissolved, and to be with Christ. Father, into thy hands I commend my spirit.

R. Lord Jesus, receive my soul.

May the blessed Virgin Mary, St. Joseph, and all the saints, pray for us to our Lord, that we may be preserved this night from sin and all evils. Amen.

Blessed St. Michael, defend us in the day of battle, that we may not be lost at the dreadful judgment. Amen.

O my good Angel, whom God, by his divine mercy, hath appointed to be my guardian, enlighten and protect me, direct and govern me this night. Amen.

May Almighty God have mercy on

us, and forgive us our sins, and bring us to life everlasting. Amen.

May the almighty and merciful Lord give us pardon, absolution, and remission of our sins. Amen.

V. Vouchsafe, O Lord, this night,
R. To keep us without sin.
V. Have mercy on us, O Lord.
R. Have mercy on us.
V. Let thy mercy, O Lord, be upon us.
R. As we have hoped in thee.
V. O Lord, hear my prayer.
R. And let my cry come to thee.

Let us Pray.

VISIT, we beseech thee, O Lord, this house and family, and drive far from it all snares of the enemy; let thy holy angels dwell herein, to keep us in peace, and let thy blessing be always upon us: through our Lord Jesus Christ. Amen.

May our Lord bless us, and preserve us from all evil, and bring us to life everlasting. And may the souls of the faithful, through the mercy of God, rest in peace. Amen.

INVOCATIONS OF THE HOLY GHOST,

PROPER BEFORE READING, OR ANY OTHER SPIRITUAL UNDERTAKING.

THE HYMN, *Veni Creator.**

COME, Holy Ghost, Creator, come,
  From thy bright heavenly throne;
Come, take possession of our souls,
  And make them all thy own.

Thou who art call'd the Paraclete,
  Best gift of God above;
The living Spring, the living Fire,
  Sweet Unction and true Love.

Thou who art sev'n-fold in thy grace,
  Finger of God's right hand;
His promise teaching little ones
  To speak and understand.

Oh! guide our minds with thy blest light,
  With love our hearts inflame;
And with thy strength, which ne'er decays,
  Confirm our mortal frame.

Far from us drive our hellish foe,
  True peace unto us bring;
And through all perils lead us safe
  Beneath thy sacred wing.

* Latin words, page 238.

Through thee may we the Father know,
  Through thee th' eternal Son,
And thee the Spirit of them both,
  Thrice blessed Three in One.

All glory to the Father be,
  With his co-equal Son,
The like to thee, great Paraclete,
  Till time itself is done.   Amen.

THE HYMN, *Veni Sancte Spiritus.**

COME, Holy Ghost, send down those
      beams,
Which sweetly flow in silent streams,
  From thy bright throne above.
Oh, come, thou Father of the poor,
Oh, come, thou Source of all our store;
  Come, fill our hearts with love.

O thou, of Comforters the best,
O thou, the soul's delightful guest,
  The pilgrim's sweet relief.
Thou art true rest in toil and sweat,
Refreshment in th' excess of heat,
  And solace in our grief.

Thrice blessed light, shoot home thy
      darts,
And pierce the centres of those hearts,
  Whose faith aspires to thee;

* Latin words, page 239.

Without thy Godhead nothing can
Have any price or worth in man,
   Nothing can harmless be.

Lord, wash our sinful stains away,
Water, from heav'n, our barren clay;
   Our wounds and bruises heal;
To thy sweet yoke our stiff necks bow;
Warm with thy fire our hearts of snow;
   Our wand'ring feet repeal.

Grant to thy faithful, dearest Lord,
Whose only hope is thy sure word,
   The seven gifts of the Spirit;
Grant us in life thy helping grace;
Grant us at death to see thy face,
   And endless joy inherit. *Amen.*

Anth. Come, Holy Spirit, fill the hearts of thy faithful, and kindle in them the fire of thy love.

V. Send forth thy Spirit, and they shall be created.

R. And thou shalt renew the face of the earth.

Let us Pray.

O GOD, who hast taught the hearts of the faithful by the light of the Holy Spirit, grant that we may, by the gift of the same Spirit, be always truly wise, and ever rejoice in his consolations. Through Jesus Christ our Lord. Amen.

Pope Pius VI. granted to all the faithful who one or more times a day should invoke the Holy Spirit with the hymn *Veni Creator Spiritus, &c.*, or the Sequence *Veni Sancte Spiritus, &c.*, with the intention of praying for peace amongst Christian princes:

1. A plenary indulgence once a month, on any one day, after confession and communion.

2. 300 days' indulgence to those who should recite the said Hymn and Sequence on Whitsunday and on each day during its octave.

3. 100 days' indulgence any other day once a day.

VENI CREATOR.

VENI Creator Spiritus,
 Mentes tuorum visita,
Imple superna gratia,
Quæ Tu creasti pectora.

 Qui diceris Paraclitus,
Altissimi Donum Dei,
Fons vivus, Ignis, Charitas,
Et spiritalis Unctio.

 Tu septiformis munere,
Digitus Paternæ dexteræ,
Tu rite promissum Patris,
Sermone ditans guttura.

Accende lumen sensibus,
Infunde amorem cordibus,
Infirma nostri corporis
Virtute firmans perpeti.

Hostem repellas longius,
Pacemque dones protinus;
Ductore sic Te prævio
Vitemus omne noxium.

Per te sciamus da Patrem,
Noscamus atque Filium,
Teque utriusque Spiritum
Credamus omni tempore.

Deo Patri sit gloria,
Et Filio, qui a mortuis
Surrexit, ac Paraclito
In sæculorum sæcula.   Amen.

VENI SANCTE SPIRITUS.

VENI Sancte Spiritus, et emitte
    cœlitus lucis tuæ radium.
Veni Pater pauperum, veni dator
    munerum, veni lumen cordium.
Consolator optime, dulcis hospes animæ, dulce refrigerium.
In labore requies, in æstu temperies,
    in fletu solatium.

O lux beatissima, reple cordis intima tuorum fidelium.
Sine tuo numine nihil est in homine, nihil est innoxium.
Lava quod est sordidum, riga quod est aridum, sana quod est saucium.
Flecte quod est rigidum, fove quod est frigidum, rege quod est devium.
Da tuis fidelibus in te confidentibus sacrum septenarium.
Da virtutis meritum, da salutis exitum, da perenne gaudium.
Amen.

V. Emitte Spiritum tuum et creabuntur.

R. Et renovabis faciem terræ.

Oremus.

DEUS qui corda fidelium sancti Spiritus illustratione docuisti: da nobis in eodem Spiritu recta sapere, et de ejus semper consolatione gaudere. Per Christum Dominum nostrum. Amen.

THE SACRAMENTS.

SHORT EXPLANATION.

[From the Catechism.]

What is a sacrament?—A sacrament is an outward sign of inward grace, ordained by Christ, by which grace is given to our souls.

Do the sacraments always give grace?—Yes; to those who receive them worthily.

Whence have the sacraments the power of giving grace?—From the merits of Christ's precious blood, which they apply to our souls.

Is it a great happiness to receive the sacraments worthily?—Yes; it is the greatest happiness in the world.

How many sacraments are there?—These seven: Baptism, Confirmation, Holy Eucharist, Penance, Extreme Unction, Holy Order, and Matrimony.

INSTRUCTION ON THE SACRAMENTS.

The Sacraments are sensible signs instituted by our Lord Jesus Christ for our sanctification. They are the means by which, as we are taught by the Council of Trent, "all justice is either begun, or when begun is increased, or when lost is recovered." Whatever degree of sanctity, therefore, any Christian may possess, it is principally to their influence that he is indebted for it. The entire efficacy of them all is derived from the passion and death of our blessed Saviour, and whatever graces they convey, are no other than the application of the said merits to our souls. Each sacrament confers a grace peculiar to itself, and in them all the wisdom and goodness of the Deity has provided appropriate helps for every stage and condition of life. 1. No sooner do we come into the world, than we are made the children of God by *baptism*. 2. As we grow up, we are fortified under the combats which we have to sustain against our spiritual enemies by *confirmation*. 3. The *Eucharist* is the daily bread, which feeds and nourishes our souls to everlasting life. 4. If unhappily we fall in the spiritual conflict, *penance* is the remedy which restores life to the soul. 5. In *matrimony* Jesus Christ has provided graces to assuage the cares and burthens of the married state. 6. *Holy orders* keep up a succession of pastors in the church, and enable them faithfully to discharge their sacred functions. And *lastly*, when sickness forewarns the Christian, that to him the figure of this world is fast passing away, and his soul is on the verge of eternity, his departing spirit is fortified and comforted by the refreshing graces of *Extreme Unction*.

Be assured, then, Christian reader, that nothing in this world is more deserving of your solicitude and care, than to be well instructed in the dispositions requisite for approaching worthily to the sacraments, that you may not, by your unworthiness, convert these instruments of grace into sources of malediction, but, on the contrary, may use them in such a manner that they may be to you abundant sources of sanctification, and may conduct you to eternal life.

THE MANNER OF LAY PERSONS BAPTIZING AN INFANT IN DANGER OF DEATH.

Take common water, pour it on the head or face of the child, and whilst you are pouring it, say the following words:

I baptize thee in the name of the Father, and of the Son, and of the Holy Ghost. Amen.

THE SACRAMENT OF PENANCE.

Penance is a sacrament instituted by Jesus Christ, by means of which the sins that we commit after baptism are forgiven, and we receive strength to enable us to avoid sin for the time to come. By this sacrament, the sanctifying grace of God, which is poured into our hearts by the Holy Ghost, cleanses the soul from all the stains of sin, restores to her the favour and friendship of God, and renders her holy and beautiful in his sight. This holy and salutary institution is grounded on the words of Jesus Christ: *Amen, I say to you, whatsoever you shall bind upon earth, shall be bound also in heaven; and whatsoever you shall loose upon earth, shall be loosed also in heaven.* Matt. xviii. 18. And, *As the Father hath sent me, I also send you. When he had said this, he breathed on them, and he said to them, Receive ye the Holy Ghost; whose sins you shall forgive, they are forgiven them; and whose sins you shall retain, they are retained.* John, xx. 21, &c. In these words Jesus Christ gave to his apostles and their lawful successors, power and authority to absolve from all sin those who sincerely repent of their offences.

A SHORT EXPLANATION.

FROM THE CATECHISM.

How many things have we to do in order to prepare for confession? Four things: 1st, We must heartily pray to God for his grace to help us. 2nd, We must carefully examine our conscience. 3rd, We must beg pardon of God, and be very sorry from our hearts for having offended him. And 4th, We must resolve to renounce our sins, and to begin a new life for the future.

What is satisfaction? It is doing the penance given us by the priest.

Let your confession be *humble*, without seeking excuses for your sins, or laying the fault on others: let it be *entire* as to the kind and number of your sins, and *such circumstances* as quite change the nature of the sin, or greatly increase its guilt. Be modest in your expressions, and take care not to name any third person.

A Prayer to implore the Divine assistance in order to make a good Confession.

O ALMIGHTY and most merciful God, who hast made me out of nothing, and redeemed me by the precious blood of thine only Son; who hast, with so much patience, borne with me to this day, notwithstanding all my sins and ingratitude; ever calling after me to return to thee from the ways of vanity and iniquity, in which I have been quite wearied out in the pursuit of empty toys and mere shadows; seeking in vain to satisfy my thirst in muddy waters, and my hunger with husks of swine: behold, O most gracious Lord, I now sincerely desire to leave all these my evil ways, to forsake the region of death, where I have so long lost myself, and to return to thee, the Fountain of life. I desire, like the prodigal child, to enter seriously into myself, and with the like resolution to arise without delay, and to go home to my Father, though I am infinitely unworthy to be called his child, in hopes of meeting with the like reception from his most tender mercy. But, O my God, though I can go astray from thee of myself, yet I cannot make one step towards returning to thee, unless thy divine grace stir me up and assist me. This grace, then, I most humbly implore, prostrate in spirit before the throne of thy mercy, I beg it for the sake of Jesus Christ, thy Son, who died upon the cross for my sins; I know thou desirest not the death of a sinner, but that he be converted and live· I know thy mercies are above all thy works; and I most confidently hope, that as in thy mercy thou hast spared me so long, and hast now given me this desire of returning to thee, so thou wilt finish the work which thou hast begun, and bring me to a perfect reconciliation with thee.

I desire now to comply with thy holy institution of the sacrament of penance; I desire to confess my sins with all sincerity to thee, and to thy minister; and therefore I desire to know myself, and to call myself to an account by a diligent examination of my conscience. But, O my God, how miserably shall I deceive myself, if thou assist me not in this great work by thy heavenly light! Oh, remove then every veil that hides any of my sins from me, that I may see them all in their true colours, and may sincerely detest them. Oh, let me not any longer be imposed upon by the enemy or by my own self-love, so as to mistake vice for virtue, to hide myself from myself, or in any way to flatter myself in my sins.

But, O my good God, what will it avail me to know my sins, if thou dost not also give me a hearty sorrow and repentance for them? without this my sins will be all upon me still, and I shall be still thine enemy and a child of hell. Thou insistest upon a change of heart, without which there can be no reconciliation with thee; and this change of heart none but thou canst give. Oh, give it me then, dear Lord, at this time. Give me a lively faith, and a firm hope, in the passion of my Redeemer; teach me to fear thee, and to love thee. Give me, for thy mercy's sake, a hearty sorrow for having offended so good a God. Teach me to detest my evil ways; to abhor all my past ingratitudes; to hate myself now with a perfect hatred for my many treasons against thee. Oh, give me a full and a firm resolution of a new life for the future, and unite me to thee with an eternal band of love, which nothing in life or death may ever break.

Grant me also the grace to make an entire and sincere confession of all my sins, and to accept of the confusion of it, as a penance justly due to my transgressions. Let not the enemy prevail upon me to pass over anything through fear or shame: rather let me die than consent to so great an evil. Let no self-love deceive me, as I fear it has done too often. Oh, grant that this confession at least may be good, and for the sake of Jesus Christ thy Son, who died for me, and for all sinners, assist me in every part of my preparation for it, that I may go through it with the same care and diligence as I should be glad to do at the hour of my death; that so being perfectly reconciled to thee, I may never offend thee more.

O blessed Virgin, Mother of my Redeemer, mirror of innocence and sanctity, and refuge of penitent sinners, intercede for me through the passion of thy Son, that I may have the grace to make a good confession. All ye blessed angels and saints of God, pray for me, a poor miserable sinner, that I may now, for good and all, turn from my evil ways, that so henceforward my heart may be for ever united with yours in eternal love, and never more go astray from the Sovereign Good. *Amen.*

This or the like prayer may be frequently repeated for some days before confession, in order to obtain of God the grace of making a good confession.

A METHOD OF
Examination of Conscience,
FOR SUCH AS CONFESS OFTEN,

ACCORDING TO THE THREEFOLD DUTY WE OWE: 1. TO GOD. 2. TO OUR NEIGHBOUR. 3. TO OURSELVES.

I. *In relation to God.*

1. Have you omitted morning or evening prayers, or neglected to make your daily examination of conscience?— Have you prayed negligently, and with wilful distractions?

2. Have you spent your time, especially on Sundays and holydays, not in sluggishly lying in bed, or in any sort of idle entertainment, but in reading, praying, or any other pious exercises; and taken care that those under your charge have done the like, and not wanted the instructions necessary for their condition, nor time for prayer, or to prepare for the sacraments?

3. Have you spoken irreverently of God and holy things? Have you taken his name in vain, or told untruths?

4. Have you omitted your duty

through human respect, interest, compliance, &c.?

5. Have you been zealous for God's honour, for justice, virtue, and truth, and reproved such as act otherwise?

6. Have you according to your means contributed towards the support of religion, and the maintenance of your pastor?

7. Have you resigned your will to God in troubles, necessities, sickness, &c.

8. Have you faithfully resisted thoughts of infidelity, distrust, presumption, impurity, &c.

II. *In relation to your Neighbour.*

1. Have you disobeyed your superiors, murmured against their commands, or spoken of them contemptuously?

2. Have you been troubled, peevish, or impatient when told of your faults, and corrected by them?—Have you scorned their good advice, or censured their proceedings?

3. Have you offended any one by injurious or threatening words or actions?

4. Or lessened their reputation by any sort of detraction, or in any matter of importance?

5. Or spread any report, true or false, that exposed your neighbour to contempt, or made him be undervalued?

6. Have you, by carrying stories backward and forward, created discord and misunderstanding between neighbours?

7. Have you been froward or peevish towards any one, in your carriage, speech, or conversation?

8. Or taken pleasure to vex, mortify, or provoke them to swear, curse, or any ways offend God?

9. Have you mocked or reproached them for their corporal or spiritual imperfections?

10. Have you been excessive in reprehending those under your care, or been wanting in giving them just reproof?

11. Have you borne with their oversights and imperfections, and given them good counsels?

12. Have you been solicitous for such as are under your charge, and provided for their souls and bodies?

13. Have you according to your power given alms, or contributed towards the relief of the poor? have you endea-

voured to promote their spiritual wellfare especially by the education of the children in your congregation?

III. *In relation to yourself.*

1. Have you been obstinate in following your own will, or in defending your own opinion, in things either indifferent, dangerous, or scandalous?
2. Have you taken pleasure in hearing yourself praised, or yielded to thoughts of vanity?
3. Have you indulged yourself in over-much ease, or in any way yielding to sensuality?
4. Has your conversation been edifying and moderate, or have you been froward, proud, or troublesome to others?
5. Have you spent over-much time in play, or useless employments, and thereby omitted, or put off your devotions, to unseasonable times?

If such as confess often fall into any of the more grievous sins, not here mentioned, their own memory will easily suggest them; since it is impossible for a tender soul to forget any mortal offence, which must of necessity afflict her, and therefore it may not be necessary for them to turn over the following table of sins, which is chiefly intended for general confessions.

AN EXAMINATION OF CONSCIENCE,

ON THE TEN COMMANDMENTS, THE COMMANDMENTS OF THE CHURCH, AND THE SEVEN DEADLY SINS.

The First Commandment.

I am the Lord thy God, who brought thee out of the land of Egypt, out of the house of bondage. Thou shalt not have strange gods before me. Thou shalt not make to thyself a graven thing, nor the likeness of any thing that is in heaven above, or in the earth beneath, nor of those things that are in the waters under the earth. Thou shalt not adore them, nor serve them. Exodus, xx.

Have you been guilty of heresy, or wilful doubting of any article of faith? Have you rashly exposed yourself to the danger of infidelity, by reading bad books, or keeping wicked company? How often?

Have you by word or deed denied your religion? Have you been ignorant of any of those things which Christians in your station are bound to know? For how long a time?

Have you been negligent in the worship of God; praying but little, or with little attention?

Have you made a bad confession or communion, by concealing some mortal sin in confession, or what you doubted might be mortal?

Have you consulted fortune-tellers, or made use of any superstitious practices; or given credit to dreams?

Have you blasphemed God or his saints, or scoffed at holy things? How often?

The Second Commandment.
Thou shalt not take the name of the Lord thy God in vain.

Have you taken God's name in vain, or used it without respect in common discourse? Have you taken a false oath, or a rash oath? Have you taken an oath to do any thing that was wicked or unlawful? or broken your lawful oaths? How often?

Have you had a custom of swearing? Have you cursed yourself or others, or any thing else? Have you been the cause of others swearing, cursing, or blaspheming? Have you broken any vow or solemn promise made to God? How often?

The Third Commandment.
Remember that thou keep holy the Sabbath day.

Have you neglected to keep the

Sunday holy? Have you, when prevented from hearing Mass on Sundays and Holy-days, supplied the omission by prayers at home, and taken care those under your charge did the same?

Have you done any servile work without necessity, or spent those days in idleness?

The Fourth Commandment.
Honour thy father and thy mother.

If a Child.—Have you been wanting in your duty to your parents, by not showing them due respect; or by disobeying them? Or have you been disobedient or disrespectful to any other lawful superiors? How often?

Have you desired your parents' death, or cursed them? Or struck them? Or provoked them to swear or offend God? Or caused them any trouble or uneasiness? How often?

Have you neglected to help your parents in their necessities, either corporal or spiritual?

If a Parent.—Have you neglected to get your children speedily baptized? Or to get them instructed in their prayers and catechism? Or to see that they go to the sacraments? Have you neglected to remove from them the occasions of sin, such as wicked companions, bad books, &c.; or allowed them to lie in the same bed with one another, with danger to their chastity? Have you given them bad example?

If a Servant.—Have you disobeyed your master or mistress? Have you been wanting in diligence or industry? Have you injured or destroyed their property through carelessness or neglect?

If a Master or Mistress.—Have you neglected to watch over the conduct of your servants? Have you refused without necessity to allow them time to hear Mass on Sundays and holy-days, or to frequent the sacraments? Have you overburdened them with work, or treated them badly?

The Fifth Commandment.
Thou shalt not kill.

Have you been guilty of anger, or violent passion, and if so, what scandal was given? Have you desired any one's death, through hatred or malice?

Have you revenged yourself of any one, or taken pleasure in the thoughts of it? How often? Have you provoked or struck others? Have you borne malice to others?

Have you procured, or thought to procure, a miscarriage? Or given any counsel, aid, or assistance thereunto? Have you desired your own death, through passion or impatience?

Have you neglected to give alms according to your ability? Have you been accessary to the sins of others? How often? And what sins?

Have you given scandal, or occasion of sin to others by lewd or irreligious discourse? by drunkenness or swearing? by immodesty of dress or behaviour, &c.?

N.B.—The circumstance of scandal is generally found in all sins that are known to others, by reason of the force of ill-example, which encourages others to sin.

The Sixth Commandment.
Thou shalt not commit adultery.

Have you been guilty of any acts of impurity? (*Under this head all sins against purity must be carefully exam-*

ined; as well as whatsoever leads to their indulgence or omission.) Have you been guilty of filthy talking? of reading immodest books? of indecency of dress? of looking at unchaste objects? of taking any dangerous or improper liberties, with yourself or with others?

N.B.—As the sins against this and the ninth commandment are most grievous, and at the same time most various, the prudent counsel of your director will assist you, if necessary, in a more particular examination.

The Seventh Commandment.

Thou shalt not steal.

Have you been guilty of stealing, or cheating, or in any way wronging your neighbour?

Have you contracted debts without design of paying them; or without any prospect of being able to pay them? Or have you refused to pay your just debts when you were able? Have you professed any art, or undertaken any business without sufficient skill or knowledge? And what injury has your neighbour suffered from it? Have you bought or received stolen goods? Have you neglected your work or business to which you were hired, or by contract obliged? Have you broken your promises in matters of consequence?

N.B.—In all sins of injustice whereby you have done any wrong to your neighbour, either in his person, or in his goods, or in his character, honour, or good name, you are strictly obliged to make full satisfaction and restitution, if it be in your power, otherwise the sin will not be forgiven.

Have you, then, neglected without just cause to make restitution, when it was in your power?

The Eighth Commandment.
Thou shalt not bear false witness against thy neighbour.

Have you been guilty of telling lies? And whether to the injury of any one? Have you entertained a bad opinion of your neighbour without grounds, or judged rashly of his actions or intentions? Have you been guilty of backbiting, or uncharitable conversation, by speaking of the known faults of your absent neighbour? How often? Have you been guilty of the sin of detraction, which consists in taking away or lessening your neighbour's reputation, by publishing his secret faults or defects? How often have you done so? From what motive, and before how many? Have you been guilty of calumny, which consists in saying of your neighbour what is false or uncertain? How often? and before how many?

In either case you are obliged to restore his character as far as you are able.

Have you willingly listened to detraction or calumny? Have you injured your neighbour's honour by reproaches and affronts, or robbed him of his peace of mind, by scoffs and derision? How often?

Have you caused misunderstanding or quarrels between others?

The Ninth Commandment.

Thou shalt not covet thy neighbour's wife.

Have you taken pleasure in any unchaste thoughts, or imaginations? Have you entertained any impure desires or feelings?

The Tenth Commandment.

Thou shalt not covet thy neighbour's goods.

Have you desired your neighbour's goods, not caring whether you had them right or wrong?

The Commandments of the Church.

1. To keep certain days holy, with the obligation of resting from servile works.
2. To hear Mass on all Sundays and Holydays of obligation.
3. To keep the days of fasting and abstinence appointed by the Church.
4. To go to confession at least once a year.
5. To receive the Blessed Sacrament at least once a year, and that at Easter or thereabouts.
6. Not to marry within certain degrees of kindred, nor to solemnize marriage at the forbidden times.

I. Have you neglected to keep holy the days of obligation?

II. Have you neglected to hear Mass on Sundays? or have you heard it with wilful distractions? Or not taken care that your children and servants should hear it? How often?

III. Have you broken the days of abstinence commanded by the Church, or eaten more than one meal on fasting days? Or been accessary to others so doing? How often?

IV. V. Have you neglected to confess your sins once a year. Or to receive the Blessed Sacrament at Easter?

VI. Have you entered into the married state at the forbidden times? Have you married within the forbidden degrees of kindred? Or with any other known impediment?

The Seven Deadly Sins.

Pride. Have you been guilty of pride, or contempt of others?

Have you been guilty of vain-glory, by doing your actions to procure esteem?

Covetousness. Have you been guilty of covetousness in desiring or loving too much the things of this world?

For the sins of Lust, see the Sixth Commandment.

For the sins of Anger, see the Fifth Commandment.

Gluttony. Have you been guilty of gluttony, by eating or drinking to excess, so as to endanger or injure your health or reason? How often, and with what scandal?

Have you made others drunk, or sought to make them so?

Envy. Have you envied your neighbour's good, either spiritual or temporal? Or rejoiced at his harm? How often? Have you been guilty of jealousy in consequence of any preference shown to others?

Sloth. Have you been guilty of sloth, or laziness of mind or body, which has prevented you from discharging your duty? How often?

Have you neglected your *Spiritual Duties,* or discharged them with tepidity or indolence? Have you studied too much your own ease, leading an unmortified and unchristian or idle life?

Have you had the desire or design of committing any sin? Of what sin. How often?

Have you gloried in any sin whatsoever? How often? And before what company? And what sin?

Here also masters and servants, husbands and wives, lawyers and physicians, ecclesiastics and magistrates, etc., ought to examine into the sins which are peculiar to their states, and how far they may have neglected the duties of their respective callings.

A Prayer for obtaining Contrition.

I HAVE now here before me, O Lord, a sad prospect of the manifold offences, by which I have displeased thy divine Majesty, and which I am assured will appear in judgment against me, if I repent not, and my soul be not disposed, by a hearty sorrow, to receive thy pardon. But this sorrow, O Lord, this repentance, must be thy free gift, and if it comes not from the hand of thy mercy, all my endeavours will be in vain, and I shall be for ever miserable. Have mercy, therefore, on me, O Father of mercies, and pour forth into my heart thy grace, whereby I may sincerely repent of all my sins; give me a true contrition, that I may bewail my past misery and ingratitude, and grieve from my heart for having offended thee so good a God. Permit me not to be deluded with a false sorrow, as, I fear, I have been too often, through my own weakness and neglect; but let it be now thy gift, descending from thee, the Father of lights, that so my repentance may be accompanied with amendment and change of life, and I may be fully acquitted from the guilt of all my sins, and once more received into the number of thy servants. Through Jesus Christ our Lord. *Amen.*

An Act of Contrition.

O MY God, who art infinitely good, and always hatest sin, I beg pardon from my heart for all my offences against thee; I detest them all and am heartily sorry for them, because they offend thy infinite goodness, and I firmly resolve by the help of thy grace never more to offend thee, and carefully to avoid the occasions of sin.

Short Act of Contrition.

O MY God, I am very sorry that I have sinned against thee, because thou art so good, and I will not sin again.

HYMN OF REPENTANT SORROW.

JESUS, my God, behold at length the time,
When I resolve to turn away from crime;
O pardon me, Jesus, thy mercy I implore,
I will never more offend thee—no, never more.

Since my poor soul thy precious blood hath cost,
Suffer me not for ever to be lost!
O pardon me, Jesus, thy mercy I implore,
I will never more offend thee—no, never more.

Kneeling, in tears, behold me at thy feet,
Like Magdalen, forgiveness I entreat,
O pardon me, Jesus, thy mercy I implore,
I will never more offend thee—no, never more.

Affections and Resolutions.

MY Lord and my All! I am confounded at the multitude and enormity of my offences against so good a God; I dare not presume even to lift up mine eyes to heaven, much less to come near thy altar, after so many treasons against thee. Alas! what shall I now do, O Lord! What shall I say! But with the humble publican, strike my breast, and cry out to thee, *O God, be merciful to me a sinner!*

My sins exceed in number the hairs of my head, and the sands of the sea, but thy mercies are more innumerable than my sins. O Ocean of mercy, have compassion on a poor miserable sinner, and make me now at least a true penitent.

Father, I have sinned against heaven, and in thy sight, and am not worthy to be called thy child: Oh! receive me as one of the least of thy servants, and never suffer me to go astray from thee any more.

It grieves me, O my good God, that I have offended thee: I am heartily sorry for all the sins which I have committed against thine infinite goodness. Oh! that I could worthily lament them, even with tears of blood.

Who will give water to my head, and a fountain of tears to mine eyes, that night and day I may weep for my sins and ingratitude?

Oh! that I had never offended my God! Oh! that I had never sinned! Happy those souls who have never lost their baptismal innocence! Ah! sweet Jesus, that I had been so happy!

Have mercy on me, O God, according to thy great mercy; and according to the multitude of thy tender mercies blot out mine iniquity. Wash me yet more from mine iniquity, and cleanse me from my sin; for I know mine iniquity, and my sin is always before me.

Oh! that I could now like Magdalen, present myself at the feet of my Saviour! Oh! that I could wash them with my tears! Oh! suffer me, dear Lord, to lay down all my sins at thy feet to be cancelled by thy precious blood.

Lord, thou hast said there is joy in heaven upon one sinner doing penance, more than upon ninety-nine just: Oh! give me now grace to be a true penitent indeed, that so heaven may rejoice at my conversion.

Thou camest, O my dear Redeemer, not to call the just, but sinners to repentance; look down upon me, a poor miserable sinner, and draw me powerfully to thee by thy grace.

I know thou willest not the death of a sinner, but that he be converted and live: Oh! let me no longer remain dead in my sins! Oh! let me now at least begin to live to thee!

Create a clean heart in me, O God; and renew a right spirit within my bowels. Oh! grant that I may now serve thee in good earnest! Oh, let this be the change of the right hand of the most High.

Thou hast made me, O my God, and redeemed me by thy precious blood. Oh! despise not the work of thy hands! Oh, let not thy blood be spilt for me in vain!

Too late have I known thee, O ancient Truth! Too late have I loved thee, O ancient Beauty! Too long have I gone astray from thee! From this moment, O my Sovereign Good, I desire to be for ever thine. Oh! let nothing in life or death ever separate me from thee any more.

O divine Lover of penitent souls, give me henceforth a contrite and humble heart! Oh! I desire from this hour to offer this sacrifice daily to thee, till the end of my life!

O divine Love, how little art thou known in this wicked world! how little art thou loved! Come now to me, and take full possession of my whole heart and soul for time and eternity.

Thy mercy hath been infinite in bearing so long with such an ungrateful sinner as I have been, and in daily heaping thy favours upon me. Add this one favour, O Lord, to all the rest, that henceforward, by thy grace, I may never offend thee more. This one thing I earnestly beg of thee, for thine infinite mercy's sake, and through the death and passion of thine only Son. Hear this one prayer, I beseech thee, and in all things else do with me what thou pleasest.

I am resolved, by thy grace, never more to return to my sins; Oh, rather let me die than offend thee wilfully any more. I am resolved to fly all evil company, and dangerous occasions; and to take proper measures for a thorough amendment of my life for the future. All this I resolve; but thou knowest my frailty, O my God; and if thou assist me not by thy grace, all my resolutions will prove ineffectual, and I shall be for ever miserable: Oh! look to me, O Lord, that I may never betray thee any more.

N. B. Here it is proper that you should think upon the measures which you must take for an entire amendment of your life for the time to come.

HOW TO GO TO CONFESSION.

Kneeling down at the side of your confessor, make the sign of the Cross, saying,

In the name of the Father, and of the Son, and of the Holy Ghost. Amen.

Then ask his blessing in these words·

Pray, Father, give me your blessing, for I have sinned.

Then say:

I confess to Almighty God, to blessed Mary ever Virgin, to blessed Michael the Archangel, to blessed John the Baptist, to the holy apostles Peter and Paul, to all the Saints, and to you, Father, that I have sinned exceedingly in thought, word, and deed, [strike your breast thrice,] *through my fault, through my fault, through my most grievous fault.*

Then say:

Since my last confession, which was so many weeks or months ago, I accuse myself, etc.

Then accuse yourself of your sins, the number of times that you have been guilty of each sin, and such circumstances as may aggravate the guilt of the sins. After you have confessed all that you can remember, say,

For these and all my other sins, which I cannot now remember, I am very sorry, and beg pardon of God, and penance and absolution of you, my ghostly father.

Therefore I beseech the blessed Mary ever Virgin, blessed Michael the Archangel, blessed John the Baptist, the holy apostles Peter and Paul, and all the Saints, and you, Father, to pray to the Lord our God for me.

Then listen to the instructions and advice of your confessor, and accept the penance he gives you, and say an Act of Contrition, page 265.

NOTE.

When the priest has not much time for hearing confessions, or when a large number of persons are waiting their turn to go to confession, he will sometimes tell the penitents not to say the *Confiteor* or *I confess*. In such cases the following form may be used.

SHORT FORM OF CONFESSION.

Kneeling down at the side of the priest, say:

Pray, Father, give me your blessing, for I have sinned.

Since my last confession, which was—(*here tell how long it is since*) I accuse myself of, &c., (*here tell the priest your sins*).

After confession, while the priest is giving you the pardon of your sins, which is called Absolution, say this

Short Act of Contrition.

O MY God, I am very sorry that I have sinned against thee, because thou art so good, and I will not sin again.

A Prayer after Confession.

O ALMIGHTY and most merciful God, who according to the multitude of thy tender mercies hast vouchsafed once more to receive this prodigal child, after so many times going astray from thee, and to admit him into this sacrament of reconciliation, I give thee thanks with all the powers of my soul, for this and all other mercies, graces and blessings bestowed on me, the most unworthy of all sinners: and prostrating myself at thy sacred feet, I offer myself now to be henceforth for ever thine. Oh! let nothing in life or death ever separate me from thee. I once more renounce with my whole soul all my treasons against thee, and all the abominations and sins of my past life. I renew my promises made in baptism, and from this moment I dedicate myself eternally to thy love and service. Oh! grant that for the time to come I may ever fly and abhor sin more than death itself, and avoid all such occasions and companies as have unhappily brought me to it. I resolve henceforth to fly them all, by thy divine grace, without which, of myself, I can do nothing. I resolve to perform such and such devotions for obtaining this grace. I resolve to fly idleness, and to set myself a regular order and method of life, for the time I have yet to come. I beg thy blessing upon these my resolutions, that they may not be ineffectual, like so many others I have formerly made: for, O Lord, without thee I am nothing but misery and sin. Supply, also, by thy mercy, whatever defects have been in this my confession. I am sensible that it hath been very imperfect, and that I was far from having that true sorrow which the heinousness of my sins required; but let the precious blood of thine only Son make up this deficiency. Accept of my poor performance, such as it is, and give me grace to be now and always a true penitent, through the same Jesus Christ thy Son. *Amen.*

A Prayer after Confession when Absolution has been deferred.

O MY God, now painful, how afflicting is it to me that I am not duly prepared to receive from thee the pardon of my sins! O Lord, I acknowledge my unworthiness, and I humbly submit to the decision of thy minister. But how long, O Lord, how long shall this afflicting separation from thee continue? Oh! assist me, I beseech thee, to begin from this moment a new life. I will endeavour by thy grace daily to excite in my heart a more sincere and earnest sorrow for my offences. I will carefully avoid all occasions of sin, and

I will faithfully put in practice the advice given me by my director. O my God, have mercy on me, and give me grace to keep these my resolutions, that so I may have the happiness to renounce all sin, and obtain from thee the full pardon of all my offences. Through Jesus Christ our Lord. *Amen.*

SATISFACTION.

JESUS CHRIST died upon the cross for our sins, and offered to his Eternal Father a full and superabundant satisfaction for them. *Jesus is the propitiation for our sins; and not for ours only, but also for those of the whole world.* 1 John, ii. 3.

When the Almighty Father, in consideration of his Son's bitter death, forgives our sins, and the eternal punishment due to them in the holy Sacrament of Penance, the order of his justice requires, that some temporal punishment should be undergone by the penitent sinner. This debt of temporal punishment may, however, be redeemed by penitential works, such as almsdeeds, prayer, and fasting, and by bearing with patience and resignation the miseries and afflictions with which Divine Providence may please to visit us in this valley of tears. Hence, before the penitent sinner is absolved from his sins, some *penance* or penitential works, such as those just mentioned, are imposed upon him by the minister of God; the performance of which is called *satisfaction*, and forms the third part of the Sacrament of Penance. The sincere penitent will therefore be careful to perform this penance in due time, and in a truly penitential spirit.

DEVOTIONS FOR HOLY COMMUNION.

Let *a man prove* (or try) *himself*, says St. Paul, 1 Cor. xi. 28, *and so let him eat of that bread, &c.* This proving or trying yourself is the first and most necessary preparation for the holy communion, and consists in looking diligently into the state of your soul, in order to discover what indispositions or sins may lie there concealed, and to apply a proper remedy to them by sincere repentance and confession: lest otherwise approaching the Holy of Holies with a soul defiled with the guilt of mortal sin, you become *guilty of the body and blood of the Lord, and receive judgment to yourself, not discerning the body of the Lord.* 1 Cor. ix. For this reason you must go to confession before communion, in order to clear your soul from the filth of sin.

Prepare yourself by acts of virtue, more especially of faith, love, and humility; that so you may approach your Lord with a firm belief of his real presence in this sacrament, and of that great sacrifice which he heretofore offered upon the cross for your redemption, of which he here makes you partaker; with an ardent affection of love to him, who has loved you so much, and who, out of pure love, gives himself to you; and with a great sentiment of your own unworthiness and sins, joined with a firm confidence in the mercies of your Redeemer.

It is a good plan to choose some particular object for which you will make your communion, and to offer it up for that intention. Then place yourself with great recollection in the presence of God, and if you find you want help to do this, read over the following acts of preparation. Take care not to read them in a hurry, but rather with your heart than your eyes, slowly and devoutly. It is not necessary to read a great many prayers in order to make a good preparation. Some of the following prayers might be read over the night before communion.

A

PREPARATORY PRAYER,

CONTAINING THE CHIEF ACTS OF DEVOTION PROPER BEFORE COMMUNION.

1. *Direct your Intention.*

O LORD Jesus Christ, King of everlasting glory, behold I desire to come to thee this day, and to receive thy body and blood in this heavenly sacrament, for thy honour and glory, and the good of my soul: I desire to receive thee, because it is thy desire, and thou hast so ordained; blessed be thy name for ever. I desire to come to thee like Magdalen, that I may be delivered from all my evils, and embrace thee my only good. I desire to come to thee, that I may be happily united to thee, that I may henceforth abide in thee, and thou in me, and that nothing in life or death may ever separate me from thee.

2. *Commemorate the Passion of Christ.*

I desire, in these holy mysteries, to commemorate, as thou hast commanded, all thy sufferings, thine agony and bloody sweat; thy being betrayed and apprehended; all the reproaches and calumnies—all the blows and buffets which thou hast endured for me; thy being scourged, crowned with thorns, and loaded with a heavy cross for my sins, and those of the whole world; thy crucifixion and death, together with thy glorious resurrection and triumphant ascension. I adore thee, and give thee thanks for all that thou hast done and suffered for us; and for giving us in this blessed sacrament, this pledge of our redemption, this victim of our ransom, this body and blood which were offered for us.

3. *Make an Act of Faith.*

I most firmly believe, that in this holy sacrament thou art present verily and indeed; that here are thy body and blood, thy soul and thy divinity. I believe that thou, my Saviour, true God and true man, art really here, with all thy treasures; that here thou communicatest thyself to us, makest us partakers of the fruit of thy passion, and givest us a pledge of eternal life. I believe that there cannot be a greater happiness than to receive thee worthily, nor a greater misery than to receive thee unworthily. All this I most steadfastly believe, because it is what thou hast taught us by thy word, and by thy church.

4. *Conceive a great Fear, and humble yourself.*

But, O my God, how shall I dare approach to thee, so wretched a worm to so infinite a Majesty? so filthy a sinner to such infinite purity and sanctity? alas! my soul is covered with a universal leprosy, and how shall I presume to embrace thee? My whole life hath been nothing but misery and sin, and it is only thy mercy that I have not been long since in hell, which I have deserved a thousand times; and how shall I venture so much as to lift up mine eyes to thee, how much less to receive thee within my breast? I tremble at the sentence of thine apostle, that *He that receiveth unworthily, receiveth his own damnation;* for I cannot but acknowledge myself infinitely unworthy: nor should I dare ever to come to thee, were I not incited by the most loving and pressing invitation, and encouraged by thine infinite goodness and mercy. It is in this mercy, which is above all thy works, I put my whole trust; and it is in this confidence alone that I presume to approach to thee. Oh! grant that it may be with a contrite and humble heart, for this, I know, thou wilt not despise.

5. *Make an Act of Contrition.*

O Lord, I detest, with my whole heart, all the sins by which I have ever offended thy divine Majesty, from the first moment that I was capable of sinning to this very hour. I desire to lay them all at thy feet, to be cancelled by thy precious blood. What can I do for them, but humbly confess and lament them all my life; and this I heartily desire to do, and from this moment continually to cry to thee for mercy. Hear me, O Lord, by that infinite love, by which thou hast shed thy blood for me; Oh, let not that blood be shed in vain! All my sins displease me now exceedingly, because they have offended thine infinite goodness. By thy grace I will never commit them any more: I am sorry for them, and I will be sorry for them as long as I live; and according to the best of my power, will do penance for them. Forgive me, dear Lord, for thy mercy's sake: pardon me all that is past; and be thou my keeper for the time to come, that I may never more offend thee.

6. *Make an Act of Divine Love.*

O sweet Jesus, the God of my heart, and the life of my soul, as the hart panteth after the fountains of water, so doth my soul pant after thee, the fountain of life, and the ocean of all good. I am overjoyed at the hearing of these happy tidings, that I am to go into the house of our Lord; or rather that our Lord is to come into my house, and take up his abode with me. O happy moments, when I shall be admitted to the embraces of the living God, for whom my poor soul languisheth with love! Oh! come, dear Jesus, and take full possession of my heart for ever! I offer it to thee without reserve. I desire to consecrate it eternally to thee. I love thee with my whole soul above all things; at least I desire so to love thee. It is nothing less than infinite love that bringeth thee to me; Oh! teach me to make a suitable return of love.

7. *Humbly beg God's Grace.*

But, O my God, thou knowest my great poverty and misery, and that of myself I can do nothing; thou knowest how unworthy I am of this infinite favour, and thou alone canst make me worthy. Oh! since thou art so good as to invite me thus to thyself, add this one bounty more to all the rest, to prepare me for thyself. Cleanse my soul from its stains—clothe it with the nuptial garment of charity, adorn it with all virtues, and make it a fit abode for thee. Drive sin and the devil far from this dwelling, which thou art here pleased to choose for thyself, and make me one according to thy own heart; that this heavenly visit which thou designest for my salvation may not, by my unworthiness, be perverted to my damnation. Oh! never let me be guilty of thy body and blood, by an unworthy communion; for the sake of this same precious blood, which thou hast shed for me, deliver me from so great an evil. Oh, rather let me die ten thousand deaths, than thus presume to crucify thee again.

8. *Implore the prayers of the Blessed Virgin and of the Saints.*

O all ye blessed angels and saints of God who see him face to face, whom I here receive under these humble veils; and thou most especially, ever-blessed Virgin, Mother of this same God and Saviour, in whose womb he was conceived and borne for nine months; I most humbly beg the assistance of your prayers and intercession, that I may in such manner receive him here, in this place of banishment, as to be brought one day to enjoy him with you in our true country, and there to praise him and love him for ever.

The Manner of Receiving Communion.

Before you receive the most holy Sacrament of the Body and Blood of Jesus Christ, you must cleanse your conscience from any mortal sin by the Sacrament of Penance. You must fast from the midnight before. When the time for Holy Communion is come, go up to the altar respectfully, kneel down there, take the cloth into your hands and hold it before your breast, do not wipe your mouth with it; let your head be raised up, the eyes shut, the mouth open, the tongue forward and resting on the under lip. Shut your mouth after receiving the Blessed Sacrament, and when it is a little moistened on your tongue swallow it. If it stops on the roof of your mouth, do not remove it with your hand, but with your tongue. Pray for at least a quarter of an hour after Holy Communion.

During the whole day, after your communion, you ought to be more than ordinarily retired, and perform more devotions than usual.

Aspirations after Communion.

BEHOLD, O Lord, I have thee now, who hast all things; I possess thee. who possessest all things, and who canst do all things: take off my heart then,

O my God and my All, from all other things but thee, in all which there is nothing but vanity and affliction of spirit: let my heart be fixed on thee alone, let me ever repose in thee, where alone my treasure is, the sovereign truth, true happiness, and happy eternity.

Let my soul, O Lord, feel the sweetness of thy presence. Let me taste how sweet thou art, O Lord; that being allured by thy love, I may never more hunt after worldly joys; for thou art the joy of my heart, and my portion for ever.

Thou art the physician of my soul, who healest all our infirmities by thy sacred blood; I am that sick man, whom thou camest from heaven to heal: Oh, heal my soul, for I have sinned against thee.

Thou art the good shepherd, who hast laid down thy life for thy sheep; behold I am that sheep that was lost, and yet thou vouchsafest to feed me with thy body and blood; take me now upon thy shoulders to carry me home. What canst thou deny me, who hast given me thyself? Govern me, and I shall want nothing in the place of pasture where thou hast put me, until thou bringest me to the happy pastures of life eternal.

O true light, which enlightenest every man that cometh into this world, enlighten my eyes, that I may never sleep in death.

O fire, ever burning, and never decaying, behold how tepid and cold I am; inflame my reins and my heart, that they may burn with thy love; for thou camest to cast fire upon earth, and what dost thou desire but that it be enkindled?

O king of heaven and earth, rich in mercy, behold I am poor and needy, thou knowest what I stand most in need of; thou alone canst assist and enrich me. Help me, O God, and out of the treasures of thy bounty succour my needy soul.

O my Lord and my God, behold I am thy servant; give me understanding, and excite my affections, that I may know and do thy will.

Thou art the Lamb of God, the Lamb without spot, who takest away the sins of the world Oh, take away from me whatever is hurtful to me and displeasing to thee, and give me what thou knowest to be pleasing to thee and profitable to me.

Thou art my love and all my joy; thou art my God and my All; thou art the portion of my inheritance, and of my chalice: thou art he that will restore my inheritance to me.

O my God and my All, may the sweet flame of thy love consume my soul, that so I may die to the world for the love of thee, who hast vouchsafed to die upon the cross for the love of me.

Acts of Devotion, Praise, and Thanksgiving after Communion.

O MY sweet Jesus, my Creator, and my Redeemer, my God and my All, whence is this to me, that my Lord, and so great a Lord, whom heaven and earth cannot contain, should come into this poor cottage, this house of clay of my earthly habitation! Oh, that I could give thee a hearty welcome! Oh, that I could entertain thee as I ought! Thy loving kindness inviteth me to thine embraces, and I would willingly say with the spouse in the Canticle, I have found him whom my soul loveth, I have held him, and will not let him go: but the awe of so great a majesty checks me, and the sense of my great unworthiness and innumerable sins keeps me back. No, my soul, it is only the feet of thy Saviour that thou canst presume to embrace; it is there thou must present thyself, like Magdalen, and wish that, like her, thou couldst wash them with thy tears. Oh, that thou couldst be so happy!

But first bow down thyself with all thy powers, to adore the Sovereign Majesty which hath vouchsafed to come to visit thee: pay him the best homage thou art able as to thy first beginning and thy last end; and perfectly annihilate thyself in the presence of this eternal, immense, infinite Deity. Then pour thyself forth in his presence, in praise and thanksgiving, in the best manner thou art able, and invite all heaven and earth to join with thee in magnifying their Lord and thine, for his mercy and bounty to thee.

Oh! what return shall I make thee, O Lord, for all that thou hast done for me! Behold, when I had no being at all, thou hast created me; and when I was gone astray, and lost in my sins, thou hast redeemed me, by dying for me; all that I have, all that I am is thy gift; and now, after all other favours, thou hast given me thyself: blessed be thy name for ever. Thou art great, O Lord, and exceedingly to be praised; great are thy works, and of thy wisdom there is no end: but thy tender mercies, thy bounty and goodness to me, are above all thy works; these I desire to confess and extol for ever. Bless, then, thy Lord, O my soul, and let all that is within thee praise and magnify his name. Bless thy Lord, O my soul, and see thou never forget all that he hath done for thee. O all ye works of the Lord, bless the Lord, praise and glorify him for ever. O all ye angels of the Lord, bless the Lord, praise and glorify his holy name. Bless the Lord, all ye saints, and let the whole church of heaven and earth join in praising and giving him thanks for all his mercies and graces to me; and so, in some measure, supply for what is due from me. But as all this still falleth short of what I owe thee for thine infinite love, I offer to thee, O eternal Father, this same Son of thine, whom thou hast given me, and his thanksgiving, which is of infinite value; and this I am sure thou wilt accept. Look not then upon my insensibility and ingratitude, but upon the face of thy Christ, and with him, and through him, receive this offering of my poor self, which I desire to make thee.

N. B. Here also might be recited the *Canticle of the Three Children*, the *Te Deum*, and some of the *Psalms of Praise* which are found among the Devotions for Sundays.

An Oblation after Communion.

O FATHER of mercies, and God of all consolation, how hast thou loved us, to whom thou hast given thine only-begotten Son, once for our ransom, and daily for the food of our souls! What can I, a wretched creature, return to thee for this infinite charity? Verily nothing else but this same beloved Son of thine, whom thou hast given me, and surely thou couldst give nothing greater or more worthy of thyself. Him then

I offer to thee, O heavenly Father, with whom thou art always well pleased; him whom thou hast lovingly delivered up to death for me, and given me in this most holy sacrament, which we frequent for the everlasting memorial of his death. He is our high priest and victim; he is the propitiation for the sins of the whole world; he is our advocate and intercessor. Look down then upon him, and for his sake look down upon me, and upon us all. Remember all his sufferings, which he endured here in this mortal life; his bitter anguish, his agony and bloody sweat: all the injuries and affronts, all the blows and stripes, all the bruises and wounds that he received for us. Remember his death, which thou wast pleased should be the fountain of our life: and, for the sake of his sacred passion, have mercy on us. Receive, O holy Father, almighty and everlasting God, this holy and unspotted victim, which I here offer thee, in union with that love with which he offered himself to thee upon the altar of the cross, receive him for the praise and glory of thy name; in thanksgiving for all the benefits bestowed on me, and on all mankind; in satisfaction also for all my sins; for the benefit of thy whole church, and the refreshment and comfort of all thy faithful, living and dead; through the same Lord, Jesus Christ, thy Son.

And turning myself to thee, O my dear Lord and Saviour, who hast here given me thyself, I would gladly make some suitable return to thee for this infinite love; I would gladly make thee some offering in acknowledgment of this rich present which thou hast made me. But, alas! thou knowest my poverty, thou knowest I have nothing worthy of thine acceptance, nothing but what, upon a thousand titles, is already thine. But, O my God, such is thy goodness, thou wilt be content with the little that I can give thee, though it be thine own already; thou askest nothing but my heart, and this I here most willingly offer thee. Oh! be pleased to accept of it, and make it wholly thine for ever. I offer thee here my whole being, my body with its senses, and my soul with all its powers: that as thou hast at present honoured them both by thy presence, so they may both be thy temple for ever. Oh, sanctify and consecrate eternally to thyself this mansion, which thou hast this day chosen for thine abode. I give thee my memory, that it may be for ever recollected in thee; my understanding, that it may be always enlightened and directed by thy truth; and my will, that it may be ever conformable to thine, and ever burn with the love of thee. Oh, take me entirely into thy hands, with all that I have, and all that I am; and let nothing henceforward in life or death, ever separate me any more from thee. *Amen.*

Petitions after Communion.

O MOST merciful Saviour, behold I have presumed to receive thee this day into my house, relying on thine infinite goodness and mercy, and hoping, like Zacheus, to obtain thy benediction. But, alas! with how little preparation! with how little devotion! From my heart I beg pardon for my great unworthiness, and for my innumerable sins, which I detest for the love of thee, and I desire to detest them for ever!

Oh! wash them all away with thy precious blood; for thou art the Lamb of God, who takest away the sins of the world; and one drop of this blood, which thou hast shed for us, is more than enough to cancel the sins of ten thousand worlds.

Thou seest, O Searcher of hearts, all my maladies, and all the wounds of my soul! thou knowest how prone I am to evil, and how backward and sluggish to good. Thou seest this self-love, that tyrannizes over my soul, which is so deeply rooted in my corrupt nature, and branches out into so many vices; so much pride and vanity; so much passion and envy; so much covetousness and worldly solicitude; so much sensuality and concupiscence. Oh, who can heal all these my evils, but thou, the true physician of my soul, who givest me thy body and blood in this blessed sacrament, as a sovereign medicine for all my infirmities, and a sovereign balsam for all my wounds. Dispel the darkness of ignorance and error from my understanding, by thy heavenly light; drive away the corruption and malice of my will, by the fire of divine love and charity; restrain all the motions of concupiscence, and all the irregular sallies of passion, that they may no more prevail over me; strengthen my weakness with heavenly fortitude; destroy this hellish monster of self-love, with its many heads; or at least chain down this worst of all my enemies, that it may no longer usurp the empire of my soul, which belongeth to thee, and which thou hast taken possession of this day; cut off the heads of this beast, and particularly that which annoyeth me most, and which is my predominant passion; stand by me henceforward in all my temptations, that I may never more be overcome; remove from me all dangerous occasions, and grant me this one favour, that I may rather die a thousand deaths, than live to offend thee mortally.

O my Jesus, thou art infinitely rich, and all the treasures of divine grace are locked up in thee; these treasures thou bringest with thee; when thou dost visit us in this blessed sacrament, and thou takest an infinite pleasure in opening them to us, to enrich our poverty. This gives me the confidence now to present my petitions to thee, and to beg of thee those graces and virtues, which I very much stand in need of, as thou knowest. Oh! increase and strengthen my belief of thy heavenly truths, and grant that henceforward I may ever live by faith, and be guided by the maxims of thy gospel. Teach me to be poor in spirit, and take off my heart from the love of these transitory things, and fix it upon eternity: teach me, by thy divine example, and by thy most efficacious grace, to be meek and humble of heart, and in my patience to possess my soul. Grant that I may ever keep my body and soul chaste and pure from the corruption of lust; that I may ever bewail my past sins, and, by a daily mortification, restrain all irregular inclinations and passions for the future. Above all things, teach me to love thee, to be ever recollected in thee, and to walk always in thy presence: teach me to love my friends in thee, and my enemies for thee; grant me grace to persevere to the end in this love, and so to come one day to that happy place, where I may love and enjoy thee for ever.

Have mercy also on my parents, friends, and benefactors, and on all those for whom I am in any way bound to pray, that we may all love thee and faithfully serve thee. Have mercy on thy whole church, and on all the clergy, and religious men and women, that all may live up to their callings, and sanctify thy name. Give thy grace and blessing to all princes and magistrates, and to all Christian people; convert all unbelievers and sinners, and bring all strayed sheep back to thy fold: particularly have mercy on N. and N. &c.

O blessed Virgin, Mother of my God and Saviour, recommend all these my petitions to thy Son. O all ye angels and saints, citizens of heaven, join also your prayers with mine; you ever stand before the throne, and see him face to face, whom I here receive under veils; be ever mindful of me, and obtain from him, and through him, that with you I may bless him, and love him for ever. *Amen.*

INVOCATIONS OF S. IGNATIUS,

To be said after hearing Mass, or receiving Holy Communion, or at any other time.

ANIMA CHRISTI SANCTIFICA ME.

SOUL of my Saviour, sanctify my breast;
His blessed body be my saving guest.
Blood of my Jesus, bathe me in thy tide;
Wash me, ye waters streaming from his side.
O Cross, O Death of Jesus, soothe my fears!
Jesus! O hear my sighs, regard my tears;
O hide me in thy wounds; there may I stay,
And never, never more be torn away.
Save me, O save me from my deadly foe;
Call me at death from off my bed of woe,
And take me to thy arms to hymn thy praise,
Among thy Saints in heaven through endless days.

Indulgences: 300 days every time they are said. Also, 7 years and 7 quarantines to all who say them after Communion. Also, a plenary indulgence, after confession and communion, to all who say them at least once a day for a month.

A PRAYER

To which is annexed a Plenary Indulgence,

Applicable to the souls in purgatory, which all the faithful may obtain, who, after having confessed their sins with contrition, received the Holy Communion, and prayed for the intentions of the Sovereign Pontiff, shall devoutly recite it before an image or representation of Christ crucified.

LOOK down upon me, good and gentle Jesus, while before thy face I humbly kneel, and with burning soul pray and beseech thee to fix deep in my heart most lively sentiments of faith, hope, and charity, true contrition for my sins, and firm purpose of amendment, the while I contemplate with great love and tender pity thy five wounds, pondering over them within me whilst I call to mind the words which David thy prophet said of thee: "They pierced my hands and my feet; they numbered all my bones."

DEVOTIONS FOR THE SICK.

A Prayer proper to be daily repeated in time of Sickness.

LORD Jesus Christ, behold I receive this sickness, with which thou art pleased to visit me, as coming from thy fatherly hand. It is thy will it should be thus with me, and therefore I submit: thy will be done on earth as it is in heaven. May this sickness be to the honour of thy holy name, and for the good of my soul. For this end, I here offer myself with an entire submission to all thine appointments, to suffer whatever thou pleasest, as long as thou pleasest, and in what manner thou pleasest; for I am thy creature, O Lord, who have most ungratefully offended thee; and since my sins have a long time cried aloud to heaven for justice, why should I now complain if I feel thy hand upon me? No, my God, thou art just in all thy ways; I have truly deserved thy punishment, and therefore I have no reason to complain of thee, but only of my own wickedness.

But rebuke me not, O Lord, in thy fury, nor chastise me in thy wrath; but have regard to my weakness. Thou knowest how frail I am; that I am nothing but dust and ashes: deal not with me, therefore, according to my sins, neither punish me according to mine iniquities: but, according to the multitude of thy most tender mercies, have compassion on me. Oh! let thy justice be tempered with mercy, and let thy heavenly grace come in to my assistance, to support me under this my illness. Confirm my soul with strength from above, that I may bear with a true Christian patience, all the uneasiness, pains, disquiets, and difficulties of my sickness, and that I may cheerfully accept them as the just punishment of my offences. Preserve me from all temptations, and be thou my defence against all the assaults of the enemy, that in this illness I may in no way offend thee; and if this is to be my last, I beg of thee so to direct me by thy grace, that I may in no way neglect or be deprived of those helps which thou hast, in thy mercy, ordained for the good of my soul, to prepare it for its happy passage into eternity; that, being perfectly cleansed from all my sins, I may believe in thee, put my whole trust in thee, love thee above all things, and, through the merits of thy death and passion, be admitted into the company of the blessed, where I may praise thee for ever. Amen.

Shorts Acts of the most necessary virtues proper to be inculcated in the time of Sickness.

LORD, I accept this sickness from thy hands, and entirely resign myself to thy blessed will, whether it be for life or death. Not my will, but thine be done; thy will be done on earth, as it is in heaven.

Lord, I submit to all the pains and uneasiness of this my illness; my sins have deserved infinitely more. Thou art just, O Lord, and thy judgment is right.

Lord, I offer up to thee all that I now suffer, or may have yet to suffer, to be united to the sufferings of my Redeemer, and sanctified by his passion.

I adore thee, O my God and my All, as my first beginning and last end; and I desire to pay thee the best homage I am able, and to bow down all the powers of my soul to thee.

Lord, I desire to praise thee for ever, in sickness as well as in health; I desire to join my heart and voice with the whole church of heaven and earth, in blessing thee for ever.

I give thee thanks from the bottom of my heart, for all thy mercies and blessings bestowed upon me and thy whole church, through Jesus Christ thy Son; and above all, for thy having loved me from all eternity, and redeemed me with his precious blood. Oh! let not that blood be shed for me in vain.

Lord, I believe all those heavenly truths which thou hast revealed, and which thy holy Catholic church believes and teaches. Thou art the sovereign Truth, who neither canst deceive, nor be deceived: and thou hast promised the Spirit of Truth, to guide thy church into all truth. I believe in God the Father Almighty, &c. In this faith, I resolve, through thy grace, both to live and die. O Lord, strengthen and increase this my faith.

O my God, all my hopes are in thee: and through Jesus Christ, my Redeemer, and through his passion and death, I hope for mercy, grace, and salvation from thee. In thee, O Lord, have I put my trust; Oh, let me never be confounded!

O sweet Jesus, receive me into thine arms, in this day of my distress: hide me in thy wounds, bathe my soul in thy precious blood.

I love thee, O my God, with my whole heart and soul, above all things; at least, I desire so to love thee. Oh, come now and take full possession of my whole soul, and teach me to love thee for ever.

I desire to be dissolved, and to be with Christ.

Oh, when will thy kingdom come? O Lord, when wilt thou perfectly reign in all hearts? When shall sin be no more?

I desire to embrace every neighbour with perfect charity for the love of thee. I forgive, from my heart, all who have in any way offended or injured me, and ask pardon of all whom I have in any way offended.

Have mercy on me, O God, according to thy great mercy; and according to the multitude of thy tender mercies, blot out mine iniquity.

Oh, who will give water to my head, and a fountain of tears to mine eyes, that night and day I may weep for all my sins?

Oh, that I had never offended so good a God! Oh, that I had never sinned! Happy those souls that have always preserved their baptismal innocence!

Lord, be merciful to me a sinner: sweet Jesus, Son of the living God, have mercy on me.

I commend my soul to God my Creator, who made me out of nothing; to Jesus Christ, my Saviour, who redeemed me with his precious blood; to the Holy Ghost, who sanctified me in baptism. Into thy hands, O Lord, I commend my spirit.

I renounce from this moment, and for all eternity, the devil and all his works; and I abhor all his suggestions and temptations. Oh, suffer not, O Lord, this mortal enemy of my soul to have any power over me, either now or at my last hour. Oh, let thy holy angels defend me from all the powers of darkness.

O holy Mary, Mother of God, pray for us sinners now, and at the hour of our death. O all ye blessed angels and saints of God, pray for me, a poor sinner.

It may be proper also, in time of sickness, to read to the sick person leisurely, and as he is able to bear it, the passion of Christ, or some meditations on his passion; the Miserere, and other penitential psalms, devout acts of contrition, &c. but not too much at once; for that might fatigue him, and do him harm.

The Holy Viaticum.

THE Viaticum is the Holy Eucharist received with the intention of preparing the Sick for death. This blessed Sacrament is indeed the bread of life, which the pious Christian frequently receives, it is to be hoped, with great profit during health: but when the soul is about to pass from this to an immortal life, there arises a new and peculiar obligation of receiving it again. This obligation is founded on the abundant graces which this holy sacrament above all the rest is capable of imparting, and which are at that time so necessary. It is the safeguard that must preserve the soul on its journey to heaven, it is the pledge of immortal glory. *He that eats this bread shall live for ever,* St. John, vi. And so urgent is the obligation of receiving it at the approach of death, that the church dispenses in behalf of those who are dangerously sick, and allows them to communicate after having broken their fast. The sick person will therefore use his best endeavour to make a worthy preparation for this blessed Sacrament.

A Short Exercise in Preparation for Death, which may be used every Day.

MY heart is ready, O God, my heart is ready; not my will, but thine be done. O my Lord, I resign myself entirely to thee, to receive death at the time, and in the manner, it shall please thee to send it.

2. I most humbly ask pardon for all my sins committed against thy sovereign goodness, and repent of them all from the bottom of my heart.

3. I firmly believe whatsoever the holy Catholic Church believes and teaches; and by thy grace I will die in this belief.

4. I hope to possess eternal life by thy infinite mercy, and by the merits of my Saviour Jesus Christ.

5. O my God, I desire to love thee as my sovereign good above all things, and to despise this mis-

erable world: I desire to love my neighbour as myself, for the love of thee, and to forgive all injuries from my heart.

6. O my divine Jesus, how great is my desire to receive thy sacred body! Oh, come now into my soul, at least, by a spiritual communion! Oh, grant that I may worthily receive thee before my death! I desire to unite myself to all the worthy communions which shall be made in thy holy church, even to the end of the world.

7. Grant me the grace, O my divine Saviour, perfectly to efface all the sins I have committed by any of my senses, by applying daily to my soul thy blessed merits, and the holy unction of thy precious blood.

8. Holy Virgin, Mother of God, defend me from my enemies in my last hour, and present me to thy divine Son. Glorious St. Michael,

prince of the heavenly host, and thou my angel guardian, and you my blessed patrons, intercede for me, and assist me in this my last and dreadful passage.

9. O my God, I renounce all the temptations of the enemy, and in general whatsoever may displease thee. I adore and accept of thy divine appointments with regard to me, and entirely abandon myself to them as most just and equitable.

10. O Jesus, my divine Saviour, be thou a Jesus to me, and save me. O my God, hiding myself with an humble confidence in thy dear wounds, I give up my soul into thy divine hands. Oh, receive it into the bosom of thy mercy. Amen.

THE Sacrament of Extreme Unction.

Our Lord and Saviour Jesus Christ, in his tender solicitude for those whom he has redeemed by his precious blood, has been pleased to institute another Sacrament, to help us at that most important hour on which eternity depends, the hour of death. This sacrament is called Extreme Unction, or the last anointing.

Of this blessed Sacrament, Saint James, the apostle, thus speaks: *Is any man sick among you? Let him bring in the priest of the church, and let them pray over him, anointing him with oil in the name of the Lord. And the prayer of faith shall save the sick man, and the Lord shall raise him up, and if he be in sins, they shall be forgiven him.* v. 14, 15. These words show the great and salutary graces bestowed by this sacrament.

The priest in administering this sacrament anoints the five principal senses of the body: the eyes, the ears, the nostrils, the lips, the hands, and the feet, because these may have been employed during life in offending God. At each anointing he pronounces these words: May the Lord by this holy anointing, and by his own most tender mercy, pardon thee whatever sin thou hast committed by thy sight, hearing, &c.

The sick person should endeavour to prepare himself to receive this sacrament by acts of sincere contrition for all his sins, by great confidence in the tender mercies of his Redeemer, and by a perfect resignation of himself to the holy will of God.

A Prayer before Extreme Unction.

Thou hast mercifully provided remedies, O Lord, for all our necessities: grant me thy grace so to make use of them, that my soul may receive all those good effects, which thou hast appointed in their institution. Now I desire to be anointed, as thou hast commanded by thine apostle; grant, I beseech thee, that by this holy unction, and the prayers of the church, I may partake of that spirit, with which Christ suffered on the cross, for thy glory, and for the destruction of sin. Give me true patience to support all the pains and trouble of my distemper; give me an inward strength to resist all the temptations of the enemy; give me grace for the pardon of all my failings; give me that true light, by which I may be conducted through the shadow of death, to eternal happiness: and if my health be expedient for thy glory, let this be the means to restore it. Behold

I approach to this holy ordinance with a firm faith and confidence in thy goodness, that thou wilt not forsake me in this time of my distress, but that thou wilt stand by me with thy grace, and defend me from all evil, and now prepare my soul for a happy passage.

* My eyes have seen vanities, but now let them be shut to the world, and open to thee alone, my Jesus; and pardon me all the sins which I have committed by my seeing.

My ears have been open to detraction, profaneness, and unprofitable discourses: let me now give ear to thy word, to thy commandments, and thy calls, and pardon me, O Jesus, all the sins which I have committed by my hearing.

I have taken delight in the perfumes of this world, which are nothing but corruptions: now let my heart and prayers ascend like incense in thy sight,

---

* *While the Priest is administering the sacrament to the sick person, one of the assistants may, before each anointing, read one of the above short prayers, corresponding to the organ of sense that is next to be anointed, that it may be repeated by the sick person.*

and pardon me all the sins which I have committed by my smelling.

My tongue hath in many ways offended both in speaking and tasting, now let its whole business be to cry for mercy: pardon me, dear Jesus, all the sins which I have committed by words, or by any excess in eating or drinking.

My hands have offended in contributing to many follies, injurious to myself and my neighbour: now let them be lifted up to heaven, in testimony of a penitent heart: and pardon me, O Lord, all the sins which I have committed by the ill use of my hands.

My feet have gone astray in the paths of vanity and sin: now let me walk in the way of thy commandments: and forgive me, O Lord, all the sins which I have committed by my disordered steps.

By this holy anointing and the power of thy grace, O God, forgive me all my sins, and convert my heart wholly to thee, that I may cheerfully submit to death, in punishment of my offences, and so enter into thine eternal rest. Amen.

A Prayer after Extreme Unction.

O MY God, it is by thee that I have been created, redeemed, and sanctified: it is thou who hast preserved me from many dangers, both of soul and body; it is thou who hast nourished me with the adorable sacrament of thy body and blood, and granted me the grace to receive the rites of thy church, preferably to so many others, who are carried off by a sudden death, without being favoured with such succours and graces as thou hast bestowed upon me, a most ungrateful sinner. For these and all other blessings, I return thee innumerable thanks. Oh, that I had the heart and tongues of all men and angels, how willingly would I employ them all in praising, loving, and glorifying thee! To thee I resign my heart. Into thy hands, O Lord, I commend my spirit. Receive me, O dear Jesus, in thy mercy, into those loving arms which were extended on the cross for my redemption, and admit me into the embraces of thine infinite charity. I desire not to be freed from my pains, since thou knowest what is best for me. Suffer me never to murmur, but grant me patience to bear whatever thou wilt, and as long as thou pleasest. Should it be thy will to inflict greater punishments on my weak body and languishing soul, than those which I now suffer, my heart is ready, O Lord, to accept them and to suffer in whatever manner and measure may be most conformable to thy divine will.

This one grace I most humbly beg of thee, that I may die the death of the just, and be admitted, after the sufferings and tribulations of this transitory and sinful life, into the kingdom of thy glory, there to see and enjoy thee in the company of the blessed, for a never-ending eternity. Amen.

THE LAST BLESSING AND PLENARY INDULGENCE.

As the hour of death approaches, that awful hour on which so much depends, the pious Christian should fervently prepare to receive the Last Blessing and Plenary Indulgence granted to those who are near their end. For our Lord Jesus Christ promised to St. Peter, (Matt. xvi.) *the keys of the kingdom of heaven,* assuring him that, *whatsoever he should bind on earth, should be bound in heaven, and whatsoever he should loose on earth, should be loosed also in heaven.* By this power of binding and loosing, derived from St. Peter to his successors, and by them communicated to the pastors of souls, the latter are authorized to grant a Plenary Indulgence, together with a solemn Blessing to all such as are in or near their last agony. But then the dying Christian should remember well, that in order to receive the benefit of this Plenary Indulgence and Blessing, it is requisite that he concur on his part, by renouncing and detesting all his sins, both known and unknown, mortal and venial; by accepting with patience and resignation whatever he may have yet to suffer, and offering up his pains and death, in union with the sufferings and death of his Redeemer, in satisfaction for his sins.

During the time the Priest is conferring this solemn Blessing, the following prayer may be repeated.

O MY God, I once more renounce and detest all my sins. Have mercy on me, O God, according to thy great mercy. I cast myself into the arms of thy holy love, and I resign myself to thy blessed will. Receive me, I beseech thee, into the number of thy servants, that I may praise thee for ever. Father, into thy hands I commend my spirit. Lord Jesus, receive my soul. Amen.

HOW TO ASSIST THE DYING.

When the soul is about to leave the body, then all those who are around the sick man's bed should kneel down and pray earnestly for him. If the dying man be unable to speak, the name of Jesus should constantly be invoked, and such words as the following should be frequently repeated in his ear:

Into thy hands, O Lord, I commend my spirit.
O Lord Jesus Christ, receive my soul.
Holy Mary, pray for me.
Holy Mary, Mother of Grace, Mother of Mercy, do thou defend me from the enemy, and receive me at the hour of death.

All present may join together in saying the Litany of Jesus, page 350; or the Litany of the Blessed Virgin, page 184; or 5 Our Fathers and 5 Hail Marys for the dying person.

The Soul being departed, the following Responsory is to be said.

COME to his assistance, all ye saints of God: meet him, all ye angels of God: receive his soul and present it now before its Lord. May Jesus Christ receive thee, and the angels conduct thee to thy place of rest. May the angels of God receive his soul, and present it now before its Lord.

V. Eternal rest give to him, O Lord; and let perpetual light shine upon him.

R. May the angels of God present him now before his Lord,

V. Lord, have mercy on him.
R. Christ, have mercy on him.
V. Lord, have mercy on him.
Our Father, &c.
V. And lead us not into temptation.
R. But deliver us from evil. Amen.
V. Eternal rest give to him, O Lord.
R. And let perpetual light shine upon him.
V. From the gates of hell,
R. Deliver his soul, O Lord.
V. May he rest in peace. R. Amen.
V. O Lord, hear my prayer.
R. And let my cry come to thee.

Let us Pray.

TO thee, O Lord, we recommend the soul of thy servant N. that being dead to this world he may live to thee, and whatever sins he hath committed in this life through human frailty, do thou in thy most merciful goodness pardon: through our Lord Jesus Christ, &c.

Then for a conclusion may be added the following Prayer for those who are present.

GRANT, O God, that while we lament the departure of this thy servant, we may always remember that we are most certainly to follow him. Give us grace to prepare for that last hour by a good life, that we may not be surprised by a sudden and unprovided death, but be ever watching, that when thou shalt call we may with the bridegroom enter into eternal glory. Through Jesus Christ our Lord. Amen.

"It is therefore a holy and wholesome thought to pray for the dead, that they may be loosed from sins." 2 Machabees xii. 42.

"Have pity on me, have pity on me, at least you my friends; because the hand of the Lord hath touched me." Job xix. 21.

The Litany for the Dead.

LORD, have mercy on us.
Lord, have mercy on us.
Christ, have mercy on us.
Christ, have mercy on us.
Lord, have mercy on us.
Lord, have mercy on us.
Jesus, receive our prayers.
Lord Jesus, grant our petitions.

O God the Father, Creator of the world, *Have mercy on the souls of the faithful departed.*

O God the Son, Redeemer of mankind, *Deliver the souls of the faithful departed.*

O God the Holy Ghost, perfecter of the elect, *Accomplish the bliss of the souls of the faithful departed.*

O sacred Trinity, three persons and one God, *Give rest to the souls of the faithful departed.*

Blessed Virgin Mary, who by a special privilege of grace, wast triumphantly assumed into the kingdom of thy Son,

Blessed angels, who ordering aright the first act of your will, were immediately settled in an unchangeable state of felicity,

Blessed patriarchs, whose spirits were filled with joy, when the desired of all nations brought redemption to your long captivity,

Blessed prophets, who, having patiently awaited the coming of the Messias, were at length refreshed with the happy visit of his divine person,

O all you blessed saints, who, after the glorious resurrection of your Saviour, were by him translated from the bosom of Abraham to the clear vision of God,

Blessed apostles, who, at the last

Pray for the souls of the faithful departed.

and terrible day shall sit on the twelve thrones, judging the tribes of Israel,

Blessed disciples of our Lord, who, following his sacred steps in the narrow path of perfection, went straight on to the heavenly Jerusalem,

Blessed martyrs, who, passing through the Red Sea of your own blood, without journeying through a tedious wilderness, entered immediately into the Land of Promise,

Blessed confessors, who, despising the vanities here below, and placing your affections entirely on the joys above, are already arrived at the full possession of all your wishes,

Blessed virgins, who, watching continually with your lamps prepared, were ready at the first voice of the chaste spouse of heaven, to enter with him into the marriage chamber,

O all ye holy saints, who, not retaining at your death the least irregular adherence to any creature, were perfectly capable of an immediate union with your Creator,

Pray for the souls of the faithful departed.

Be merciful, O Lord, *and pardon their sins.*

Be merciful, O Lord, *and hear our prayers.*

From the shades of death, where they sit deprived of the blissful light of thy countenance,

From the evils to which their defective mortifications in this world have exposed them in the other,

From thine anger, which now too late they grieve to have provoked by their negligence and ingratitude,

From the bonds of sin, wherein they remain entangled by the disorder of their affections,

From the pains of purgatory, justly inflicted on them as the proper effects of their sins,

From that dreadful prison, whence there is no release till they have paid the last farthing,

From all their torments, incomparably greater than the sharpest pains of this life,

By the multitude of thy mercies, which have always shown compassion on the frailties of human nature,

By the infinite merits of thy death

Deliver them, O Lord.

upon the cross, where thou reconciledst the world to thy Father,

By thy victorious descent into hell, to break asunder the chains of death, and free such as were imprisoned,

By thy glorious resurrection from the grave, when thou openedst the kingdom of heaven to believers,

By thy triumphant ascension into heaven, when thou ledst captivity captive, and promisedst to prepare a place for thy servants,

By thy dreadful coming to judge the world, when the works of every one shall be tried by fire,

Deliver them, O Lord.

We sinners *beseech thee hear us,*

That it would please thee to hasten the day of visiting thy faithful detained in the receptacles of sorrow, and transport them to the city of eternal peace,

That it would please thee to shorten the time of expiation of their sins, and graciously admit them into thy holy sanctuary, where no unclean thing can enter,

That it would please thee, through the prayers and alms of thy church,

We beseech thee hear us.

and especially the inestimable sacrifice of thy holy altar, to receive them into the tabernacles of rest, and crown their longing hopes with everlasting fruition,

That the blessed vision of Jesus may comfort them, and the glorious light of his cross shine upon them,

That thy holy angels may bring them into the land of the living, and the glorious queen of saints present them before thy throne,

That the venerable patriarchs may meet them, and all the ancient prophets rejoice to see them,

That the sacred college of apostles may open to them the gates of bliss, and the victorious army of martyrs conduct them to thy palace,

That the blessed company of confessors may place them in seats of eternal glory, and the chaste train of virgins, with heavenly anthems, congratulate their reception,

That the whole triumphant church may celebrate the jubilee of their deliverance; and all the choirs of angels sing hymns of joy, for their new and never-ending felicity,

We beseech thee hear us.

That in the midst of all these triumphs, the souls that are delivered may themselves adore the glorious Author of their happiness, and in their white robes eternally sing Alleluia! salvation to our God, who sitteth upon the throne, and to the Lamb that redeemed us by his blood, and made us kings to reign with him for ever, *We beseech thee hear us.*

Son of God, *We beseech thee hear us.*

O Lamb of God, who wilt come with glory to judge the living and the dead, *Give rest to the souls of the faithful departed.*

O Lamb of God, at whose presence the earth shall be moved, and the heavens melt away, *Give rest to the souls of the faithful departed.*

O Lamb of God, in whose blessed book of life all their names are written, *Give eternal rest to the souls of the faithful departed.*

The Antiphon.

DELIVER us, O Lord, and all thy faithful, in that day of terror, when the sun and moon shall be darkened, and the stars fall down from heaven; in that day of calamity and amazement, when heaven itself shall shake, the pillars of the earth be moved, and the glorious majesty of Jesus come with innumerable angels to judge the world by fire.

V. Deliver us, O Lord, in that dreadful day.

R. And place us with the blessed at thy right hand for ever.

V. O Lord, hear my prayer.

R. And let my cry come to thee.

ALMIGHTY God, with whom do live the spirits of the perfect, and in whose holy custody are deposited the souls of all those that depart hence in an inferior degree of thy grace, who being by their imperfect charity rendered unworthy of thy presence, are detained in a state of grief, and suspended hopes: as we bless thee for the saints already admitted to thy glory, so we humbly offer our prayers for thy afflicted servants, who continually wait and sigh after the day of their deliverance: pardon their sins, supply their unpreparedness, and wipe away the tears from their eyes:

that they may see thee, and in thy glorious light eternally rejoice, through Jesus Christ, &c.

O ETERNAL God, who, besides the general precept of charity, hast commanded a particular respect to parents, kindred, and benefactors; grant, we beseech thee, that as they were the instruments by which thy providence bestowed on us our birth, education, and innumerable other blessings, so our prayers may be the means to obtain for them a speedy release from their excessive sufferings, and free admittance to thine infinite joys. Through Jesus, &c.

See Prayers for the Dead, &c. p. 332.

MOST wise and merciful Lord, who hast ordained this life as a passage to the future, confining our repentance to the time of our pilgrimage here, and reserving for hereafter the state of punishment and reward: vouchsafe us thy grace, who are yet alive, and still have opportunity of reconciliation with thee, so to watch over all our actions, and correct every least deviation from the true way to heaven, that we be neither surprised with our sins uncancelled, nor with our duties imperfect; but when our bodies go down into the grave, our souls may ascend to thee, and dwell for ever in the mansions of eternal felicity. Through Jesus Christ our Lord and only Saviour: Amen.

Prayers for the Dead.

Psalm cxxix. *De profundis.*

OUT of the depths I have cried to thee, O Lord; Lord, hear my voice.

Let thine ears be attentive to the voice of my supplication.

If thou, O Lord, wilt mark iniquities; Lord, who shall stand it?

For with thee there is merciful forgiveness: and by reason of thy law I have waited for thee, O Lord.

My soul hath relied on his word; my soul hath hoped in the Lord.

From the morning watch even until night, let Israel hope in the Lord.

Because with the Lord there is mercy, and with him plentiful redemption.

And he shall redeem Israel from all his iniquities.

Eternal rest give to them, O Lord: and let perpetual light shine upon them.

A Prayer for all the Faithful departed.

O GOD, the Creator and Redeemer of all the faithful, give to the souls of thy servants departed the remission of all their sins; that, through pious supplications, they may obtain the pardon which they have always desired: who livest and reignest world without end. Amen. May they rest in peace. Amen.

A Prayer upon the day of a Person's Decease or Burial.

O GOD, whose property is always to have mercy and to spare, we humbly beseech thee for the soul of thy servant N. which thou hast this day called out of the world, that thou wouldst not deliver it up into the hands of the enemy, nor forget it unto the end; but command it to be received by thy holy angels, and to be carried to

Paradise, its true country; that as in thee it had faith and hope, it may not suffer the pains of hell, but may take possession of everlasting joys; through our Lord Jesus Christ.

Another.

WE beseech thee, O Lord, admit the soul of thy servant N. which this day hath departed out of this world, into the fellowship of thy saints, and pour forth upon it the dew of thy eternal mercy: through our Lord Jesus Christ.

On the Anniversary-day.

O LORD, the God of mercy and pardon, grant to the soul of thy servant N. whose anniversary we commemorate, the seat of refreshment, the happiness of rest, and the brightness of light: through our Lord, &c.

A Prayer for one lately deceased.

ABSOLVE, we beseech thee, O Lord, the soul of thy servant N. that, being dead to the world, he may live to thee: and whatever he hath committed in this life through human frailty, do thou of thy most merciful goodness forgive: through our Lord, &c.

A Prayer for a Bishop or a Priest.

O GOD, who amongst thy apostolic priests hast raised up thy servant N. to the dignity of a bishop (or a priest) grant, we beseech thee, that he may also be admitted in heaven to their everlasting fellowship: through Jesus Christ our Lord.

For Father and Mother.

O GOD, who hast commanded us to honour our father and mother, have mercy on the souls of my father and mother; and grant that I may see them in the glory of eternity: through our Lord, &c.

For Brethren, Relations, and Benefactors.

O GOD, the giver of pardon, and lover of the salvation of mankind, we beseech thy clemency in behalf of our brethren, relations, and benefactors, who have departed this life; that the blessed Mary ever Virgin and all thy saints interceding for them, they may come to the fellowship of eternal happiness: through our Lord Jesus Christ.

For all that lie in the Church or Church-yard.

O GOD, by whose mercy the souls of the faithful find rest, grant to all thy servants here and elsewhere, that have slept in Christ, the full pardon of their sins; that being discharged from all guilt, they may rejoice with thee for all eternity: through the same Lord Jesus Christ.

For many deceased.

O GOD whose property is always to have mercy and to spare, be favourably propitious to the souls of thy servants, and grant them the remission of all their sins; that being delivered from the bonds of this mortal life, they may be admitted to life everlasting: through our Lord Jesus Christ, thy Son. &c.

Litany for a Happy Death.

[From the Raccolta.]

Indulgences: 100 days once a day. Plenary, with the usual conditions, and applicable to the dead, once a month, for those who have recited this Litany daily during the month.

O LORD Jesus, God of goodness, and Father of mercies, I draw nigh to thee with a contrite and humble heart: to thee I recommend the last hour of my life, and that judgment which awaits me afterwards. *Merciful Jesus, have mercy on me.*

When my feet, benumbed with death, shall admonish me that my course in this life is drawing to an end, *Merciful Jesus, have mercy on me.*

When my hands, cold and trembling, shall no longer be able to clasp the crucifix, and shall let it fall against my will on my bed of suffering, *Merciful Jesus, have mercy on me.*

When my eyes, dim with trouble at the approach of death, shall fix themselves on thee, my last and only support, *Merciful Jesus, have mercy on me.*

When my lips, cold and trembling, pronounce for the last time thy adorable name, *Merciful Jesus, have mercy on me.*

When my face, pale and livid, shall inspire the beholders with pity and dismay; when my hair, bathed in the sweat of death, and stiffening on my head, shall forebode my approaching end, *Merciful Jesus, have mercy on me.*

When my ears, soon to be for ever shut to the discourse of men, shall be open to that irrevocable decree which is to fix my doom for all eternity, *Merciful Jesus, have mercy on me.*

When my imagination, agitated by dreadful spectres, shall be sunk in an abyss of anguish; when my soul, affrighted with the sight of my iniquities and the terrors of thy judgments, shall have to fight against the angel of darkness, who will endeavour to conceal from my eyes thy mercies, and to plunge me into despair, *Merciful Jesus, have mercy on me.*

When my poor heart, oppressed

with suffering and exhausted by its continual struggles with the enemies of its salvation, shall feel the pangs of death, *Merciful Jesus, have mercy on me.*

When the last tear, the forerunner of my dissolution, shall drop from my eyes, receive it as a sacrifice of expiation for my sins; grant that I may expire the victim of penance; and in that dreadful moment, *Merciful Jesus, have mercy on me.*

When my friends and relations, encircling my bed, shall be moved with compassion for me, and invoke thy clemency in my behalf, *Merciful Jesus, have mercy on me.*

When I shall have lost the use of my senses, when the world shall have vanished from my sight, when my agonizing soul shall feel the sorrows of death, *Merciful Jesus, have mercy on me.*

When my last sighs shall force my soul to issue from my body, accept them as the children of a loving impatience to come to thee, *Merciful Jesus, have mercy on me.*

When my soul, trembling on my

lips, shall bid adieu to the world, and leave my body lifeless, pale, and cold; receive this separation as a homage which I willingly pay to thy divine majesty, and in that last moment of my mortal life, *Merciful Jesus, have mercy on me.*

When at length my soul, admitted to thy presence, shall first behold the splendour of thy majesty, reject me not, but receive me into thy bosom, where I may for ever sing thy praises; and in that moment when eternity shall begin to me, *Merciful Jesus, have mercy on me.*

Let us pray.

O God, who hast doomed all men to die, but hast concealed from all the hour of their death; grant that I may pass my days in the practice of holiness and justice, and that I may be made worthy to quit this world in the peace of a good conscience, and in the embrace of thy love. Through Christ our Lord. Amen.

MASS FOR THE DEAD.

FOR THE DAY OF DECEASE OR BURIAL.

INTROIT.

REQUIEM æternam dona eis, Domine; et lux perpetua luceat eis. *Ps.* Te decet hymnus, Deus, in Sion: et tibi reddetur votum in Jerusalem. Exaudi orationem meam: ad te omnis caro veniet. Requiem, &c. *to Ps.*

GRANT them eternal rest, O Lord; and let perpetual light shine on them. *Ps.* A hymn becometh thee, O God, in Sion: and a vow shall be paid to thee in Jerusalem. O hear my prayer: all flesh shall come to thee. Grant them, &c. *to Ps.*

COLL. *Deus, cui.* O God, whose property it is always to have mercy and to spare, we humbly present our prayers to thee in behalf of the soul of thy servant N. which thou hast this day called out of the world: beseeching thee not to deliver it into the hands of the enemy, nor to forget it for ever: but command it to be received by the holy angels, and to be carried into paradise: that as it believed and hoped in thee, it may be delivered from the pains of hell, and inherit everlasting life. Through.

EPISTLE. 1 *Thess.* iv. 12, 17. *Brethren:* We will not have you ignorant concerning them that are asleep, that you be not sorrowful, even as others who have no hope. For if we believe that Jesus died and rose again, even so them who have slept through Jesus, will God bring with him. For this we say unto you in the word of the Lord, that we who are alive, who remain unto the coming of the Lord, shall not prevent them who have slept. For the Lord himself shall come down from heaven with commandment, and with the voice of an archangel, and with the trumpet of God: and the dead who are in Christ shall rise first. Then we who are alive, who are left, shall be taken up together with them in the clouds to meet Christ, into the air, and so shall we be always with the Lord. Wherefore comfort ye one another with these words.

GRAD. Grant them eternal rest, O Lord, and let perpetual light shine on them. V. The just shall be in everlasting remembrance: he shall not fear the evil hearing.

TRACT. *Absolve.* Release, O Lord, the souls of all the faithful departed from the bonds of their sins. V. And by the assistance of thy grace may they escape the sentence of condemnation. V. And enjoy the bliss of eternal light.

THE SEQUENCE OR PROSE.

DIES IRÆ.

DIES iræ, dies illa	THE day of wrath, that dreadful day
Solvet sæculum in favilla,	Shall the whole world in ashes lay,
Teste David cum Sybilla.	As David and Sybilla say.
Quantus tremor est futurus,	What horror will invade the mind,
Quando Judex est venturus,	When the strict Judge, who would be kind,
Cuncta stricte discussurus.	Shall have few venial faults to find?

Tuba mirum spargens sonum	The last loud trumpet's wond'rous sound
Per sepulchra regionum,	Must thro' the rending tombs rebound,
Coget omnes ante thronum.	And wake the nations under ground.
Mors stupebit, et natura,	Nature and death shall with surprise
Cum resurget creatura.	Behold the pale offender rise,
Judicanti responsura.	And view the Judge with conscious eyes.
Liber scriptus proferetur	Then shall with universal dread
In quo totum continetur,	The sacred mystic book be read,
Unde mundus judicetur.	To try the living and the dead.
Judex ergo cum sedebit,	The Judge ascends his awful throne,
Quidquid latet apparebit:	He makes each secret sin be known,
Nil inultum remanebit.	And all with shame confess their own.
Quid sum, miser, tunc dicturus,	O then! what int'rest shall I make,
Quem patronum rogaturus,	To save my last important stake,
Cum vix justus sit securus?	When the most just have cause to quake!

Rex tremendæ majestatis!
Qui salvandos salvas gratis,
Salva me fons pietatis.

Thou mighty formidable King!
Thou mercy's unexhausted spring!
Some comfortable pity bring.

Recordare Jesu pie,
Quod cum causa tuæ viæ,
Ne me perdas illa die.

Forget not what my ransom cost,
Nor let my dear-bought soul be lost,
In storms of guilty terror tost.

Quærens me, sedisti lassus:
Redemisti, crucem passus:
Tantus labor non sit cassus.

Thou, who for me didst feel such pain,
Whose precious blood the cross did stain:
Let not those agonies be vain.

Juste Judex ultionis,
Donum fac remissionis,
Ante diem rationis.

Thou, whom avenging pow'rs obey,
Cancel my debt (too great to pay)
Before the said accounting day.

Ingemisco tanquam reus,
Culpa rubet vultus meus;
Supplicanti parce, Deus.

Surrounded with amazing fears;
Whose load my soul with anguish bears;
I sigh, I weep: accept my tears.

Qui Mariam absolvisti,	Thou, who wast mov'd with Mary's grief,
Et latronem exaudisti,	And by absolving of the thief,
Mihi quoque spem dedisti.	Hast given me hope, now give relief.
Preces meæ non sunt dignæ :	Reject not my unworthy prayer,
Sed tu bonus fac benigne,	Preserve me from the dangerous snare,
Ne perenni cremer igne.	Which death and gaping hell prepare.
Inter oves locum præsta,	Give my exalted soul a place
Et ab hædis me sequestra,	Among the chosen right-hand race,
Statuens in parte dextra.	The sons of God, and heirs of grace.
Confutatis maledictis,	From that insatiate abyss,
Flammis acribus addictis,	Where flames devour and serpents hiss,
Voca me cum benedictis.	Promote me to thy seat of bliss.
Oro supplex et acclinis,	Prostrate, my contrite heart I rend,
Cor contritum quasi cinis,	My God, my Father, and my friend :
Gere curam mei finis.	Do not forsake me in my end.

Lacrymosa dies illa!	Well may they curse their second birth,
Qua resurget ex favilla	
Judicandus homo reus.	Who rise to a surviving death.
Huic ergo parce Deus:	Thou great Creator of mankind,
Pie Jesu Domine, dona eis requiem. Amen.	Let guilty man compassion find. Amen.

GOSPEL. *John* xi. 21, 28. *At that time:* Martha said to Jesus: Lord, if thou hadst been here, my brother had not died. But now also I know that whatsoever thou wilt ask of God, God will give it thee. Jesus saith to her: Thy brother shall rise again. Martha saith to him: I know that he shall rise again in the resurrection at the last day. Jesus said to her: I am the resurrection and the life; he that believeth in me, although he be dead, shall live. And every one that liveth, and believeth in me, shall not die for ever. Believest thou this? She saith to him: Yea, Lord, I have believed that thou art Christ the Son of the living God, who art come into this world.

OFFERT. Lord Jesus Christ, King

of glory, deliver the souls of all the faithful departed from the flames of hell, and from the deep pit. Deliver them from the lion's mouth, lest hell swallow them, lest they fall into darkness: and let the standard bearer, St. Michael, bring them into the holy light, which thou promisedst of old to Abraham and his posterity. V. We offer thee, O Lord, a sacrifice of praise and prayers: accept them in behalf of the souls we commemorate this day: and let them pass from death to life, which thou promisedst of old to Abraham and his posterity.

SECRET. Have mercy, O Lord, we beseech thee, on the soul of thy servant N., for which we offer this victim of praise, humbly beseeching thy majesty, that by this propitiatory sacrifice he (*or* she) may arrive at eternal rest. Through.

COMM. Let eternal light shine on them, O Lord, with thy saints for ever: for thou art merciful. V. Grant them, O Lord, eternal rest: and let perpetual light shine on them, with thy saints for ever: for thou art merciful.

P. Comm. *Præsta.* Grant, we beseech thee, O Almighty God, that the soul of thy servant, which this day hath departed this life, being purified and freed from sin by this sacrifice, may obtain both forgiveness and eternal rest. Through.

On the 3rd, 7th, or 30th day after Decease, the whole of the foregoing Mass is said, except

Coll. *Quæsumus.* Admit, we beseech thee, O Lord, the soul of thy servant N., (the third, seventh, *or* thirtieth day) of whose decease we commemorate, in the fellowship of thy saints, and refresh it with the perpetual dew of thy mercy. Through.

Secret. Mercifully look down, O Lord, we beseech thee, on the offerings we make for the soul of thy servant N., that being purified by these heavenly mysteries, it may find rest in thy mercy. Through.

P. Comm. *Suscipe.* Receive, O Lord, our prayers in behalf of the soul of thy servant N., that if any stains of the corruption of this world still stick to it, they may be washed away by thy forgiving mercy. Through.

Litany of the Most Holy Name of Jesus.

An Indulgence of Three Hundred Days was granted by Rescript, dated April 28, 1864, to the Faithful in England for the devout recitation of the Litany of the Most Holy Name, by our Most Holy Father Pope Pius IX., who at the same time prohibited any form but that of which the following is a translation, authorised by the Bishops:—

LORD have mercy on us.
Lord have mercy on us.
Christ have mercy on us.
Christ have mercy on us.
Lord have mercy on us.
Lord have mercy on us.
Jesus hear us.
Jesus graciously hear us.
God the Father of heaven,
God the Son, Redeemer of the world,
God the Holy Ghost,
Holy Trinity, one God,
Jesus, Son of the living God,
Jesus, splendour of the Father,
Jesus, brightness of eternal light,
Jesus, King of Glory,
Jesus, Sun of Justice,

Have mercy on us.

LITANY OF THE MOST HOLY NAME OF JESUS.

Jesus, Son of the Virgin Mary,
Jesus, most amiable,
Jesus, most admirable,
Jesus, mighty God,
Jesus, Father of the world to come,
Jesus, Angel of great counsel,
Jesus, most powerful
Jesus, most patient,
Jesus, most obedient,
Jesus, meek and humble of heart,
Jesus, lover of chastity,
Jesus, lover of us,
Jesus, God of peace,
Jesus, Author of life,
Jesus, example of virtues,
Jesus, zealous lover of souls,
Jesus, our God,
Jesus, our refuge,
Jesus, Father of the poor,
Jesus, treasure of the faithful,
Jesus, Good Shepherd,
Jesus, true light,
Jesus, eternal wisdom,
Jesus, infinite goodness,
Jesus, our way and our life,
Jesus, joy of Angels,
Jesus, King of Patriarchs,
Jesus, Master of Apostles.

Have mercy on us.

352 LITANY OF THE MOST HOLY NAME OF JESUS.

Jesus, Teacher of Evangelists,
Jesus, strength of Martyrs,
Jesus, light of Confessors,
Jesus, purity of Virgins,
Jesus, Crown of all Saints,

Have mercy on us.

Be merciful unto us, *Spare us, O Jesus.*
Be merciful unto us, *Graciously hear us, O Jesus.*

From all evil,
From all sin,
From thy wrath,
From the snares of the devil,
From the spirit of uncleanness,
From everlasting death,
From the neglect of Thy Inspirations,
Through the mystery of Thy holy Incarnation,
Through Thy Nativity,
Through Thine infancy,
Through Thy most divine life,
Through Thy labours,
Through Thine agony and passion,
Through Thy Cross and dereliction,
Through thy faintness and weariness,
Through Thy death and burial,
Through Thy resurrection,

Jesus, deliver us.

Through Thine ascension,
Through Thy joys,
Through Thy glory,
} *Jesus, deliver us.*

Lamb of God, who takest away the sins of the world,

Spare us, O Jesus.

Lamb of God, who takest away the sins of the world,

Graciously hear us, O Jesus.

Lamb of God, who takest away the sins of the world,

Have mercy on us, O Jesus.

Jesus, hear us.

Jesus, graciously hear us.

Let us pray.

O LORD Jesus Christ, who hast said: Ask, and ye shall receive; seek, and ye shall find; knock, and it shall be opened unto you; give, we beseech Thee, to us who ask, the grace of Thy most divine love, that with all our heart, words and works, we may love Thee, and never cease to praise Thee.

MAKE us, O Lord, to have a perpetual fear and love of Thy holy

Name, for Thou never failest to govern those whom Thou dost solidly establish in Thy love. Through Jesus Christ our Lord. Amen.

ST. BERNARD'S HYMN.

JESUS! the only thought of Thee
  With sweetness fills my breast:
But sweeter far it is to see,
  And on Thy beauty feast.

No sound, no harmony so gay,
  Can art or music frame;
No thoughts can reach, no words can say,
  The sweets of Thy blest Name.

Jesus, our hope when we repent,
  Sweet source of all our grace;
Sole comfort in our banishment,
  Oh! what when face to face?

Jesus! that Name inspires my mind
  With springs of life and light;
More than I ask in Thee I find,
  And languish with delight.

No art or eloquence of man
  Can tell the joys of love;
Only the Saints can understand
  What they in Jesus prove.

Thee, then, I'll seek, retired apart,
  From world and business free;
When these shall knock, I'll shut my heart,
  And keep it all for Thee.

PART II.

Before the morning light I'll come,
   With Magdalen, to find,
In sighs and tears, my Jesu's tomb,
   And there refresh my mind.

My tears upon His grave shall flow,
   My sighs the garden fill;
Then at His feet myself I'll throw,
   And there I'll seek His will.

Jesus! in Thy bless'd steps I'll tread,
   And walk in all Thy ways;
I'll never cease to weep and plead
   Till I'm restored to grace.

O King of Love! Thy blessed fire
   Does such sweet flames excite,
That first it raises the desire,
   Then fills it with delight.

Thy lovely presence shines so clear
   Through every sense and way,
That souls which once have seen Thee near,
   See all things else decay.

Come, then, dear Lord, possess my heart,
   Chase thence the shades of night;
Come, pierce it with Thy flaming dart,
   And ever shining light.

Then I'll for ever Jesus sing,
   And with the saints rejoice;
And both my heart and tongue shall bring
Their tribute to my dearest King,
   In never-ending joys.   Amen.

FAITH OF OUR FATHERS.

FAITH of our fathers! living still,
  In spite of dungeon, fire and sword;
Oh, how our hearts beat high with joy
  Whene'er we hear that glorious word!
    Faith of our fathers! holy Faith!
    We will be true to thee till death.

Our fathers chained in prisons dark,
  Were still in heart and conscience free
How sweet would be their children's fate,
  If they like them could die for thee!
    Faith of our fathers! holy Faith!
    We will be true to thee till death.

Faith of our fathers! Mary's prayers
  Shall win our country back to thee,
And through the truth that comes from God,
  Oh, then indeed shall we be free.
    Faith of our fathers! holy Faith!
    We will be true to thee till death.

Faith of our fathers! we will love
  Both friend and foe in all our strife,
And preach thee too, as love knows how,
  By kindly words and virtuous life.
    Faith of our fathers! holy Faith!
    We will be true to thee till death.

Faith of our fathers! guile and force
  To do thee bitter wrong unite;
But all our saints shall pray for us,
  And bring us back thy blessed light.
    Faith of our fathers! holy Faith!
    We will be true to thee till death.

The Jesus Psalter.

There is no other name under heaven given to men whereby we must be saved. *Acts,* iv. 12.

This Psalter consists of fifteen petitions, and the glorious Name of Jesus *being repeated ten times before each of them, the repetition is made thrice fifty times. It may be said either all at once, or at thrice, according to a person's devotion and leisure, as this sacred* Name *is not to be repeated hastily over, but with great reverence and devotion.*

PART I. *You must begin by a devout kneeling, or bowing, at the adorable Name of* Jesus, *saying,*

IN the Name of Jesus let every knee bow, of things in heaven, of things on earth, and of things under the earth; and let every tongue confess, that our Lord Jesus Christ is in the glory of God the Father. *Phil.* ii. 10.

The First Petition.

Jesus, Jesus, Jesus,
Jesus, Jesus, Jesus, } Have mercy on me.
Jesus, Jesus, Jesus,

Jesus, have mercy on me, O God of compassion, and forgive the many and great offences which I have committed in thy sight.

Many have been the follies of my life, and great are the miseries which I have deserved for my ingratitude.

Have mercy on me, dear Jesus, for I am weak; O Lord, heal me, who am unable to help myself.

Deliver me from setting my heart upon any of thy creatures, which may divert my eyes from a continual looking up to thee.

Grant me grace henceforth, for the love of thee, to hate sin; and out of a just esteem of thee, to despise all worldly vanities.

Have mercy on all sinners, Jesus, I beseech thee; turn their vices into virtues, and making them true observers of thy law, and sincere lovers of thee, bring them to bliss in everlasting glory.

Have mercy also on the souls in purgatory, for thy bitter passion, I beseech thee, and for thy glorious Name Jesus.

O blessed Trinity, one eternal God,

have mercy on me. Our Father. Hail Mary, &c.

The Second Petition.

Jesus, Jesus, Jesus, ⎫
Jesus, Jesus, Jesus, ⎬ help me.
Jesus, Jesus, Jesus, ⎭

JESUS, help me to overcome all temptations to sin, and the malice of my ghostly enemy.

Help me to spend my time in virtuous actions, and in such labours as are acceptable to thee.

To resist and repel the motions of my flesh to sloth, gluttony, and impurity.

To render my heart enamoured of virtue, and inflamed with desires of thy glorious presence.

Help me to deserve and keep a good name, by a peaceful and pious living, to thy honour, O Jesus, to my own comfort, and the benefit of others.

Have mercy on all sinners, &c., *as before.* Our Father. Hail Mary.

The Third Petition.

Jesus, Jesus, Jesus,
Jesus, Jesus, Jesus, } strengthen me
Jesus, Jesus, Jesus,

Jesus, strengthen me in soul and body, to please thee in doing such works of virtue as may bring me to thine everlasting joy and felicity.

Grant me a firm purpose, most merciful Saviour, to amend my life, and to recompense for the years past.

Those years, which I have mispent to thy displeasure in vain or wicked thoughts, words, deeds, and evil customs.

Make my heart obedient to thy will, and ready for thy love, to perform all the works of mercy.

Grant me the gifts of the Holy Ghost, which, by a virtuous life, and devout frequenting of thy most holy sacraments, may at length bring me to thy heavenly kingdom. Have mercy, &c. Our Father. Hail Mary.

The Fourth Petition.

Jesus, Jesus, Jesus,
Jesus, Jesus, Jesus, } comfort me.
Jesus, Jesus, Jesus,

JESUS, comfort me, and give me grace to place my chief, my only joy, and felicity in thee.

Send me heavenly meditations, spiritual sweetness, and fervent desires of thy glory; ravish my soul with the contemplation of heaven, where I shall everlastingly dwell with thee.

Bring often to my remembrance thine unspeakable goodness, thy gifts, and the great kindness which thou hast shown me.

And when thou bringest to my mind the sad remembrance of my sins, whereby I have so unkindly offended thee,

Comfort me with the assurance of obtaining thy grace by the spirit of perfect repentance, which may purge away my guilt, and prepare me for thy kingdom.

Have mercy, &c. Our Father. Hail Mary.

The Fifth Petition.

Jesus, Jesus, Jesus,
Jesus, Jesus, Jesus, } make me constant.
Jesus, Jesus, Jesus,

Jesus, make me constant in faith, hope, and charity, give me perseverance in all virtues, and a resolution never to offend thee.

Let the memory of thy passion, and of those bitter pains which thou sufferedst for me, strengthen my patience, and recreate me in all tribulation and adversity.

Let me always hold fast the doctrines of thy Catholic church, and render me a diligent frequenter of all holy duties.

Let no false delight of this deceitful world blind me, no fleshly temptation, or fraud of the devil, shake my heart.

My heart, which hath for ever set up its rest in thee, and resolved to undervalue all for thine eternal reward.

Have mercy on all sinners, Jesus, I beseech thee; turn their vices into virtues, and making them true observers of thy law, and sincere lovers of thee, bring them to bliss in everlasting glory.

Have mercy also on the souls in purgatory, for thy bitter passion, I beseech thee, and for thy glorious name Jesus.

O blessed Trinity, one eternal God, have mercy on me.

Our Lord Jesus Christ *humbled himself, becoming obedient unto death, even to the death of the cross.* Phil. ii. 8.

Hear these my petitions, O my most merciful Saviour, and grant me grace so frequently to repeat and consider them, that they may prove easy steps, whereby my soul may ascend to the knowledge, love, and performance of my duty to thee, and my neighbour, through the whole course of my life. Amen. Our Father. Hail Mary. I believe in God.

PART II. *Begin as before, saying,*

In the name of Jesus let every knee, &c.

The Sixth Petition.

Jesus, Jesus, Jesus, ⎫
Jesus, Jesus, Jesus, ⎬ enlighten me with spiritual wisdom.
Jesus, Jesus, Jesus, ⎭

JESUS, enlighten me with spiritual wisdom to know thy goodness, and all those things which are most acceptable to thee.

Grant me a clear apprehension of my only good, and discretion to order my life according to it.

Grant that I may wisely proceed from virtue to virtue, till at length I arrive at the clear vision of thy glorious Majesty.

Permit me not, dear Lord, to return to those sins for which I have been sorry, and of which I have purged myself by repentance and confession.

Grant me grace to benefit the souls of others by my good example, and to reduce those by good counsel, who misbehave towards me.

Have mercy, &c., *as at first.* Our Father. Hail Mary.

The Seventh Petition.

Jesus, Jesus, Jesus,
Jesus, Jesus, Jesus, } grant me grace to fear thee.
Jesus, Jesus, Jesus,

JESUS, grant me grace inwardly to fear thee, and to avoid all occasions of offending thee.

Let thy threats of the torments which

are to fall on sinners, the fear of losing thy love and thy heavenly inheritance, always keep me in awe.

Let me not dare to remain in sin, but soon return to repentance, lest, through thine anger, the dreadful sentence of endless death and damnation fall upon me.

Let the powerful intercession of thy blessed mother, and all thy saints, but above all, thy own merits and mercy, O my Saviour, be ever between thine avenging justice and my poor soul.

Enable me, O my God, to work out my salvation with fear and trembling; and let the apprehension of thy secret judgments render me a more humble and diligent suitor to the throne of thy grace.

Have mercy, &c. Our Father. Hail Mary.

The Eighth Petition.

Jesus, Jesus, Jesus,
Jesus, Jesus, Jesus, } grant me grace to love thee.
Jesus, Jesus, Jesus,

JESUS, grant me grace truly to love thee for thine infinite goodness, and those excessive bounties which I have received, and hope for ever to receive from thee.

Let the remembrance of thy kindness and patience conquer the malice and wretched inclinations of my perverse nature.

Let the consideration of my many deliverances, thy frequent calls, and continual assistance in the ways of life, make me ashamed of my ingratitude.

And what dost thou require of me for all thy mercies, or by them, but to love thee? And why dost thou require it, but because thou art my only good?

O my dear Lord, my whole life shall be nothing but a desire of thee; and because I indeed love thee, I will most diligently keep thy commandments.

Have mercy, &c. Our Father. Hail Mary.

The Ninth Petition.

Jesus, Jesus, Jesus,
Jesus, Jesus, Jesus, } grant me grace to remember
Jesus, Jesus, Jesus, my death.

JESUS, grant me grace always to remember my death and the great account which I am then to give, that so, my soul, being always well disposed, may depart out of this world in thy grace.

Then by the holy intercession of thy blessed mother, and the assistance of the glorious St. Michael, deliver me from the enemy of my soul; and thou, my good angel, I beseech thee to help me at that most important hour.

Then, dear Jesus, remember thy mercy, and turn not thy most amiable face away from me because of my offences.

Secure me against the terrors of that day, by causing me now to die daily to all earthly things, and so to have my conversation continually in heaven.

Let the remembrance of my death teach me how to esteem my life; and the memory of thy resurrection encourage me to descend cheerfully into the grave.

Have mercy, &c. Our Father. Hail Mary.

The Tenth Petition.

Jesus, Jesus, Jesus,
Jesus, Jesus, Jesus, } send me here my purgatory.
Jesus, Jesus, Jesus,

Jesus, send me here my purgatory, and so prevent the torments of that cleansing fire, which attends those souls in the next world, that have not been sufficiently purged in this.

Vouchsafe to grant me those merciful crosses and afflictions which thou seest necessary for the taking off my affections from all things here below.

Since no one can see thee that loveth anything which is not for thy sake, suffer not my heart to find any rest here, but in sighing after thee.

Too bitter, alas! will be the anguish of a soul that is separated from thee, that desireth, but cannot come to thee, being clogged with the heavy chains of sin.

Here, then, O my Saviour, keep me continually mortified to this world; that being purged thoroughly with the fire of thy love, I may immediately pass hence into thine everlasting possession.

Have mercy, &c. *as at the end of the Fifth Petition.* Our Father. Hail Mary. I believe in God.

PART III. *Begin as before, saying,*
In the name of Jesus let every knee, &c.

The Eleventh Petition.

Jesus, Jesus, Jesus, ⎫ grant me grace
Jesus, Jesus, Jesus, ⎬ to avoid bad
Jesus, Jesus, Jesus, ⎭ company.

JESUS, grant me grace to avoid bad company; or if I chance to come among such, I beseech thee, by the merits of thine incorrupt conversation among sinners, preserve me from being overcome by any temptations to mortal sin.

Cause me, O blessed Lord, to remember always with dread, that thou art present and hearest, who wilt take an account of all our words and actions, and wilt judge us according to them.

How dare I then converse with slanderers, liars, drunkards, or swearers; or with such whose discourse is either quarrelsome, dissolute, or vain?

Repress in me, dear Jesus, all inordinate affections to carnal pleasure, and to the delight of taste; grant me grace to avoid such company as would blow the fire of those unruly appetites.

Thy power defend, thy wisdom direct, thy fatherly pity chastise me, and make me live so here among men, that I may be fit for the conversation of angels hereafter.

Have mercy, &c. *as at first.* Our Father. Hail Mary.

The Twelfth Petition.

Jesus, Jesus, Jesus, } grant me grace
Jesus, Jesus, Jesus, } to call on thee
Jesus, Jesus, Jesus, } for help.

JESUS, grant me grace in all my necessities to call on thee for help, faithfully remembering thy death and resurrection for me.

Wilt thou be deaf to my cries, that wouldst lay down thy life for my ransom? or canst thou not save me, that couldst take it up again for my crown?

Whom have I in heaven but thee, O my Jesus, whose blessed mouth hath pronounced, *Call upon me in the day of trouble, and I will deliver thee?*

Thou art my sure rock of defence against all sorts of enemies; thou art my ready grace, able to strengthen me to every good work.

Therefore, in all my sufferings, weaknesses, and temptations, I will confidently call on thee; hear me, O my Jesus, and when thou hearest have mercy.

Have mercy on all sinners, &c. *as before.* Our Father. Hail Mary.

The Thirteenth Petition.

Jesus, Jesus, Jesus, } make me persevere in virtue.
Jesus, Jesus, Jesus,
Jesus, Jesus, Jesus,

JESUS, make me persevere in virtue and a good life, and never give over thy service, till thou bringest me to my reward in thy kingdom.

In all pious customs and holy duties, in my honest and necessary employments, continue and strengthen, O Lord, my soul and body.

Is my life anything but a pilgrimage on earth towards the new Jerusalem, to which, he that sitteth down, or turneth out of the way, can never arrive?

O Jesus, make me always consider thy blessed example: through how much pain, and how little pleasure, thou didst press on to a bitter death, that being the way to a glorious resurrection.

Make me, O my Redeemer, seriously weigh those severe words of thine, *he only that persevereth to the end shall be saved.*

Have mercy on all sinners, &c. *as before.* Our Father. Hail Mary.

The Fourteenth Petition.

Jesus, Jesus, Jesus, ⎫
Jesus, Jesus, Jesus, ⎬ grant me grace to fix my mind on thee.
Jesus, Jesus, Jesus, ⎭

JESUS, grant me grace to fix my mind on thee, especially in time of prayer, when I directly converse with thee.

Stop the motions of my wandering head, and the desires of my unstable heart; suppress the power of my spiritual enemies, who endeavour at that time to draw my mind from heavenly thoughts, to many vain imaginations.

So shall I, with joy and gratitude, look on thee as my deliverer from all the evils I have escaped; and as my benefactor for all the good I have ever received, or can hope for

I shall see that thou art my only good, and that all other things are but means ordained by thee, to make me fix my mind on thee, to make me love thee more and more, and, by loving thee, to be eternally happy.

O beloved of my soul, take up all my thoughts here, that mine eyes, abstaining from all vain and hurtful sights, may become worthy to behold thee face to face in thy glory for ever.

Have mercy, &c. Our Father. Hail Mary.

The Fifteenth Petition.

Jesus, Jesus, Jesus,
Jesus, Jesus, Jesus,
Jesus, Jesus, Jesus,
} give me grace to order my life towards my eternal welfare.

JESUS, give me grace to order my life towards my eternal welfare, heartily intending, and wisely designing, all the operations of my body and soul to obtain the reward of thine infinite bliss, and eternal felicity.

For what else is this world, but a school to breed up souls, and fit them for the other; and how are they fitted, but by an eager desire of enjoying God, their only end?

Break my froward spirit, O Jesus; make it humble and obedient: grant me grace to depart hence with contempt of this world and a heart filled with joy at my going to thee.

Let the memory of thy passion make me cheerfully undergo all temptations or sufferings here for thy love, whilst my soul breatheth after that blissful life and immortal glory, which thou hast prepared in heaven for thy servants.

O Jesus, let me frequently and attentively consider, that whatever I gain, if I lose thee, all is lost; and whatever I lose, if I gain thee, all is gained.

Have mercy, &c. *as in the Fifth Petition.* Our Father. Hail Mary. I believe.

STABAT MATER.

1 STABAT Mater dolorosa,
 Juxta crucem lacrymosa,
  Dum pendebat Filius.
 Cujus animam gementem,
 Contristatam et dolentem,
  Pertransivit gladius.

AT the cross her station keeping,
Stood the mournful Mother weeping,
 Close to Jesus to the last;
Through her heart, his sorrow sharing,
All his bitter anguish bearing,
 Now at length the sword had passed.

2 O quam tristis et afflicta,
Fuit illa benedicta
Mater Unigeniti!
Quæ mœrebat, et dolebat,
Pia Mater dum videbat,
Nati pœnas incliti.

O, how sad and sore distressed
Was that Mother, highly blest,
Of the Sole-begotten One!
Christ above in torment hangs;
She beneath beholds the pangs
Of her dying glorious Son.

3 Quis est homo qui non fleret,
Matrem Christi si videret,
In tanto supplicio?
Quis non posset contristari,
Christi Matrem contemplari
Dolentem cum Filio?

Is there one who would not weep,
'Whelmed in miseries so deep
Christ's dear Mother to behold?
Can the human heart refrain
From partaking in her pain,
In that Mother's pain untold?

4 Pro peccatis suæ gentis,
Vidit Jesum in tormentis
Et flagellis subditum.
Vidit suum dulcem natum,
Moriendo desolatum,
Dum emisit Spiritum.

Bruised, derided, cursed, defiled,
She beheld her tender Child,
All with bloody scourges rent;
For the sins of his own nation
Saw him hang in desolation
Till his Spirit forth he sent.

5 Eja Mater, fons amoris
  Me sentire vim doloris,
    Fac, ut tecum lugeam.
  Fac ut ardeat cor meum
  In amando Christum Deum,
    Ut sibi complaceam.

O thou Mother! fount of love!
  Touch my spirit from above,
    Make my heart with thine accord;
  Make me feel as thou hast felt;
  Make my soul to glow and melt
    With the Love of Christ my Lord.

6 Sancta Mater istud agas,
  Crucifixi fige plagas
    Cordi meo valide.
  Tui nati vulnerati,
  Tam dignati pro me pati,
    Pœnas mecum divide.

Holy Mother! pierce me through;
  In my heart each wound renew
    Of my Saviour crucified;
  Let me share with thee his pain,
  Who for all my sins was slain,
    Who for me in torment died.

7 Fac me tecum pié flere,
  Crucifixo condolere
    Donec ego vixero.
  Juxta crucem tecum stare,
  Et me tibi sociare
    In planctu desidero.

Let me mingle tears with thee,
  Mourning him who mourned for me,
    All the days that I may live:
  By the cross with thee to stay;
  There with thee to weep and pray,
    Is all I ask of thee to give.

8 Virgo virginum præ-
   clara,
  Mihi jam non sis am-
   ara,
    Fac me tecum plan-
     gere.
  Fac, ut portem Christi
   mortem,
  Passionis, fac consor-
   tem,
    Et plagas recolere.

Virgin of all virgins best!
  Listen to my fond re-
   quest:
    Let me share thy
     grief divine;
  Let me to my latest
   breath
  In my body bear the
   death
    Of that dying Son of
     thine.

9 Fac me plagis vulne-
   rari,
  Fac me cruce inebri-
   ari,
    Et cruore Filii.
  Flammis ne urar suc-
   census,
  Per te, virgo, sim de-
   fensus,
    In die judicii.

Wounded with his every
   wound,
  Steep my soul till it
   hath swooned
    In his very blood
     away;
  Be to me, O Virgin,
   nigh,
  Lest in flames I burn
   and die
    In his awful judg-
     ment-day.

10 Christe, cum sit hinc
   exire,
  Da per Matrem me
   venire
    Ad palmam victo-
     riæ,
  Quando corpus mori-
   etur,
  Fac ut animæ done-
   tur
    Paradisi gloria.
       Amen.

Christ, when thou shalt
   call me hence,
  Be thy Mother my de-
   fence,
    Be thy cross my vic-
     tory:
  While my body here
   decays,
  May my soul thy good-
   ness praise
    Safe in paradise with
     thee. *Amen.*

THE STATIONS, OR WAY OF THE CROSS.

Those who perform devoutly the *Way of the Cross*, gain all the Indulgences which have ever been granted by the Popes to the faithful who visit in person the sacred places in Jerusalem.

PRAYER BEFORE THE HIGH ALTAR.

O JESUS Christ, my Lord! with what great love thou didst pass over this painful road, which led thee to death; and I—how often I have abandoned thee! But now, I love thee with my whole soul, and because I love thee, I am sincerely sorry for having offended thee. My Jesus, pardon me, and permit me to accompany thee in this journey. Thou art going to die for the love of me, and it is my wish also, O my dearest Redeemer! to die for love of thee. O yes, my Jesus! in thy love I wish to live, in thy love I wish to die.

FIRST STATION.

Jesus is Condemned to Death.

V. We adore thee, O Christ, and praise thee.
R. Because by thy holy Cross thou hast redeemed the world.

WAY OF THE CROSS.

Consider how Jesus, after having been scourged and crowned with thorns, was unjustly condemned by Pilate to die on the Cross. *Pause awhile.*

MY adorable Jesus, it was not Pilate; no, it was my sins that condemned thee to die. I beseech thee, by the merits of this sorrowful journey, to assist my soul in her journey towards eternity. I love thee, my beloved Jesus; I love thee more than myself; I repent with my whole heart of having offended thee. Never permit me to separate myself from thee again. Grant that I may love thee always; and then do with me what thou wilt.

Our Father. Hail Mary. Glory, &c.

O Jesus! who, for love of me,
Didst bear thy cross to Calvary;
In thy sweet mercy grant to me
To suffer and to die with thee.

SECOND STATION.
Jesus is made to bear his Cross.

V. We adore thee, O Christ, and praise thee.
R. Because by thy holy Cross thou hast redeemed the world.

Consider how Jesus, in making this journey with the Cross on his shoulders, thought of us and offered for us to his

Father the death he was about to undergo. *Pause awhile.*

MY most beloved Jesus, I embrace all the tribulations thou hast destined for me until death. I beseech thee, by the merits of the pain thou didst suffer in carrying thy cross, to give me the necessary help to carry mine with perfect patience and resignation. I love thee, Jesus, my love, above all things; I repent with my whole heart of having offended thee. Never permit me to separate myself from thee again. Grant that I may love thee always; and then do with me what thou wilt.

Our Father. Hail Mary. Glory, &c.

O Jesus! who, for love of me, &c., p. 379.

THIRD STATION.

Jesus falls the first time under his Cross.

V. We adore thee, O Christ, and praise thee.

R. Because by thy holy Cross thou hast redeemed the world.

Consider this first fall of Jesus under his Cross, his flesh was torn by the scourges, his head crowned with thorns, and he had lost a great quantity of blood. He was so weakened he could scarcely walk, and yet he had to carry this great load upon his shoulders. The soldiers struck him rudely, and thus he fell several times. *Pause awhile.*

MY Jesus, it is not the weight of the Cross, but of my sins, which has made thee suffer so much pain. Ah! by the merits of this first fall, deliver me from the misfortune of falling into mortal sin. I love thee, O my Jesus, I repent with my whole heart of having offended thee. Never permit me to separate myself from thee again. Grant that I may love thee always; and then do with me what thou wilt.

Our Father. Hail Mary. Glory, &c.

O Jesus! who, for love of me, &c., p. 379.

FOURTH STATION.

Jesus meets his afflicted Mother.

V. We adore thee, O Christ, and praise thee.
R. Because by thy holy Cross thou hast redeemed the world.

Consider the meeting of the Son and the Mother, which took place on this journey. Their looks became like so many arrows to wound those hearts which loved each other so tenderly. *Pause awhile.*

MY sweet Jesus, by the sorrow thou didst experience in this meeting, grant me the grace of a truly devoted love for thy most holy Mother. And thou, my Queen, who wast overwhelmed with sorrow, obtain for me, by thy intercession, a continual and tender remembrance of the passion of thy Son. I love thee, Jesus, my love, above all things; I repent of ever having offended thee. Never permit me to separate myself from thee again. Grant that I may love thee always; and then do with me what thou wilt.

Our Father. Hail Mary. Glory, &c.

O Jesus! who, for love of me, &c., p. 379.

FIFTH STATION.

The Cyrenian helps Jesus to carry his Cross.

V. We adore thee, O Christ, and praise thee.

R. Because by thy holy Cross thou hast redeemed the world.

Consider how the Jews, seeing that at each step Jesus was on the point of expiring, and fearing he would die on the way, when they wished him to die the ignominious death of the Cross, constrained Simon the Cyrenian to carry the Cross behind our Lord. *Pause awhile.*

MY most beloved Jesus, I will not refuse the Cross as the Cyrenian did; I accept it; I embrace it. I accept in particular the death thou hast destined for me, with all its pains; I unite it to thy death, I offer it to thee. Thou hast died for love of me; I will die for love of thee. Help me by thy grace. I love thee, Jesus, my love, above all things; I repent with my whole heart of having offended thee. Never permit me to separate myself from thee again. Grant that I may love thee always; and then do with me what thou wilt.

Our Father. Hail Mary. Glory, &c.

O Jesus! who, for love of me, &c., p. 879.

SIXTH STATION.
Veronica wipes the Face of Jesus.

V. We adore thee, O Christ, and praise thee.
R. Because by thy holy Cross thou hast redeemed the world.

Consider how the holy woman named Veronica, seeing Jesus so ill used, and his face bathed in sweat and blood, presented him with a towel, with which he wiped his adorable face, leaving on it the impression of his holy countenance
Pause awhile.

MY most beloved Jesus, thy face was beautiful before, but in this journey it has lost all its beauty, and wounds and blood have disfigured it. Alas! my soul also was once beautiful, when it received thy grace in baptism; but I have disfigured it since by my sins; thou alone, my Redeemer, canst restore it to its former beauty. Do this by thy passion, O Jesus! I repent with my whole heart of having offended thee. Never permit me to separate myself from thee again. Grant that I may love thee always; and then do with me what thou wilt.

Our Father. Hail Mary. Glory, &c.

O Jesus! who, for love of me, &c., p. 379.

SEVENTH STATION.

Jesus falls the second time.

V. We adore thee, O Christ, and praise thee.

R. Because by thy holy Cross thou hast redeemed the world.

Consider the second fall of Jesus under the Cross; a fall which renews the pain of all the wounds of his head and members. *Pause awhile.*

MY most sweet Jesus, how many times thou hast pardoned me, and how many times have I fallen again, and begun again to offend thee. Oh! by the merits of this second fall, give me the necessary helps to persevere in thy grace until death. Grant that in all temptations which assail me, I may always commend myself to thee. I love thee, Jesus, my love, above all things; I repent with my whole heart of having offended thee. Never permit me to separate myself from thee again. Grant that I may love thee always; and then do with me what thou wilt.

Our Father. Hail Mary. Glory, &c.

O Jesus! who, for love of me, &c., p. 379.

EIGHTH STATION.

Jesus speaks to the daughters of Jerusalem.

V. We adore thee, O Christ, and praise thee.

R. Because by thy holy Cross thou hast redeemed the world.

Consider how these women wept with compassion at seeing Jesus in such a pitiable state, streaming with blood as he walked along. "My children," said he, "weep not for me, but for your children." *Pause awhile.*

MY Jesus, laden with sorrows, I weep for the offences I have committed against thee, because of the pains they have deserved, and still more because of the displeasure they have caused thee, who hast loved me so much. It is thy love, more than the fear of Hell, which causes me to weep for my sins. My Jesus, I love thee more than myself; I repent with my whole heart of having offended thee. Never permit me to separate myself from thee again. Grant that I may love thee always; and then do with me what thou wilt.

Our Father. Hail Mary. Glory, &c.

O Jesus! who, for love of me, &c., page 379.

NINTH STATION.

Jesus falls the third time.

V. We adore thee, O Christ, and praise thee.

R. Because by thy holy Cross thou hast redeemed the world.

Consider the third fall of Jesus Christ. His weakness was extreme, and the cruelty of his executioners excessive, who tried to hasten his steps when he could scarcely move. *Pause awhile.*

AH! my outraged Jesus, by the merits of the weakness thou didst suffer in going to Calvary, give me strength sufficient to conquer all human respect, and all my wicked passions, which have led me to despise thy friendship. I love thee, Jesus, my love, above all things; I repent with my whole heart of having offended thee. Never permit me to separate myself from thee again. Grant that I may love thee always; and then do with me what thou wilt.

Our Father. Hail Mary. Glory, &c.
O Jesus! who, for love of me, &c., page 379.

TENTH STATION.

Jesus is stripped of his Garments.

℣. We adore thee, O Christ, and praise thee.
℞. Because by thy holy Cross thou hast redeemed the world.

Consider the violence with which the executioners stripped Jesus. His inner garments adhered to his torn flesh, and they dragged them off so roughly that the skin came with them. Compassionate your Saviour thus cruelly treated. *Pause awhile.*

MY innocent Jesus, by the merits of the torment thou hast felt, help me to strip myself of all affection to things of earth, in order that I may place all my love in thee, who art so worthy of my love. I love thee, O Jesus, above all things; I repent with my whole heart of having offended thee. Never permit me to separate myself from thee again. Grant that I may love thee always; and then do with me what thou wilt.

Our Father. Hail Mary. Glory, &c.

O Jesus! who, for love of me, &c., page 379.

ELEVENTH STATION.

Jesus is nailed to the Cross.

V. We adore thee, O Christ, and praise thee.
R. Because by thy holy Cross thou hast redeemed the world.

Consider how Jesus, after being thrown on the Cross, extended his hands, and offered to his eternal Father the sacrifice of his life for our salvation. These barbarians fastened him with nails, and then, securing the Cross, allowed him to die with anguish on this infamous gibbet. *Pause awhile.*

MY Jesus, loaded with contempt, nail my heart to thy feet, that it may ever remain there to love thee, and never quit thee again. I love thee more than myself; I repent with my whole heart of having offended thee. Never permit me to separate myself from thee again. Grant that I may love thee always; and then do with me what thou wilt.

Our Father. Hail Mary. Glory, &c.

O Jesus! who, for love of me, &c., page 379.

TWELFTH STATION.

Jesus dies on the Cross.

V. We adore thee, O Christ, and praise thee.
R. Because by thy holy Cross thou hast redeemed the world.

Consider how Jesus, after three hours' agony on the Cross, consumed with anguish, abandoned himself to the weight of his body, bowed his head, and died. *Pause awhile.*

O MY dying Jesus! I kiss devoutly the Cross on which thou didst die for love of me. I have merited by my sins to die a miserable death, but thy death is my hope. Ah! by the merits of thy death, give me grace to die embracing thy feet, and burning with love to thee. I commit my soul into thy hands. I love thee, O Jesus, above all things; I repent of ever having offended thee. Permit not that I ever offend thee again. Grant that I may love thee always; and then do with me what thou wilt.

Our Father. Hail Mary. Glory, &c.
O Jesus! who, for love of me, &c., page 379.

THIRTEENTH STATION.

Jesus is taken down from the Cross.

V. We adore thee, O Christ, and praise thee.
R. Because by thy holy Cross thou hast redeemed the world.

Consider how our Lord, having expired, two of his disciples, Joseph and Nicodemus, took him down from the Cross, and placed him in the arms of his afflicted Mother, who received him with unutterable tenderness, and pressed him to her bosom. *Pause awhile.*

O MOTHER of sorrow, for the love of this Son, accept me for thy servant, and pray for me. And thou, my Redeemer, since thou hast died for me, permit me to love thee; for I wish but thee, and nothing more. I love thee, my Jesus, above all things; I repent of ever having offended thee. Never permit me to offend thee again. Grant that I may love thee always; and then do with me what thou wilt.

Our Father. Hail Mary. Glory, &c.
O Jesus! who, for love of me, &c., page 879.

FOURTEENTH STATION.
Jesus is placed in the Sepulchre.

V. We adore thee, O Christ, and praise thee.
R. Because by thy holy Cross thou hast redeemed the world.

Consider how the disciples carried the body of Jesus to bury it, accompanied by his holy Mother, who arranged it in the sepulchre with her own hands. They then closed the tomb, and all withdrew. *Pause awhile.*

AH! my buried Jesus, I kiss the stone that encloses thee. But thou didst rise again the third day. I beseech thee, by thy resurrection, to make me rise glorious with thee at the last day, to be always united with thee in heaven, to praise thee and love thee for ever. O Jesus, I love thee, and I repent of ever having offended thee. Permit not that I ever offend thee again. Grant that I may love thee: and then do with me what thou wilt.

Our Father. Hail Mary. Glory, &c.
O Jesus! who for love of me, &c., page 379.
   Finally say, *Our Father. Hail Mary. Glory, &c.*, five times, to gain other Indulgences.

PRAYER OF ST. IGNATIUS.

RECEIVE, O Lord, my memory, my will, my understanding, and entire liberty. Thou hast given me all I have, and I surrender all to thy Divine will, that thou mayest dispose of me as it shall please thee. Give me only thy love and thy grace, and I shall be happy, and shall have no more to ask!

JESUS CRUCIFIED.

O COME and mourn with me awhile;
    See, Mary calls us to her side:
O come and let us mourn with her;
    Jesus, our Love, is crucified!

Have we no tears to shed for Him,
    While soldiers scoff and Jews deride?
Ah! look how patiently He hangs;
    Jesus, our Love, is crucified!

How fast His hands and feet are nailed,
    His blessed tongue with thirst is tied,
His failing eyes are blind with blood,
    Jesus, our Love, is crucified!

His Mother cannot reach His face,
   She stands in helplessness beside;
Her heart is martyred with her Son's;
   Jesus, our Love, is crucified!

Seven times He spoke, seven words of love,
   And three long hours His silence cried
For mercy on the souls of men,
   Jesus, our Love, is crucified!

What was Thy crime, my dearest Lord?
   By earth, by heaven, Thou hast been tried,
And guilty found of too much love;
   Jesus, our Love, is crucified!

DEVOTIONS
TO THE SACRED HEART OF JESUS.

THE ACT OF CONSECRATION.

TO thee, O Sacred Heart of Jesus! to thee I devote and offer up my life, thoughts, words, actions, pains, and sufferings. May the least part of my being be no longer employed, save only in loving, serving, honouring, and glorifying thee. Wherefore, O most sacred Heart! be thou the sole object of my love, the protector of my life, the pledge of my salvation, and my secure refuge at the hour of my death. Be thou, O most bountiful Heart! my justification at the throne of God, and screen me from his anger, which I have so justly merited. In thee I place all my confidence, and, convinced as I am of my own weakness, I rely entirely on thy bounty. Annihilate in me all that is displeasing and offensive to thy pure eye. Imprint thyself like a divine seal on my heart, that I may ever remember my obligations never to be separated from thee. May my name also, I beseech thee by thy tender bounty, ever be fixed and engraved in thee, O Book of Life! and may I ever be a victim consecrated to thy glory, ever burning with the flames of thy pure love, and entirely penetrated with it for an eternity. In this I place all my happiness, this is all my desire, to live and die in no other quality, but that of thy devoted servant. Amen.

LITANY OF
THE SACRED HEART OF JESUS.

LORD, have mercy on us.
Christ, have mercy on us.
Lord, have mercy on us.
Christ, hear us.
Christ, graciously hear us.
God the Father of heaven,
God the Son, Redeemer of the world,
God the Holy Ghost,
Holy Trinity, one God,
Heart of Jesus,
Heart of Jesus, formed in the womb of the most Blessed Virgin,
Heart of Jesus, hypostatically united to the eternal Word,
Heart of Jesus, Sanctuary of the Divinity,

Have mercy on us,

SACRED HEART OF JESUS. 395.

Heart of Jesus, Tabernacle of the most holy Trinity,
Heart of Jesus, Temple of all Sanctity,
Heart of Jesus, Fountain of all Graces,
Heart of Jesus, most meek,
Heart of Jesus, most humble,
Heart of Jesus, most obedient,
Heart of Jesus, most chaste,
Heart of Jesus, Furnace of Love,
Heart of Jesus, Source of Contrition,
Heart of Jesus, Treasure of Wisdom,
Heart of Jesus, Ocean of Bounty,
Heart of Jesus, Throne of Mercy,
Heart of Jesus, Abyss of all Virtues,
Heart of Jesus, sorrowful in the Garden,
Heart of Jesus, spent with a bloody Sweat,
Heart of Jesus, glutted with reproaches,
Heart of Jesus, consumed for our sins,
Heart of Jesus, made obedient even unto the Death of the Cross,
Heart of Jesus, pierced through with a lance,
Heart of Jesus, Refuge of Sinners,
Heart of Jesus, Fortitude of the Just,
Heart of Jesus, comfort of the afflicted,
Heart of Jesus, main strength of the tempted,
Heart of Jesus, Terror of the Devils,
Heart of Jesus, sanctification of Hearts,
Heart of Jesus, Perseverance of the good,
Heart of Jesus, hope of the dying,
Heart of Jesus, joy of the blessed,
Heart of Jesus, the delight of all the Saints,

Have mercy on us.

Lamb of God, who takest away the sins of the world, *Spare us, O Jesus!*

Lamb of God, who takest away the sins of the world, *Hear us, O Jesus!*

Lamb of God, who takest away the sins of the world, *Have mercy on us, O Jesus!*

V. O most sacred Heart of Jesus, have mercy on us.

R. That we may worthily love thee with our whole hearts.

Let us pray.

O GOD! who out of thy immense love hast given to the faithful the most Sacred Heart of thy Son our Lord, as the object of thy tender affection; grant, we beseech thee, that we may so love and honour this pledge of thy love on earth, as by it to merit the love of both thee and thy gift, and be eternally loved by thee and this most blessed Heart in heaven. Through the same Jesus Christ our Lord thy Son, who livest and reignest with thee in the unity of the Holy Ghost one God, world without end. Amen.

THROUGH thy Sacred Heart, O Jesus, overflowing with all sweetness, we recommend to thee ourselves, and all our concerns, our friends, benefactors, parents, and relations, our superiors, and enemies; take under thy protection this house, city, and kingdom; extend this thy care to all such as are under any affliction, and to those who labour in the agony and pangs of death; cast an eye of compassion on the obstinate sinner, and more particularly on the poor suffering souls in purgatory, as also on those who are engaged and united with us in the holy confederacy of honouring and worshipping thee.—Bless these in particular, O bountiful Jesus! and bless them according to the extent of thy infinite goodness, mercy, and charity. Amen.

AN ACT OF REPARATION

To the Sacred Heart, to be made on the Feast itself, or at any other time, in the presence of the Blessed Sacrament.

O MOST amiable and adorable heart of Jesus! centre of all hearts, glowing with charity, and inflamed with zeal for the interest of thy Father, and the salvation of mankind! O Heart ever sensible of our misery, and ever in motion to redress our evils; the real victim of love in the Holy Eucharist, and a propitiatory sacrifice for sin on the altar of the cross! Seeing that the generality of Christians make no other return for these thy mercies, than contempt of thy favours, forgetfulness of their own obligations, and ingratitude to the best of benefactors,—is it not just, that we thy servants, penetrated with the deepest sense of the like indignities, should enter upon a due and satisfactory reparation of honour to thy most sacred majesty? Prostrate, therefore, in body, and humbled in mind, before heaven and earth, we solemnly declare our utter detestation and abhorrence of such a conduct. Inexpressible, we know, was the bitterness which the multitude of our sins brought upon thy tender heart; insufferable the weight of our iniquities, which pressed thy face to the earth in the Garden of Olives; and unsurmountable thy anguish, when expiring with love, grief, and agony, on Mount Calvary, in thy last breath thou wouldst reclaim sinners to their duty and repentance. This we know, O dear Redeemer! and would most willingly redress these thy sufferings by our own, or share with thee in thine.

O MERCIFUL Jesus! ever present on our altars, and with a heart open to receive all who *labour and are burdened!* O adorable heart of Jesus, source of true contrition! impart to our hearts the true spirit of penance, and to our eyes a fountain of tears, that we may bewail and wash off our sins, and those of the world. Pardon, divine Jesus! all the injuries, reproaches, and outrages done thee through the course of thy holy life and bitter passion. Pardon all the impieties, irreverences, and sacrileges, which have been committed against thee in the sacrament of the Eucharist, from its first institution. Graciously receive the small tribute of our sincere repentance, as an agreeable offering in thy sight, and in requital for the benefits we daily receive from the altar, where thou art a living and continual sacrifice, and in union of that bloody holocaust, thou didst present to thy eternal Father on Mount Calvary from the Cross.

SWEET Jesus! give thy blessing to the ardent desire we now entertain, and the holy resolution we have taken of ever loving and adoring thee after a proper manner, in the

sacrament of love, the Eucharist; thus to
repair by a true conversion of heart, and a
becoming zeal for thy glory, our past negligence
and infidelity. Be thou, O adorable Heart!
who knowest the clay of which we are formed,
be thou our mediator with thy heavenly Father,
whom we have so grievously offended; strengthen
our weakness, confirm our resolution, and with
thy charity, humility, meekness, and patience,
cover the multitude of our iniquities; be thou
our support, our refuge, and our strength, that
nothing henceforth in life or death may separate
us from thee. Amen.

LITTLE CHAPLET AND PRAYERS TO THE SACRED HEART OF JESUS.

[Indulgences : i. 300 days, once a day, for reciting the following prayers.

ii. A plenary indulgence, once a month, to all who say them once a day for an entire month; to be gained on that day, when, after confession and communion, they shall pray for the intention of the Sovereign Pontiff.]

V. Incline unto mine aid, O God.
R. O Lord, make haste to help me.
Glory be to the Father, &c.

I. My most loving Jesus, my own heart is glad when I think upon thy most Sacred Heart, all tenderness and sweetness for sinners, and I am filled with confident hope of thy kind welcome. But O, my sins! how many and how great are they! Grieving now, like Peter and like Magdalene, I bewail and abhor them, because they are an offence to thee, my sovereign good. O, grant me pardon for them all. Would that I might die before I offend thee again. I pray thee, by thy Sacred Heart, that I may live only to requite thy love.

Say the Our Father once, and the Glory be to the Father five times, in honour of the Sacred Heart, then say,

Sweet Heart of my Jesus,
Make me love thee ever more and more.

II. My Jesus, I bless thy most humble heart: and I give thanks unto thee, who by making it my model, dost not only give me strong and urgent inducement to imitate it, but also, at the cost of so many humiliations, dost vouchsafe thyself to point out and to smooth for me the way to follow thee. Foolish and ungrateful that I am, how have I wandered far away from thee! Pardon me, my Jesus! Take from me all hateful pride and ambition, that with lowly heart I may follow thee, my Jesus, amidst humiliations, and so obtain peace and salvation. Strengthen me, thou who canst, and I will ever bless thy Sacred Heart.

Say the Our Father once, and the Glory be to the Father five times; then say,

Sweet Heart of my Jesus,
Make me love thee ever more and more.

III. My Jesus, I admire thy most patient Heart, and I give thee thanks for all the wondrous examples of unwearied patience which thou hast left us. It grieves me that these examples still have to reproach me for my extraordinary delicacy, which shrinks from every little pain. Pour, then, into my heart, O dear Jesus, a fervent and constant love of suffering and the cross, of mortification and of penance, that, following thee to Calvary, I may with thee attain to glory, and the joys of paradise.

Say the Our Father once, and the Glory be to the Father five times.

> Sweet Heart of my Jesus
> Make me love thee ever more and more.

IV. Dear Jesus, when I look first upon thy most gentle Heart, and then upon my own, I shudder to see how unlike mine is to thine. How I am wont to fret and grieve when a hint, a look, or a word thwarts me! Pardon for the future all my violence, and give me grace to imitate in every contradiction thy unalterable meekness, that so I may enjoy an everlasting and holy peace.

Say the Our Father once, and the Glory be to the Father five times; then say,

> Sweet Heart of my Jesus
> Make me love thee ever more and more.

V. Let me sing praises to Jesus for his most generous Heart, the conqueror of death and hell; for well it merits every praise. I am more than ever confounded whilst I look upon my coward heart, which dreads even a rough word or injurious taunt. But it shall be so with me no more. My Jesus, I pray thee for such strength that, fighting and conquering on earth, I may one day rejoice triumphantly with thee in heaven.

Say the Our Father once, and the Glory be to the Father five times; then say,

> Sweet Heart of Jesus,
> Make me love thee ever more and more.

Let us now have recourse to Mary; and dedicating ourselves wholly to her, and trusting in her maternal heart, let us say: By all the virtue of thy most sweet heart obtain for us, great Mother of God, our Mother Mary, a true and enduring devotion to the Sacred Heart of Jesus, thy Son, that, bound up in every thought and affection in union with his Heart, we may fulfil all our duties, serving our Jesus evermore with readiness of heart, and especially this day.

V. Heart of Jesus, burning with love of us,
R. Inflame our hearts with love of thee.

Let us pray.

Lord, we beseech thee, let thy holy Spirit kindle in our hearts that fire of charity which our Lord Jesus Christ, thy Son, sent forth from his inmost heart upon this earth, and willed that it should be kindled exceedingly. Who liveth and reigneth with thee in the unity of the same Holy Spirit, God for ever and ever. Amen.

HYMN TO THE SACRED HEART OF JESUS.

TO Jesu's Heart all burning
  With fervent love for men,
My heart with fondest yearning
  Shall raise its joyful strain.

Chorus.—While ages course along,
    Blest be with loudest song
    The Sacred Heart of Jesus
    By every heart and tongue.

O Heart, for me on fire
  With love no tongue can speak,
My yet untold desire
  God gives me for thy sake.
          While ages, &c.

Too true I have forsaken
   Thy Heart by wilful sin;
Yet let me now be taken
   Back to my home again.
            While ages, &c.

As thou art meek and lowly
   And ever pure of heart,
So may my heart be wholly
   Of thine the counterpart.
            While ages, &c.

Would that to me were given,
   The pinions of the dove!
I'd pierce the highest heaven
   My Jesus' love to prove.
            While ages, &c.

When life away is flying,
   And earth's false glare is done,
Still, Sacred Heart, in dying,
   I'll say, " I'm all thine own."
            While ages, &c.

THE LIVING ROSARY.

To enable all to join the more readily in the recitation of the Rosary, an association has been instituted called the " Living Rosary," the members of which, by reciting daily one decade, enjoy certain privileges. It is thus arranged: Fifteen persons form themselves into a circle, and divide amongst them by lot the fifteen mysteries. Each recites his Our Father and ten Hail Marys daily; and by this means the entire Rosary is gone through by the circle every month. The association was confirmed by a brief of Gregory XVI., January, 1832.

THE ROSARY OF
THE BLESSED VIRGIN.

The Method of saying the Rosary of our Blessed Lady, as it was ordered by his Holiness Pope Pius V.

THE FIVE JOYFUL MYSTERIES,

Assigned for Mondays and Thursdays throughout the Year, the Sundays in Advent, and after Epiphany till Lent.

IN the name of the Father, and of the Son, and of the Holy Ghost. Amen.

Blessed be the holy and undivided Trinity, now, and for evermore. Amen.

Invocation of the Holy Ghost.

Come O Holy Spirit, fill the hearts of thy Faithful, and kindle in them the fire of thy love.

V. Send forth thy Spirit, and they shall be created.

R. *And thou wilt renew the face of the earth.*

LET US PRAY.

O GOD, who by the light of the Holy Ghost didst instruct the hearts of the Faithful, grant us in the same Holy Spirit, a love and relish of what is right, and the constant enjoyment of his consolations. Through Jesus Christ our Lord. Amen.

V. Incline unto mine aid, O God.
R. O Lord! make haste to help me.
V. Glory be to the Father, &c.
R. As it was in the beginning, &c.

I. *The Annunciation.*

LET us contemplate in this mystery, how the angel Gabriel saluted our blessed Lady with the title, Full of grace, and declared unto her the incarnation of our Lord and Saviour Jesus Christ.

Our Father, &c., *once;* Hail Mary, &c., *ten times;* Glory, &c., *once.*

Let us pray.

O HOLY Mary, Queen of Virgins, by the most high mystery of the incarnation of thy beloved Son, our Lord Jesus Christ, by which our salvation was so happily begun; obtain for us, by thy intercession, light to know this so great benefit which he hath bestowed upon us, vouchsafing in it to make himself our brother, and thee, his own most beloved Mother, our Mother also. Amen.

II. *The Visitation.*

LET us contemplate in this mystery, how the Blessed Virgin Mary, understanding from the angel, that her cousin St. Elizabeth had conceived, went with haste into the mountains of Judea to visit her, and remained with her three months.

Our Father, &c., &c., *as before.*

Let us pray.

O HOLY Virgin, most spotless mirror of humility, by that exceeding charity which moved thee to visit thy holy cousin, St. Elizabeth, obtain for us, by thy intercession, that our hearts may be so visited by thy most holy Son, that being free from all sin, we may praise him and give him thanks for ever. Amen.

III. *The Nativity.*

LET us contemplate in this mystery, how the Blessed Virgin Mary, when the time of her delivery was come, brought forth our Redeemer Christ Jesus, at midnight, and laid him in a manger, because there was no room for him in the inns at Bethlehem. Our Father, &c.

Let us pray.

O MOST pure Mother of God, by thy virginal and most joyful delivery, by which thou gavest unto the world thy only Son our Saviour; we beseech thee, obtain for us, by thy intercession grace, to lead so pure and holy a life in this world, that we may worthily sing without ceasing, both by day and night, the mercies of thy Son, and his benefits to us by thee. Amen.

IV. *The Presentation.*

Let us contemplate in this mystery, how the most Blessed Virgin Mary, on the day of her purification presented the Child Jesus in the temple, where holy Simeon, giving thanks to God with great devotion, received him into his arms. Our Father, &c., &c.

Let us pray.

O Holy Virgin, most admirable mistress and pattern of obedience, who didst present in the temple the Lord of the temple: obtain for us, of thy beloved Son, that with holy Simeon and devout Anna, we may praise and glorify him for ever. Amen.

V. *The finding of the Child Jesus in the Temple.*

Let us contemplate in this mystery, how the Blessed Virgin Mary, after having lost, without any fault of hers, her beloved Son in Jerusalem, sought him for the space of three days, and at length found him the third day in the temple, in the midst of the doctors, disputing with them, being of the age of twelve years. Our Father, &c., &c.

Let us pray.

MOST Blessed Virgin, more than martyr in thy sufferings, and yet the comfort of such as are afflicted; by that unspeakable joy wherewith thy soul was ravished at finding thy beloved Son in the temple, in the midst of the doctors, disputing with them, obtain of him that we may so seek him, and find him in the Holy Catholic Church, as to be never more separated from him. Amen.

Salve Regina.

HAIL, holy Queen, Mother of Mercy, our life, our sweetness, and our hope; to thee do we cry, poor banished sons of Eve; to thee do we send our sighs, mourning and weeping in this vale of tears: turn then, most gracious advocate, thine eyes of mercy towards us, and after this our exile ended, show unto us the blessed fruit of thy womb, Jesus. O most clement, most pious, and most sweet Virgin Mary.

V. Pray for us, O holy Mother of God,
R. That we may be made worthy of the promises of Christ.

Let us pray.

O God, whose only-begotten Son, by his life, death, and resurrection, hath purchased for us the rewards of eternal life; grant, we beseech thee, that meditating upon these mysteries, in the most holy Rosary of the Blessed Virgin Mary, we may imitate what they contain, and obtain what they promise. Through the same Christ our Lord. Amen.

PART II.

THE FIVE SORROWFUL MYSTERIES,

For Tuesdays and Fridays throughout the year, and the Sundays in Lent.

In the name of the Father, &c., *as before,* p. 404.

I. *The Prayer and Bloody Sweat of our blessed Saviour in the Garden.*

Let us contemplate in this mystery, how our Lord Jesus was so afflicted for us in the Garden of Gethsemani, that his body was bathed in a bloody sweat.

which ran trickling down in great drops upon the ground.

Our Father, &c., &c.

Let us pray.

MOST holy Virgin, more than martyr, by that ardent prayer which thy beloved Son poured forth unto his Father in the Garden, vouchsafe to intercede for us, that our passions being reduced to the obedience of reason, we may always, and in all things, conform and subject ourselves to the will of God. Amen.

II. *The Scourging of our Blessed Lord at the Pillar.*

Let us contemplate in this mystery, how our Lord Jesus Christ, being delivered up by Pilate to the fury of the Jews, was most cruelly scourged at a pillar. Our Father, &c., &c.

Let us pray.

O Mother of God, overflowing fountain of patience, through those stripes which thine only and most beloved Son vouchsafed to suffer for us; obtain of him for us grace, that we may know how to mortify our rebellious senses, and cut off all occasions of sinning, with that sword of grief and compassion which pierced thy most tender soul. Amen.

III. *The Crowning of our blessed Saviour with Thorns.*

Let us contemplate in this mystery, how those cruel ministers of Satan platted a crown of sharp thorns, and most cruelly pressed it on the most sacred head of our Lord Jesus Christ.

Our Father, &c., &c.

Let us pray.

O Mother of our eternal prince and king of glory, by those sharp thorns wherewith his most holy head was pierced, we beseech thee that, through thine intercession, we may be delivered from all motions of pride, and, in the day of judgment, from that confusion which our sins deserve. Amen.

IV. *Jesus carrying his Cross*

Let us contemplate in this mystery, how our Lord Jesus Christ, being sentenced to die, bore, with the most amazing patience, the cross, which was laid upon him for his greater torment and ignominy. Our Father, &c., &c.

Let us pray.

O Holy Virgin, example of patience, by the most painful carrying of the cross in which thy Son our Lord Jesus Christ bore the heavy weight of our sins, obtain for us, of him, through thine intercession, courage and strength to follow his steps and bear our cross after him, to the end of our lives. Amen.

V. *The Crucifixion of our Lord Jesus Christ.*

Let us contemplate in this mystery, how our Lord Jesus Christ, being come to Mount Calvary, was stripped of his clothes, and his hands and feet most cruelly nailed to the cross in the presence of his most afflicted Mother.

Our Father, &c., &c.

Let us pray.

O Holy Mary, Mother of God, as the body of thy beloved Son was for us stretched on the Cross, so may our desires be daily more and more extended in his service, and our hearts wounded with compassion for his most bitter passion; and thou, O most blessed Virgin, graciously vouchsafe, by thy powerful intercession, to help us to accomplish the work of our salvation. Amen.

The Salve Regina. Hail, holy Queen, &c., with the verse and prayer, page 408.

PART III.

THE FIVE GLORIOUS MYSTERIES,

For Wednesdays and Saturdays throughout the year, and the Sundays from Easter till Advent.

IN the name of the Father, &c., as before, p. 404.

I. *The Resurrection.*

Let us contemplate in this mystery, how our Lord Jesus Christ, triumphing gloriously over death, rose again the third day, immortal and impassible.

Our Father, &c., &c.

Let us pray.

O GLORIOUS Virgin Mary, by that unspeakable joy which thou receivedst in the resurrection of thine only Son, we beseech thee obtain of him, for us, that our hearts may never go astray after the false joys of this world, but may. be ever and wholly employed the pursuit of the only true and solid joys of heaven. Amen.

II. *The Ascension of Christ into Heaven.*

Let us contemplate in this mystery, how our Lord Jesus Christ, forty days after his resurrection, ascended into heaven, attended by angels, in the sight and to the great admiration of his most holy Mother, and his holy apostles and disciples. Our Father, &c., &c.

Let us pray.

O MOTHER of God, comfort of the afflicted, as thy beloved Son, when he ascended into heaven, lifted up his hands, and blessed his apostles, so vouchsafe, most holy Mother, to lift up thy pure hands to him for us, that we may enjoy the benefits of his blessing, and thine also on earth, and hereafter in heaven. Amen.

III. *The descent of the Holy Ghost on the Apostles.*

Let us contemplate in this mystery, how our Lord Jesus Christ, being seated on the right hand of God, sent, as he had promised, the Holy Ghost upon his apostles, who, after he was ascended, returning to Jerusalem, continued in prayer and supplication with the blessed Virgin Mary, expecting the performance of his promise. Our Father, &c., &c.

Let us pray.

O SACRED Virgin, tabernacle of the Holy Ghost, we beseech thee, obtain by thine intercession, that this most sweet Comforter, whom thy beloved Son sent down upon his apostles (filling them thereby with spiritual joy) may teach us, in this world, the true way to salvation, and make us walk in the paths of virtue and good works. Amen.

IV. *The Assumption of the Blessed Virgin Mary into Heaven.*

Let us contemplate in this mystery, how the glorious Virgin, twelve years after the resurrection of her Son, passed out of this world unto him, and was by him assumed into heaven, accompanied by the holy angels. Our Father, &c., &c.

Let us pray.

O MOST prudent Virgin, who entering the heavenly palace didst fill the holy angels with joy, and man with hope, vouchsafe to intercede for us at the hour of our death, that being delivered from the illusions and temptations of the devil, we may joyfully and securely pass out of this temporal state, to enjoy the happiness of eternal life. Amen.

V. *The Coronation of the most Blessed Virgin Mary in Heaven.*

Let us contemplate in this mystery, how the glorious Virgin Mary was, to the great jubilee and exultation of the whole court of heaven, and particular glory of all the saints, crowned by her Son with the brightest diadem of glory.

Our Father, &c., &c.

Let us pray.

O GLORIOUS Queen of all the heavenly citizens, we beseech thee, accept this Rosary which as a crown of roses we offer at thy feet; and grant, most gracious Lady, that, by thine intercession, our souls may be inflamed with so ardent a desire of seeing thee so gloriously crowned, that it may never die in us until it shall be changed into the happy fruition of thy blessed sight Amen.

The Salve Regina. Hail, holy Queen, &c., with the verse and prayer, as before, p. 408.

Let us pray.

HEAR, O merciful God, the prayers of thy servants, that we, who meet together in the society of the most holy Rosary of the Blessed Virgin, Mother of God, may, through her intercession, be delivered by thee from the dangers that continually hang over us. Through Jesus Christ our Lord. Amen.

ACT OF CONSECRATION
TO THE SACRED HEART OF MARY.

O HOLY mother of God, glorious Queen of heaven and earth! I choose thee this day for my mother, my queen, and my advocate at the throne of thy divine Son. Accept the offering which I here make of my heart; may it be irrevocable. It never can be out of danger whilst at my own disposal; it never can be secure but in thy hands.

Ye Choirs of Angels, witnesses of this my oblation, bear me up in the day of judgment; and, next to Jesus and Mary, be ye propitious to me should the enemy of my salvation have any claim upon me. Obtain for me at present the gift of a true repentance, and those graces I may afterwards stand in need of for the gaining of life everlasting. Amen.

THE TE DEUM.

We praise thee, O God; we acknowledge thee to be our Lord.

Thee the Father everlasting, all the earth doth worship.

To thee the angels, to thee the heavens, and all the powers,

To thee the cherubim and seraphim cry out without ceasing:

Holy, Holy Holy, Lord God of Sabbaoth:

Full are the heavens and the earth of the majesty of thy glory.

Thee the glorious choir of the apostles,

Thee the laudable company of the prophets,

Thee the white-robed army of martyrs doth praise.

Thee the holy Church throughout the world doth confess,

The Father of incomprehensible Majesty,

Thine adorable, true, and only Son,

And the Holy Ghost the Paraclete.

Thou, O Christ, art the King of Glory,

Thou art the everlasting Son of the Father.

Thou being to take upon thee to deliver man, didst not disdain the Virgin's womb.

Thou having overcome the sting of death, hast opened to believers the kingdom of heaven.

Thou sittest at the right hand of God, in the glory of the Father.

Thee we believe to be the Judge to come.

We beseech thee therefore, help thy servants, whom thou hast redeemed with thy precious blood.

Make them to be numbered with thy saints in eternal glory.

O Lord, save thy people, and bless thine inheritance.

And govern them, and exalt them for ever.

Every day we bless thee.

And we praise thy name for ever and ever.

Vouchsafe, O Lord, to keep us this day without sin.

Have mercy on us, O Lord, have mercy on us.

Let thy mercy, O Lord, be upon us; as we have put our trust in thee.

In thee, O Lord, have I put my trust: let me not be confounded for ever.

THE THIRTY DAYS' PRAYER

To the Blessed Virgin Mary, in honour of the sacred Passion of our Lord Jesus Christ, by the devout recital of which, for the above space of time, we may confidently hope to obtain our lawful request. It is particularly recommended as a proper devotion for every day in Lent, and all the Fridays throughout the year.

EVER glorious and Blessed Mary, Queen of virgins, Mother of mercy, hope and comfort of all dejected and desolate souls; through that sword of sorrow which pierced thy tender heart, whilst thine only Son, Christ Jesus our Lord, suffered death and ignominy on the cross;

through that filial tenderness and pure love he had for thee, grieving in thy grief, whilst from his cross he recommended thee to the care and protection of his beloved disciple, St. John; take pity, I beseech thee, on my poverty and necessities; have compassion on my anxieties and cares; assist and comfort me in all my infirmities and miseries. Thou art the Mother of mercies; the sweet consolatrix and refuge of the needy and the orphan, of the desolate and the afflicted. Look, therefore, with pity on a miserable forlorn child of Eve, and hear my prayer; for since, in just punishment of my sins, I am encompassed with evils, and oppressed with anguish of spirit, whither can I fly for more secure shelter, O amiable Mother of my Lord and Saviour Jesus Christ, than to thy maternal protection? Attend, therefore, I beseech thee, with pity and compassion to my humble and earnest request. I ask it through the infinite merits of thy dear Son; through that love and condescension wherewith he assumed our nature, when, in compliance with the Divine will, thou gavest thy consent; and whom, after the expiration of nine months, thou didst bring forth from the chaste enclosure of thy womb, to visit this world, and to bless it with his presence. I ask it through that anguish of mind wherewith thy beloved Son, my dear Saviour, was overwhelmed on Mount Olivet, when he besought his Eternal Father to remove from him, if possible, the bitter chalice of his future passion. I ask it through the threefold repetition of his prayer in the garden, from whence afterwards, with dolorous steps and mournful tears, thou didst accompany him to the doleful theatre of his death and sufferings. I ask it through the stripes and wounds of his virginal flesh, occasioned by the cords and whips wherewith he was bound and scourged, when stript of his seamless garment, for which his executioners afterwards cast lots. I ask it through the scoffs and ignominies by which he was insulted; the false accusations and unjust sentence by which he was condemned to death, and which he bore with heavenly patience. I ask it through his bitter tears and bloody sweat; his silence and resignation; his sadness and grief of heart. I ask it through the blood which trickled from his royal and sacred head, when struck with the sceptre of a reed, and pierced with his crown of thorns. I ask it through the excruciating torments he suffered, when his hands and feet were fastened with gross nails to the tree of the cross. I ask it through his vehement thirst and bitter potion of vinegar and gall. I ask it through his dereliction on the cross, when he exclaimed, *My God! My God! why hast thou forsaken Me?* I ask it through the mercy extended to the good thief; and through his recommending his precious soul and spirit into the hands of his Eternal Father before he expired, saying, ALL IS FINISHED. I ask it through the blood mixed with water, which issued from his sacred side when pierced with a lance, and whence a flood of grace and mercy has flowed to us. I ask it through his immaculate life, bitter passion, and ignominious death on the cross, at which nature itself was thrown into convulsions by the bursting of rocks, rending of the veil of the temple, the earthquake, and darkness of the sun and moon. I ask it through his descent into hell, where he comforted the saints of the old law with his presence, and led captivity captive. I ask it through his glorious victory over death, when he arose again into life on the third day; and through the joy which his appearance for forty days after gave thee, his blessed Mother, his apostles, and the rest of his disciples; and when, in thy presence and in theirs, he miraculously ascended into heaven. I ask it through the grace of the Holy Ghost, infused into the hearts of his disciples, when he descended upon them in the form of fiery tongues, and by which they were inspired with zeal in the conversion of the world when they went to preach the gospel. I ask it through the awful appearance of thy Son at the last dreadful day, when he shall come to judge the living and the dead, and the world by fire. I ask it through the compassion he bore thee in this life, and the ineffable joy thou didst feel at thine assumption into heaven, where thou art eternally absorbed in the sweet contemplation of his divine perfections.

O glorious and ever-blessed Virgin, comfort the heart of thy supplicant by obtaining for me [*Here mention the particular favour you desire.*] And as I am persuaded my divine Saviour honours thee as his beloved mother, to whom he can refuse nothing, let me speedily experience the efficacy of thy powerful intercession, according to the tenderness of thy maternal affection, and his filial loving heart, who mercifully grantest the requests and compliest with the desires of those who love and fear him. O most blessed Virgin, besides the object of my present petition, and whatever else I may stand in need of, obtain for me of thy Divine Son, our Lord and our God, lively faith, firm hope, perfect charity, true contrition, a horror of sin, love of God and my neighbour, contempt of the world, and patience and resignation under the trials and afflictions of this life. Obtain likewise for me, O sacred mother of God, the great gift of final perseverance, and grace to receive the last sacraments worthily at the hour of my death. Lastly, obtain, I beseech thee, for the souls of my parents, brethren, relations, and benefactors, both living and dead, life everlasting. Amen.

LOOK DOWN, O MOTHER MARY.

LOOK down, O Mother Mary,
   From thy bright throne above;
Cast down upon thy children
   One only glance of love.
And if a heart so tender
   With pity flows not o'er,
Then turn away, O Mother,
   And look on us no more.
       Look down, &c.

See how ingrate and guilty
  We stand before thy Son;
His loving heart reproaches
  The evil we have done.
But if thou wilt appease Him,
  Speak for us but one word;
Thou only canst obtain us
  The pardon of our Lord.
        Look down, &c.

O Mary, dearest Mother!
  If thou wouldst have us live,
Say that we are thy children,
  And then He will forgive.
Our sins make us unworthy
  That title still to bear,
But thou art still our Mother!
  Then show a mother's care.
        Look down, &c.

Open to us thy mantle,
  There stay we without fear;
What evil can befall us
  If, Mother, thou art near?
O sweetest, dearest Mother!
  Thy sinful children save;
Look down on us with pity,
  Who thy protection crave.
        Look down, &c.

IMMACULATE! IMMACULATE!

O MOTHER! I could weep for mirth,
  Joy fills my heart so fast;
My soul to-day is heaven on earth,
  O could the transport last!

I think of thee, and what thou art,
    Thy majesty, thy state;
And I keep singing in my heart—
    Immaculate! Immaculate!

When Jesus looks upon thy face,
    His Heart with rapture glows,
And in the Church by His sweet grace,
    Thy blessed worship grows.
        I think of thee, &c.

The angels answer with their songs,
    Bright choirs in gleaming rows;
And saints flock round thy feet in throngs,
    And heaven with bliss o'erflows.
        I think of thee, &c.

Immaculate conception! far
    Above all graces blest;
Thou shinest like a royal star
    On God's eternal breast.
        I think of thee, &c.

PRAYERS IN HONOUR OF OUR LADY OF PERPETUAL SUCCOUR.

O Mother of Perpetual Succour, pray for us thy children. Obtain for us that we may continually have recourse to thee.

O HOLY Virgin Mary, who, in order to inspire us with an unbounded confidence, hast been pleased to take the sweet name of Mother of Perpetual Succour, I implore thee to come to my succour always and in all places, in my temptations and after my falls, in my afflictions and trials, and in all the sorrows of this miserable life, but especially at the hour of my death. Obtain for me, O loving Mother, the grace of ever having recourse to thee, for if I am only faithful in calling upon thee, thou wilt always be faithful in coming to my assistance. Obtain then for me this grace of graces, the grace of ever having recourse to thee with a childlike confidence, that, by means of my faithful prayers, I may ever merit thy perpetual succour, and final perseverance. Bless me, O most loving and compassionate Mother, pray for me, and succour me now and at the hour of my death. Amen.

EJACULATORY PRAYER.

O Mother of Perpetual Succour, lend me thy all-powerful aid, and may I ask this favour of thee without ceasing. Amen.

TRIDUUM, OR THREE DAYS PRAYER TO OUR LADY OF PERPETUAL SUCCOUR.

FIRST DAY.

BEHOLD at thy feet, O Mother of Perpetual Succour, a miserable sinner, who has recourse to thee, and puts his trust in thee. O Mother of Mercy, have pity upon me! I hear thee called by all the refuge and the hope of sinners; be then my refuge and my hope. Succour me, for the love of Jesus Christ; stretch forth thy hand to a fallen wretch who recommends himself to thee, and who dedicates himself to thee as thy perpetual servant. I bless and thank God for having in His mercy given to me this confidence in thee, the pledge, as I believe, of my eternal salvation. Alas! too often in past times have I miserably fallen because I had not recourse to thee. I know that with thy help I shall conquer; I know that thou wilt help me if I recommend myself to thee; but I fear lest in the occasions of falling I should cease to call upon thee, and so should lose my soul. This, then, is the grace I seek from thee; and I conjure thee, as far as I know how and can, to obtain it for me, namely, in the assaults of hell always to have recourse to thee, and to say to thee, O Mary, help me; Mother of Perpetual Succour, suffer me not to lose my God.

Five Hail Marys.

℣. Pray for us, O Holy Mother of God.

℞. That we may be made worthy of the promises of Christ.

Let us pray.

Almighty and merciful God, who, to succour the human race, didst will the Blessed Virgin Mary to be the Mother of thine only-begotten Son, grant, we beseech thee, that through her intercession we may shun the infection of the devil, and serve thee with a true mind. Through the same Christ our Lord. Amen.

SECOND DAY.

O MOTHER of Perpetual Succour, grant that I may always invoke thy most powerful name, for thy name is help in life, salvation in death. Ah, Mary most pure, Mary most sweet, let thy name henceforth be the breath of my life. Tarry not, O Lady, to come to my succour whenever I call upon thee: for in all the temptations which shall assail me, in all the wants which shall befall me, I will never cease to call upon thee, and to repeat again and again, Mary, Mary. What comfort, what sweetness, what confidence, what tenderness, does my soul feel in the mere mention of thy name, in the very thought of thee. I thank the Lord for having given thee for my good this name, so sweet, so amiable, so powerful. But merely to pronounce thy name is not enough for me. I wish to do so out of love; I wish that love may remind me to call thee always Mother of Perpetual Succour.

Five Hail Marys and the prayer as before.

THIRD DAY.

O MOTHER of Perpetual Succour, thou art the dispenser of all the graces which God bestows upon us wretched creatures; and for this end has he made thee so powerful, so rich, so kind, in order that thou mayest succour us in our miseries. Thou art the advocate of the most miserable and abandoned criminals who have recourse to thee; help me, then, who recommend myself to thee. I place my eternal salvation in thy hands, to thee I consign my soul. Number me amongst thy more special servants, take me under thy protection, and I am satisfied; yes, for if thou helpest me, I fear nothing; neither my sins, since thou wilt obtain for me the pardon of them; nor the devils, for thou art more powerful than all hell; nor even Jesus, my very Judge, because by one prayer of thine he will be appeased. My only fear is that through my own negligence I should cease to recommend myself to thee, and should thus be lost. Obtain for me, my Lady, the pardon of my sins, the love of Jesus, final perseverance, and the grace of ever having recourse to thee, O Mother of Perpetual Succour.

Five Hail Marys and the prayer as before.

[His Holiness Pope Pius IX., by a decree of the Sacred Congregation of Rites, dated May 17, 1866, graciously approved the preceding prayers, and granted to all the faithful who should recite them with contrition and devotion an Indulgence of 100 days once in the day for each prayer. The said Indulgences are applicable also to the holy souls in purgatory.]

THE SEVEN SORROWS OF OUR LADY.

[A perpetual Indulgence of 300 days, applicable to the dead, every time this exercise is recited in honour of the sorrowful heart of the most Blessed Virgin.]

℣. O God, stretch forth to aid me.
℟. O Lord, make haste to help me.
Glory be to the Father.

1. O most sorrowful Mary, I compassionate the grief of thy tender heart at the prophecy of the holy old man Simeon. O beloved Mother, through that afflicted heart obtain for me the virtue of humility and the gift of the holy fear of God. Hail Mary, &c.

2. O most sorrowful Mary, I compassionate those afflictions which thy most sensitive heart endured during the flight into Egypt and the dwelling there. O beloved Mother, by that afflicted heart obtain for me the virtue of liberality, specially towards the poor, and the gift of piety. Hail Mary, &c.

3. O most sorrowful Mary, I compassionate that intense distress which thine anxious heart experienced in the loss of thy dearest Jesus. O beloved Mother, by that deeply troubled heart obtain for me the virtue of chastity and the gift of knowledge. Hail Mary, &c.

4. O most sorrowful Mary, I compassionate the

consternation which thy maternal heart experienced when thou didst meet Jesus bearing his cross. O beloved Mother, by that deep distress of thy tender heart obtain for me the virtue of patience and the gift of fortitude. Hail Mary, &c.

5. O most sorrowful Mary, I compassionate that martyrdom which thy generous heart endured in witnessing the last agony of Jesus. O beloved Mother, by that martyred heart obtain for me the virtue of temperance and the gift of counsel. Hail Mary, &c.

6. O most sorrowful Mary, I compassionate that wound which thy mournful heart endured from the lance which tore the side of Jesus, and wounded his most lovely heart. O beloved Mother, by thy pierced heart obtain for me the virtue of fraternal charity and the gift of understanding. Hail Mary, &c.

7. O most sorrowful Mary, I compassionate the convulsion which thy most loving heart experienced at the burial of Jesus. O beloved Mother, by this extreme grief of thy sacred heart obtain for me the virtue of diligence and the gift of wisdom. Hail Mary, &c.

℣. Pray for us, O most sorrowful Virgin.

℟. That we may be made worthy of the promises of Christ.

Let us pray.

Grant, we beseech thee, O Lord Jesus Christ, that the Blessed Virgin Mary, thy Mother, may intercede for us with thy clemency, now and at the hour of our death, who at the hour of thy passion was pierced in her most holy soul by the sword of sorrow; grant this, O Jesus Christ, Saviour of the world, who, with the Father, and the Holy Ghost, liveth and reigneth, world without end. Amen.

LITANY OF ST. JOSEPH.

LORD, have mercy on us.
Christ, have mercy on us.
Lord, have mercy on us.
Jesus receive our prayers.
Lord Jesus, grant our petition.
O God the Father, Creator of the world, *Have mercy on us.*
O God the Son, Redeemer of mankind, *Have mercy on us.*
Holy Ghost, perfecter of the elect, *Have mercy on us.*
Holy Trinity, one God, *Have mercy on us.*
Holy Mary, spouse of St. Joseph, *Pray for us.*
St. Joseph, advocate of the humble,
St. Joseph, blessed amongst men,
St. Joseph, defender of the meek,
St. Joseph, exiled with Christ into Egypt,
St. Joseph, favourite of the King of heaven,
St. Joseph, guardian of the Word incarnate,
St. Joseph, honoured amongst men,
St. Joseph, pattern of humility and obedience,
St. Joseph, kind intercessor for the afflicted,
St. Joseph, lily of chastity and temperance,
St. Joseph, example of silence and resignation,
St. Joseph, nursing father to the Son of God,
St. Joseph, the just and perfect man,
St. Joseph, pattern of the industrious and innocent,
St. Joseph, endowed with all virtue,
St. Joseph, ruler of the family of Jesus,

St. Joseph, spouse of the ever-blessed Virgin,
St. Joseph, possessed of all glorious privileges,
St. Joseph, union of all Christian perfections,
St. Joseph, protector of the dying,
St. Joseph, our dear pattern and defender,

Pray for us.

O Lamb of God, that takest away the sins of the world, *Spare us, O Lord.*

O Lamb of God, that takest away the sins of the world, *Hear us, O Lord.*

O Lamb of God, that takest away the sins of the world, *Have mercy on us.*

V. Pray for us, O holy St. Joseph,

R. That we may be made worthy of the promises of Christ.

Let us pray.

O GOD, who didst make choice of holy St. Joseph, to be the spouse of the Blessed Virgin Mary, the nurse and guardian of thy beloved Son Jesus, we humbly beseech thee to grant us, through his intercession, purity both of soul and body, that being free from all sin, and adorned with the wedding garment, we may be admitted to the nuptials of the Lamb in eternal glory, through the same Lord Jesus Christ, thy Son, who liveth and reigneth, &c.

SORROWS AND JOYS OF ST. JOSEPH.

[Indulgences: 100 days each time; 300 days on Wednesdays; 300 days on each day of the two Novenas before his Feast and his Patronage; plenary on those two Feasts; plenary once a month for daily recital; 300 days for each Sunday when recited on seven consecutive Sundays. Applicable to the dead.]

1. O glorious St. Joseph, most pure spouse of thy most holy Mary, even as the trouble and anguish of thy heart was great in the perplexity of abandoning thy most chaste and stainless spouse, so, too, inexplicable was thy delight when by the angel was revealed to thee the sovereign mystery of the Incarnation.

Through this sorrow and this joy of thine, we pray thee, now and in our last agony, to comfort our soul with the joy of a good life, and of a holy death, like unto thine between Jesus and Mary.

Our Father, Hail Mary, and Glory be to the Father.

2. O glorious St. Joseph, most blessed patriarch, who wast selected for the office of reputed father of the Word made Man, the grief which thou didst feel at seeing the child Jesus born in such great poverty was suddenly changed for thee into heavenly exultation at hearing the angelic harmony, and seeing the glories of that most resplendent night.

Through this sorrow and this joy of thine we beseech thee to obtain for us that, after the journey of this life is over, we may pass hence to hear the angelic praises, and to enjoy the splendours of the glory of heaven.

Our Father, Hail Mary, and Glory be to the Father.

3. O glorious St. Joseph, who didst fulfil most obediently all God's commands, the most precious blood which the child Redeemer shed in the circumcision struck death into thy heart, but the name of Jesus revived it and filled it full of joy.

Through this sorrow and this joy of thine, obtain for us that, all vices having been taken from us during life, we may expire in exultation with the most holy name of Jesus in our hearts and upon our lips.

Our Father, Hail Mary, and Glory be to the Father.

4. O most glorious St. Joseph, most faithful saint, who wast a partaker in the mysteries of our redemption, if Simeon's prophecy of that which Jesus and Mary were to suffer caused thee a mortal pang, it filled thee also with a blessed joy at the salvation and glorious resurrection of innumerable souls, which he at the same time foretold would thence proceed.

Through this sorrow and this joy of thine, obtain for us that we may be of the number of those who, through the merits of Jesus, and at the intercession of the Virgin Mother, are to rise again in glory.

Our Father, Hail Mary, and Glory be to the Father.

5. O glorious St. Joseph, most watchful guardian and familiar attendant of the incarnate Son of God, how much didst thou suffer in supporting and in serving the Son of the Most High, particularly in the flight which thou hadst to make into Egypt; but how much again didst thou rejoice at having always with thee that same God, and at seeing the idols of Egypt fall to the ground.

Through this sorrow and this joy of thine, obtain for us that, by keeping far from us hell's tyrant, especially by flying from dangerous occasions, every idol of earthly affection may fall from our hearts; and that, wholly occupied in the service of Jesus and of Mary, we may live for them alone, and die a happy death.

Our Father, Hail Mary, and Glory be to the Father.

6. O glorious St. Joseph, angel of the earth, who didst marvel at beholding the King of Heaven subject to thy commands, if thy consolation at bringing him back from Egypt was disturbed by the fear of Archelaus, yet, assured by the angel, thou didst with Jesus and Mary dwell in joy at Nazareth.

Through this sorrow and this joy of thine, obtain for us that our heart, unclouded by hurtful fears, may enjoy peace of conscience, and that we may live secure with Jesus and Mary, and with them may also die.

Our Father, Hail Mary, and Glory be to the Father.

7. O glorious St. Joseph, model of all holiness, when, without fault of thine, thou hadst lost the child Jesus, thou didst seek him for three days in the greatest sorrow, until with joyful heart thou didst possess again thy life, finding him in the temple among the doctors.

Through this sorrow and this joy of thine, with fervent sighs we supplicate thee to interpose in our behalf, that so it may never befall us to lose Jesus by mortal sin; but that, if unhappily we ever lose him, we may seek him again with unwearied sorrow, until once more we find his favour, especially at the moment of our death, that so we may pass to the enjoyment of him in heaven, and there with thee sing his divine mercies for all eternity.

Our Father, Hail Mary, and Glory be to the Father.

Ant. Jesus himself was beginning about his thirtieth year, being (as it was supposed) the son of Joseph.

℣. Pray for us, O holy Joseph.

℟. That we may be made worthy of the promises of Christ.

Let us pray.

O God, who by thy ineffable providence didst vouchsafe to choose the blessed Joseph for the spouse of thy most holy Mother; grant, we beseech thee, that he whom we venerate as our protector on earth may be our intercessor in heaven; who livest and reignest for ever and ever. Amen.

HYMN TO SAINT JOSEPH.

Hail! holy Joseph, hail!
Sweet spouse of Mary, hail!
Chaste as the lily flow'r
In Eden's peaceful vale.

Hail! holy Joseph, hail!
Comrade of angels, hail!
Cheer thou the hearts that faint,
And guide the steps that fail.

Hail! holy Joseph, hail!
Father of Christ esteem'd!
Father be thou to those
Thy Foster Son redeem'd!

Hail! holy Joseph, hail!
God's choice wert thou alone;
To thee the Word made flesh
Was subject as a Son.

Hail! holy Joseph, hail!
Prince of the house of God!
May His best graces be
By thy sweet hands bestow'd.

Hail! holy Joseph, hail!
Teach us our flesh to tame;
And, Mary, keep the hearts
That love thy husband' name.

Mother of Jesus! bless,
And bless, ye Saints on high,
All meek and simple souls
That to St. Joseph cry.

V. He made him lord over His house.
R. And prince of all that was His.

Let us pray.

GUARDIAN of Virgins and Father, holy Joseph, to whose faithful custody Christ Jesus, very Innocence, and Mary, Virgin of Virgins, were committed; I pray and beg of thee, by these dear pledges Jesus and Mary, free me from all uncleanness, and make me, with spotless mind, pure heart, and chaste body, ever most chastely to serve Jesus and Mary all the days of my life. Amen.

BONA MORS;

OR,

Prayers to obtain the grace of a happy Death, through the Passion of Jesus Christ.

OPEN, O Lord, our mouths, to bless thy holy name; cleanse our hearts from all vain and distracting thoughts; enlighten our understandings, inflame our wills, that we may worthily perform this holy exercise with attention and devotion, and may deserve to be heard in the presence of thy divine Majesty; through Christ our Lord. Amen.

Lord, have mercy on us.
Christ, have mercy on us.
Lord, have mercy on us.
Holy Mary, *Pray for us.*
All ye holy Angels and Archangels,
St. Abel,
All ye choirs of just souls,
St. Abraham,
St. John the Baptist,
All ye holy Patriarchs and Prophets,
St. Peter,
St. Paul,
St. Andrew,
St. John,
All ye holy Apostles and Evangelists,
All ye holy Disciples of our Lord,
All ye holy Innocents,
St. Stephen,
St. Lawrence,
All ye holy Martyrs,

Pray for us.

St. Silvester,
St. Gregory,
St. Augustine,
All ye holy Bishops and Confessors, *Pray for us.*
St. Benedict,
St. Francis,
All ye holy Monks and Hermits,
St. Mary Magdalen,
St. Lucy,
All ye holy Virgins and Widows,
All ye Saints of God, *Make intercession for us.*
Be merciful unto us, *Spare us, O Lord.*
Be merciful unto us, *Hear us, O Lord.*
Be merciful unto us, *O Lord, deliver us.*
From thy anger, *O Lord, deliver us.*
From the perils of death,
From an unprovided death,
From the pains of hell,
From all evil,
From the power of the Devil, *O Lord, deliver us.*
By thy nativity,
By thy cross and passion,
By thy death and burial,
By thy glorious resurrection,
By thy admirable ascension,
By the grace of the Holy Ghost the Comforter,
In the day of Judgment,
We sinners, *Beseech thee to hear us*
That thou wilt spare us, *We beseech thee to hear us.*
Lord, have mercy on us.
Christ have mercy on us.
Lord, have mercy on us.

Let us pray.

MAY thy clemency vouchsafe, O God, so to confirm thy servants in thy holy grace, that at the hour of death the enemy may not prevail over them, and that with thy angels they may deserve to pass into life everlasting; through our Lord Jesus Christ. Amen.

ALMIGHTY and most gracious God, who for thy thirsting people didst bring forth from the rock a stream of living water, draw forth from the hardness of our hearts tears of compunction, that we may bewail our sins, and receive remission of them from thy mercy; through Christ our Lord. Amen.

An Act of Contrition.

O LORD Jesus Christ, Redeemer of the world, behold prostrate at thy feet a most ungrateful and perfidious creature! My God, I have offended thee exceedingly, in thought, word, and deed. My heinous crimes fixed thee to the bloody cross. To rescue me from eternal damnation, thou didst agonize three hours on Mount Calvary. But oh! how much am I displeased with myself! how grieved for having offended thee,—a God of infinite goodness, of infinite charity! I am astonished and confounded at thy unwearied patience in supporting a most provoking sinner. From the bottom of my heart I detest all my sins; and because I love thee, and will love thee and rather to die than commit one mortal sin. Amen.

The Stations of the Sacred Passion.

O Most sweet Jesus! praying to thy Father in the garden, sorrowful even unto death, and sweating blood in an agony of grief, have mercy on us.

℞. Have mercy on us, O Lord, have mercy on us.

O most sweet Jesus! delivered by the traitor's kiss into the hands of thine enemies, seized and bound like a thief, and abandoned by thy disciples, have mercy on us.

℞. Have mercy on us, O Lord, have mercy on us.

O most sweet Jesus! by the unjust verdict of the Jews found guilty of death, brought like a malefactor before the tribunal of Pilate, scorned and derided by the impious Herod, have mercy on us.

℞. Have mercy on us, O Lord, have mercy on us.

O most sweet Jesus! stripped of thy garments, and most cruelly scourged at the pillar, have mercy on us.

℞. Have mercy on us, O Lord, have mercy on us.

O most sweet Jesus! crowned with thorns, blindfolded, buffeted, struck with a reed, clothed in derision with a purple garment, and many other ways scorned and overwhelmed with reproaches, have mercy on us.

℟. Have mercy on us, O Lord, have mercy on us.

O most sweet Jesus! reputed more criminal than Barabbas the murderer, rejected by the Jews, and unjustly condemned to the death of the cross, have mercy on us.

℟. Have mercy on us, O Lord, have mercy on us.

O most sweet Jesus! loaded with a heavy cross, and led like an innocent lamb to the place of execution, have mercy on us.

℟. Have mercy on us, O Lord, have mercy on us.

O most sweet Jesus! numbered amongst thieves, derided, blasphemed, made to taste vinegar and gall, and crucified in dreadful torments from the sixth to the ninth hour, have mercy on us.

℟. Have mercy on us, O Lord, have mercy on us.

O most sweet Jesus! dead upon the cross, and in thy holy Mother's presence pierced by a lance in thy side, whence issued forth blood and water, have mercy on us.

℟. Have mercy on us, O Lord, have mercy on us.

O most sweet Jesus! taken down from the cross, and bathed with the tears of thy most sorrowful Mother, have mercy on us.

℟. Have mercy on us, O Lord, have mercy on us.

O most sweet Jesus! covered with bruises, marked with five wounds, embalmed with spices, and laid in the sepulchre, have mercy on us.

℟. Have mercy on us, O Lord, have mercy on us.

℣. He truly bore our sorrows.

℟. And he carried our grief.

Let us pray.

O God! who, for the redemption of the world, didst vouchsafe to be born, to be circumcised, to be rejected by the Jews, to be betrayed with a kiss, to be bound like a malefactor, and like an innocent lamb, to be led to slaughter; to be ignominiously brought before Annas, Caiphas, Pilate, and Herod; to be accused by false witnesses, scourged with whips, buffeted, spit upon, struck with a reed, crowned with thorns, stripped of thy garments, nailed to a cross, and placed between two thieves; to have vinegar and gall given thee to drink; to have thy side pierced through with a spear. Do thou, O Lord, by these most grievous pains, which I, thy unworthy servant, commemorate, and by thy most holy cross and death, deliver me from the pains of hell, and conduct me whither thy mercy did conduct the good thief crucified with thee, who, together with the Father and the Holy Ghost, livest and reignest for ever. Amen.

Devotions to the Five Wounds of our Saviour.

O LORD Jesus Christ! I humbly adore the most sacred wound in thy left foot. I thank thee for that cruel pain, suffered with so much love and charity. I feelingly compassionate thy torments, and the excessive grief of thy most afflicted Mother. I humbly beg pardon for all my sins, which I deplore beyond all imaginable evils, because they offend thee, O infinite goodness! and I resolve never more to sin. O bring with me all sinners to a true conversion, and give them light to know the heinousness and enormity of mortal sin.

Our Father. Hail Mary. Glory, &c.

O LORD Jesus Christ! I humbly adore the most sacred wound of thy right foot. I give thee thanks for that cruel pain, suffered with so great love and charity. I feelingly condole with thee in thy torments, and with thy most afflicted Mother. Grant me strength against all temptations, and prompt obedience in the execution of thy divine will. Comfort, O Jesus! all poor, miserable, afflicted, tempted, and persecuted persons. Most just Judge! govern those who administer justice, and assist all labourers in the care of souls, whether amongst Christians or infidels.

Our Father. Hail Mary. Glory, &c.

O LORD Jesus Christ! I humbly adore the most sacred wound of thy left hand. I render thee thanks for that cruel pain, endured for me with so much love and charity. I condole with thee in thy sufferings, and with thy most afflicted Mother. Deliver me from the pains of hell; grant me patience in the adversities of this life, and conformity in all things to thy blessed will. I offer to thee all my sufferings of body and soul, in satisfaction for my sins, which have so often deserved eternal torments. Pardon all my enemies, and all those who bear ill-will against me. Grant patience to the sick, and restore them to health, and support with thy assisting grace all who are in their agony, that they may not perish.

Our Father. Hail Mary. Glory, &c.

O LORD Jesus Christ! I humbly adore the most sacred wound of thy right hand. I thank thee for that cruel pain, endured for me with so much love and charity. I condole with thee in thy sufferings, and with thy most afflicted Mother. Grant me a firm and resolute will in all things relating to my salvation. Bless me with final perseverance in grace, that I may secure the enjoyment of that glory which was purchased at the price of thy most precious blood. Grant also, my Jesus! speedy peace and repose to the souls in purgatory, and daily advance towards perfection thy holy servants in this world, especially those who are of this confraternity.

Our Father. Hail Mary. Glory, &c.

O LORD Jesus Christ! I humbly adore the most sacred wound in thy blessed side. I thank thee for the immense love manifested towards us at the opening of thy inflamed heart. Grant me a pure and perfect charity; that, loving thee above all things, I may breathe my last in the purest sentiments of divine love. Protect thy holy Catholic Church, direct thy governing Vicar on earth, and all ecclesiastical orders and pious persons who are instrumental in bringing souls to their duty. Preserve in thy happy service all Christian kings and princes. Bring into the way of salvation all those who are gone astray, whether through malice or ignorance, and subject unto thy sweet yoke all infidels, heretics, and all the enemies of thy holy name.

Our Father. Hail Mary. Glory, &c.

Let us pray.

O LORD Jesus Christ! God of my heart! by those five wounds which thy love for us inflicted on thee, succour thy servants, whom thou hast redeemed with thy precious blood. Amen.

Most merciful Redeemer! I humbly beseech thee by those unspeakable torments, and the immense grief which thou wast pleased to suffer for me, especially when thy blessed soul was separated from thy body, that thou wilt secure my poor soul at the hour of its departure, and comfort me then as thou didst the good thief with the blessed assurance that I shall be with thee in Paradise. Amen.

Let us say *thrice* the Our Father, and the Hail Mary, in memory of the three hours our dear Redeemer hung upon the cross, for the souls of the faithful departed of this congregation.—*Our Father, &c. Hail Mary, &c.*

Let us say *once* the Our Father and the Hail Mary, for such as are in the lamentable state of mortal sin.

Our Father, &c. Hail Mary, &c.

Let us likewise say *once* the Our Father and the Hail Mary, for the person in this congregation that is to die next, that he may be prepared, and depart happily, fortified with the holy sacraments of the Church.—*Our Father, &c. Hail Mary, &c.*

Let us dispose ourselves, by acts of perfect contrition, and pure love of God, to receive worthily the benediction of our Lord and Saviour, in the adorable sacrament of the altar.

MERCIFUL Redeemer, and holy God of infinite patience! great is my confusion to appear in thy divine presence, having so frequently preferred contemptible creatures to thee, the omnipotent Creator of the universe. I utterly detest my presumption in sinning in thy most pure sight; I acknowledge myself a criminal, and I plead guilty at the bar of thy dread tribunal. Thou mightest have been glorified in thy justice, by striking me suddenly dead, and condemning me to eternal flames, for base indignities offered to thee; but thou wast pleased to be glorified in the high prerogative of thy mercy, in calling me back to repentance. I abhor all my crimes of thought, word, and deed; not only for the hope of reward, or fear of punishment, but for thy own sake, and because thou dost infinitely abominate them. O God of majesty and mercy! look upon those sacred marks in thy hands, feet, and side, which thou still retainest in thy glorified body, to plead my pardon. By that tender love which induced thee to create, redeem, and sanctify me, unite the abyss of thy merits to the abyss of my misery. Strengthen my weakness, confirm this my resolution of never offending thee more; O rather let me lose everything, with life itself, than lose thy favour by mortal sin. My heart was created for thee, and I love thee more than myself. Every aspiration of my life, especially the last, shall be a protestation of my pure and sincere love of thy divine majesty. Sweet Saviour of perishing mankind! who openest thy hand and fillest every creature with benediction, give me now such a blessing as thou didst bestow on thy beloved disciples when ascending in triumph from Mount Olivet, that I may live and die in this happy disposition. Amen.

LITANY OF THE PASSION OF JESUS.

BY the blood that flowed from Thee
  In Thy bitter agony,
By the scourge so meekly borne,
By thy purple robe of scorn—
  Jesu, Saviour, hear our cry,
    Thou wert suffering once as we;
  Hear the loving Litany
    We Thy children sing to Thee.

By the thorns that crowned Thy head,
By Thy sceptre of a reed,
By Thy footstep, faint and slow,
Weighed beneath Thy cross of woe—
    Jesu, &c.

By the nails and pointed spear,
By Thy people's cruel jeer,
By Thy dying prayer which rose,
Begging mercy for Thy foes—
    Jesu, &c.

By the darkness, thick as night,
Blotting out the sun from sight;
By the cry with which in death
Thou didst yield Thy parting breath—
    Jesu, &c.

By Thy weeping Mother's woe,
By the sword that pierced her through,
When in anguish standing by
On the cross she saw Thee die—
    Jesu, &c.

J. M. J.

ASSOCIATION OF PRAYER, IN HONOUR OF THE SACRED THIRST AND AGONY OF JESUS, TO REPRESS INTEMPERANCE.

Approved of by His Holiness Pope Pius IX.

"Afterwards, Jesus said, I thirst; and they gave him vinegar to drink mingled with gall."—S. John xix. 28; and S. Matt. xxvii. 34.

OBJECT.—This Association has for its object, the union of all the faithful, *especially those who are in the friendship of God*, in devotion to the Sacred Thirst and Agony of Jesus, and the Compassionate Heart of Mary, to obtain the repression of the vice of intemperance, which, as S. John Chrysostom tells us, is the "joy of demons, and the parent of ten thousand evils." (Hom. 27.) On its extirpation depend the education of children, and, therefore, the future of society itself, the peace of families, the conversion of many sinners, and even their happiness for eternity.

MEANS.—I. Each member shall recite daily "Our Father" once, and "Hail Mary" three times, in honour of the Sacred Thirst and Agony of Jesus, and of the Compassionate Heart of Mary, for the intentions of the Association, and the repression of this awful vice.—II. All are requested to offer their other good works for this purpose, especially Holy Communion on the second Sunday of the month. This offering, far from taking away or diminishing the efficacy of these good works for other intentions, will greatly increase it. —III. As "prayer is good with fasting and alms," (Tobias xii. 8,) the zealous are recommended to add some small act of mortification, especially in the use of drinks on Fridays, or oftener if their devotion suggests it.

ADVANTAGES.—His Holiness has granted (July 28th, 1868,) to this work of charity the following Indulgences.

PARTIAL.—For every good work done for the Association, accompanied by prayer, 100 days. Thus, to enrol a member and say one "Hail Mary," will gain 100 days. To enrol ten members, 7 years and 7 quarantines, on the same condition.

PLENARY, on the usual conditions, and provided that the prayers for the intentions of the Church are said in the church in which Communion has been received, on the following Feasts: the Sacred Heart of Jesus, the Precious Blood, the Exaltation of the Holy Cross, the Holy Name of Jesus, the Five Wounds, the Most Pure Heart of Mary, the Espousals of the Blessed Virgin and St. Joseph, Auxilium Christianorum (May 24), Our Lady of the Sacred Heart (May 31), St. Patrick, Patron of Ireland, St. George, Patron of England, and St. Andrew, Patron of Scotland.

RICHARDSON AND SONS, PRINTERS, DERBY.

PRAYER OF ST. BERNARD.

REMEMBER, O most Holy Virgin Mary, that no one ever had recourse to thy protection, implored thy help, or sought thy mediation, without obtaining relief. Confiding, therefore, in thy goodness, behold me. a penitent sinner, sighing out my sins before thee, beseeching thee to adopt me for thy son, and to take upon thee the care of my eternal salvation.

Despise not, O Mother of Jesus, the petition of thine humble client, but hear and grant my prayer. Amen.

AVE MARIS STELLA.

Hail, Queen of Heaven, the ocean star,
  Guide of the wanderer here below,
Thrown on life's surge, we claim thy care,
  Save us from peril and from woe.
      Mother of Christ, star of the sea,
      Pray for the wanderer, pray for me.

O pious, chaste, and spotless maid,
  We sinners make our prayers through thee,
Remind thy Son that He has paid
  The price of our iniquity.
      Virgin most pure, star of the sea,
      Pray for the sinner, pray for me.

Sojourners in this vale of tears,
  To thee, blest advocate, we cry,

Pity our sorrows, calm our fears,
  And soothe with hope our misery.
    Refuge in grief, star of the sea,
    Pray for the mourner, pray for me.

And while to Him who reigns above,
  In Godhead one, in persons three,
The source of life, of grace, of love,
  Homage we pay on bended knee,
    Do thou, bright Queen, star of the sea,
    Pray for thy children, pray for me.

LOVE OF THE SACRED HEART.

I rise from dreams of time,
And an angel guides my feet,
To the sacred altar-throne,
Where Jesu's Heart doth beat.

The lone lamp softly burns,
And a wondrous silence reigns,
Only with a low still voice
The Holy One complains.

"Long! long, I've waited here,
And though thou heed'st not Me,
The Heart of God's own Son,
Beats ever on for thee."

In the womb of Mary meek,
In the cradle, on the tree:
Heart of pure undying love,
It lived, loved, bled for me.

Ever pleading, day and night,
Thou canst not from us part;
O veiled and wondrous Son!
O love of the Sacred Heart!

www.ingramcontent.com/pod-product-compliance
Lightning Source LLC
Chambersburg PA
CBHW022139300426
44115CB00006B/263